0065363

D0385992

WITHDRAWN

DATE DUE

Rogues' Gallery

Rogues' Gallery

America's Foes
from George III to Saddam Hussein

LARRY HEDRICK

BRASSEY'S (US), INC.
A Division of Maxwell Macmillan, Inc.

WASHINGTON • NEW YORK • LONDON

Brassey's (US), Inc.

Editorial Offices	*Order Department*
Brassey's (US), Inc.	Brassey's Book Orders
8000 Westpark Drive	c/o Macmillan Publishing Co.
First Floor	100 Front Street, Box 500
McLean, Virginia 22102	Riverside, New Jersey 08075

Brassey's (US), Inc., books are available at special discounts for bulk purchases for sales promotions, premiums, fund-raising, or educational use through the Special Sales Director, Macmillan Publishing Company, 866 Third Avenue, New York, New York 10022.

Library of Congress Cataloging-in-Publication Data
Hedrick, Larry.
   Rogues' gallery : America's foes from George III to Saddam Hussein
/ Larry Hedrick.
      p.   cm.
   Includes bibliographical references and index.
   ISBN 0-02-881000-7 : $24.00 (approx.)
   1. United States—History, Military.   I. Title.
E181.H43   1992
973—dc20

92-9912
CIP

10 9 8 7 6 5 4 3 2 1

Printed in the United States of America

To My Mother and Father

Contents

Acknowledgments

I owe a particular debt of gratitude to the academic specialists who read and commented on my individual chapters. They include Charles D. Ameringer, Lamar Cecil, Edward M. Cook, Jr., Ken de Bevoise, Lloyd C. Gardner, J. Arch Getty, William Hauser, Peter Hayes, Michael H. Hunt, and Steve Ireton. Their combined efforts allowed me to clarify a number of obscurities; any remaining problems are, of course, entirely my own.

At the University of Washington libraries, the burdens of research were lightened by the expertise of Madeline Copp, Thomas Deardorff, Marino Lundin, Glenda Pearson, and Mark Young. Those who kindly helped me in the Kitsap library system include Millie Kirk, Lisa Muldoon, and Patty Puzon.

Many thanks for the kindness and consideration of Ron and Connie Hedrick, Joyce Gruenewald, Jamie and Todd Kooy, and Candace Young; also to Dan Bentley, Chuck and Dawn Braithwaite, Pat Danford, Betty Hicks, Diane Kelly, and the inimitable Neil Venard.

Dale Head volunteered his time to customize my word-processing software. John Lathourakis and Vicki Chamlee patiently initiated me into the mysteries of copy editing. The enthusiasm and insight of Judith Meyers also deserve recognition; she carefully read the manuscript and made useful suggestions for the better ordering of the prose.

At Brassey's (US), Don McKeon handled my work with the kind of care that authors pray for nightly. More than any other single factor, it was his judicious sponsorship that transformed the manuscript of this book into a published reality.

1

Enemies of the American Order

The journalist who coined the phrase "manifest destiny," John L. O'Sullivan, saw the United States as "the nation of human progress." In the 1840s he rhetorically asked, "Who will, what can, set limits to our onward march?"[1] There would be far more answers to that question than O'Sullivan anticipated. Possessed by a world vision from the earliest days of the Republic, Americans have found no shortage of foreign competitors with world visions of their own. Inevitably, the United States experienced its foes as the enemies of enlightened government. They were, as Senator Albert Beveridge of Indiana would put it in 1908, "infidels to the gospel of liberty."[2]

Like all other nationalists, we Americans have tended to overlook our own shortcomings and concentrate on the evil in our adversaries. But there is some truth behind our sense of being crusaders against despotism. A review of the historical record shows that Saddam Hussein is hardly the first brutal militarist with whom we have come to blows. Although the United States has never declared war on another democracy, it has shown a distinct tendency to attract the hostility of the world's less savory regimes. By any reasonable standard, it is easier to discover nobility of character in Thomas Jefferson than in Yusuf Karamanli of Tripoli, in James Polk than in General Santa Anna of Mexico, in Woodrow Wilson than in Kaiser Wilhelm II of Germany, in Franklin Roosevelt than in Hideki Tojo of Japan.

Lack of moral scruples has never given our foes a decisive advantage, for aggressors have a habit of overreaching. The United States has exploited their overconfidence to score victory after victory. But many of our enemies have offered us strenuous challenges, and by doing so they have unwittingly introduced us to our own strengths. The misrule of George III helped to inspire our original sense of nationhood and challenged us to fight for independence. Reacting to the piratical fleet of Yusuf Karamanli, we built a navy and projected our power into the Mediterranean world for the first time. Santa Anna inadvertently served up Texas and the vast reaches of the West, giving us the gold of golden California. Kaiser Wilhelm II's rash actions taught us that the United States, as a child of European enlightenment, could also be its savior; Hitler confirmed that lesson.

It is difficult to exaggerate the importance of foreign foes in the creation of America's national unity from such a racially and culturally diverse population. The lesson has been clear from 1776 onward: nothing unifies a people like a threat from abroad. Unsurprisingly, the greatest part of our foundation document, the Declaration of Independence, is a catalogue of the wrongs visited on America by its last king.

The power of foreign opposition to bring Americans together has been demonstrated time and again in the course of U.S. history, but never so graphically as by the Japanese in December 1941. A month after the bombing of Pearl Harbor, Franklin Roosevelt reported that "the spirit of the American people was never higher than it is today—the Union was never more closely knit together—this country was never more deeply determined to face the solemn tasks before it."[3] Hideki Tojo might have expected such a result. As Arnold Toynbee generalized in his *Study of History,* a violent attack on an essentially healthy civilization is "not destructive but positively stimulating."[4]

Yet the process of rising through the hostility of other nations has been costly and painful. The sense of vulnerability caused by Pearl Harbor alone has yet to dissipate entirely. The U.S. role in the nuclear arms race shows what World War II did to us: It left us with a need to make ourselves formidable above all other nations. By 1962, the year of the Cuban missile crisis, thoughtful observers around the world were beginning to wonder if weapons of mass destruction would lead not only to the failure of the American experiment but the extermination of the human race. The cold war threatened to culminate with the planet under a pall of radioactive ashes; as John Kennedy observed near the end of his life, "Domestic issues can only lose elections, but foreign policy issues can kill us all."[5] The lack of a world order had become a matter of life and death.

U.S. diplomacy has usually responded to genuine threats with rational reactions. But just as important, it has also responded to its own sense of national mission. The success of the American Revolution was accepted as proof that God had blessed our experiment in liberty from its very beginnings. The expansion of the U.S. sphere was therefore seen as providential and inevitable. A new people—strong, democratic, and generous—had been chosen to create a new age and, with the passage of time, our work would be brought to fruition. Willingly or unwillingly, the world would be remade in our image.

Embracing this type of nationalism with religious fervor, every generation of Americans has been ready to rally 'round the flag when the nation's leaders have led them into war, and essentially every U.S. military expedition has been seen as part of an effort to bring light to yet another benighted corner of the planet.

But a strong strain in the American character has resisted any attempt to hurry the coming of the American heyday or to force U.S. hegemony on the world. The mission of the United States was to set an example, not forge an empire. Using armed force to extend the dominion of democracy might well backfire, dooming popular rule at home. John C. Calhoun expressed the sentiment most clearly in 1848, cautioning Americans to hold themselves aloof from foreign adventures—thereby doing "more for liberty, not only for ourselves, but for the example of mankind, than can be done by a thousand victories. . . ."[6]

For many decades the question of the American role in the world was largely beside the point: We were just too busy settling our own broad continent to seek offshore challenges. Prosperous and secure behind wide oceans, the United States belittled its own army. As Barbara Tuchman reported, "Troop trains on the railroads rated after freight cars in priority and had to wait on sidings to let passenger and freight trains go by. The public attitude was such that Congress felt required in 1911 to provide a $500 fine for any public place of entertainment that discriminated against men in uniform."[7] This antimilitarism was fated to fade, for the United States rose to power in a world that was armed to the teeth.

In 1914, as Europe threw itself into the butchery of World War I, Americans looked on in horror. It was now more obvious than ever that the nations needed American guidance. "Too proud to fight," President Woodrow Wilson aimed to remain neutral so that he could take the lead in restoring peace to the world. As Richard Barnet has pointed out, Wilson believed that "If the United States stayed above the fray, at the right moment its power could be used to usher in a new world order. . . ."[8] But Wilson's good offices were not enough to end the war by negotiation, and when the United States entered the fighting, his administration engineered the nation's first major military buildup since the Civil War.

The possession of so much offensive force positioned the United States to bring its full influence to bear on the international stage for the first time. A convinced globalist, Wilson sought to exploit this new power to remake the world in America's image. Hailed as the man who had saved Europe from Kaiser Wilhelm's insatiable imperialism, Wilson presented his Fourteen Points in an atmosphere of unprecedented hope for the future. Wilson called for worldwide acceptance of democratic self-determination as well as new economic arrangements that would insure universal prosperity. All nations were meant to join in an international organization that would guarantee the security of people everywhere.

When he presented the Treaty of Versailles to the Senate for ratification in the summer of 1919, Wilson said that the United States had finally come of age: "There can be no question of our ceasing to be a world power. The only question is whether we can refuse the moral leadership that is offered us, whether we shall accept or reject the confidence of the world."[9] To Wilson's chagrin, the Senate could and did reject his particular vision of America's international role, and the president's idealistic desires were frustrated by his own inflexibility and the nation's postwar disillusionment. The new world order was not to be. But even if the Senate had voted for the treaty, the European powers were in no mood to see national self-determination get out of hand. In 1920, Great Britain alone controlled a fifth of the earth's land surface and ruled a quarter of its peoples, and London was in no hurry to bid its empire farewell.

After a halfhearted attempt to strangle Vladimir Illyich Lenin's brand of communism in its cradle at the end of World War I, the United States largely left the European world order to its own devices. This policy of disengagement was not a success; combined with severe dislocations in the global economy, it only speeded the rise of Benito Mussolini and Adolf Hitler. As the "arsenal of democracy" entered World War II, Franklin Roosevelt told Congress that the United States would not repeat the same mistakes that it had committed after World War I. The American crusade would not be completed until the nation had achieved "the objective of establishing and securing freedom of speech, freedom of religion, freedom from want, and freedom from fear everywhere in the world."[10] So the dreams of Woodrow Wilson were alive and well in the White House of FDR. At Roosevelt's behest, the United Nations was established; but after his death, his version of the new world order would prove vulnerable to the bipolar split of the emerging cold war.

Even before the birth of the Soviet Union, U.S. policymakers had been bedeviled by the threat of Marxism, which forthrightly claimed to be the unstoppable wave of the future. Following World War II, the United States put its armed forces on a permanent war footing for the first time in its history. Though U.S. military personnel occupied 275 major military bases in thirty-one countries at the height of the cold war, a sense of national security escaped the American elite. When Marxism in the person of Fidel Castro succeeded in taking control of Cuba, fears of an eventual Communist encirclement intensified, and military spending soared to new heights.

Many Americans resisted the militarized vision of its leaders, but it seemed fairly obvious that the future of civilization was being decided by the struggle between communism and capitalism. In the depths of the cold war, the aura of romance that hung around rampant Marxists like Mao Zedong sent shudders through capitalists like John Foster Dulles, President Dwight Eisenhower's first secretary of state. Describing Marxism as "the gravest threat that has ever faced what we call western civilization," Dulles preached that containing the spread of communism would not be enough: "It is only by keeping alive the hope of liberation . . . that we will end this terrible peril which dominates the world."[11] As it happened, global realities would demand that the United States spend most of the postwar era trying to stop the spread of communism, not effecting its rollback. This effort would lead to places like Vietnam, where America would meet its most successful enemy, Ho Chi Minh.

Throughout its national existence, attempts by the United States to spread its vision have been stymied by the brute facts of an anarchic world. U.S. military adventures have typically been followed by profound disillusionment as the limits of American power became clear even in the midst of exceptional triumphs. Kaiser Wilhelm was defeated, but the next European war would be even more devastating. Hitler was crushed, but Joseph Stalin inherited Eastern Europe and Soviet troops remained there for over forty years. Japan was subdued, but Mao came to power in China. The disillusionment of the American people about the results of the war against Saddam Hussein is remarkably characteristic of how their forebears have reacted to past wars. Orgies of patriotism generally lead to a major indulgence of pessimism. Dazzling displays of U.S. military might finally seem to represent more razzle-dazzle than real power.

Regardless of the mood of the American public, the world has seen a surfeit of ambitious leaders who know how to disguise their intentions until their imperial designs are well advanced. And more than economic forces, more than geographical facts, it is such individuals who make history. As Václav Havel testified in 1991, "I realize again and again how terribly important the personal characteristics of politicians are, their relationships and mutual animosities, what an immense political influence their good and bad qualities can have on the lives of millions of people."[12]

All too often, it is the bad qualities that exert the greatest influence on suffering humanity, if only because the struggle for political power in every country tends to bring amoral schemers to the top of the heap. Certainly, all of the enemies of the United States treated in this book were devious men. But so were all of the U.S. leaders who opposed them. For there are no innocents in the intrigue-laden world of international politics. American statesmen have had to develop intricate strategies for confronting foreign foes, and the fortunes of war add a strain of uncertainty to every decision that is taken.

In the historical record, a country's enemies are more impressive than its allies; conflict is, after all, more dramatic than cooperation. The adversarial process tends to breed obsessions, and those obsessions usually become focused on one man, the chief of the enemy state, whether he be George III or Santa Anna, Adolf Hitler or Fidel Castro. This book is a study of those obsessions.

2

The Royal Brute of Britain

On July 9, 1776, George Washington's troops in New York City were treated to a reading of the Declaration of Independence and turned loose to celebrate the birth of their new nation. They joined the local revolutionaries in a rampage that carried them to the houses of Loyalists, where no window was left unshattered. Satisfied on that score, they moved on to a symbol that was dear to every Loyalist's heart: the huge equestrian statue of George III that occupied a pedestal just off Broadway in Bowling Green.

Though made of lead, the statue was coated with gold from top to bottom—and served as an impressive monument to the power of the British crown. In a flash the revelers hurdled the railing that surrounded the statue and looped ropes around the royal rider and his mount. When the tugging was over and George III was cast down, a man with a saw stepped out of the crowd and cut through the soft metal of the neck, decapitating the fallen monarch.

The next day Washington's headquarters recognized that "the persons who pulled down and mutilated the statue in the Broadway last night were actuated by zeal in the public cause." But the commander in chief wished that the king had been brought low in a more orderly fashion. In the future, he decreed, "such things shall be avoided by the soldiers and be left to be executed by proper authority."[1] Whether Washington approved or not, the king's leaden head was presented to a party of American troops, who put it on a spike in the Blue Bell Tavern in north Manhattan. Later, two Loyalists staged a midnight raid on the tavern and carried off the prize, which eventually fell into the hands of the British. But the torso and horse were delivered to a munitions factory in Ridgefield, Connecticut, where they were melted down and molded into 42,088 bullets.

Ammunition loomed large in American minds during the summer of 1776, for George III's army and navy were already on hand to begin the reconquest of New York. Masses of British tents crowded each other on the hillsides of Staten Island, and six weeks after the fall of the king's statue, New York Bay harbored a formidable British armada of 37 men-of-war and 400 transports. Gen. Sir William Howe, George III's commander of land forces in America, had 24,000 soldiers at his disposal, including 8,000 German mercenaries. Washington could muster only 15,000 troops, largely unseasoned, to counter Howe's force of professionals—and up to 20 percent of the American army were suffering from dysentery.

It was a pity that Washington could not send his recruiting sergeants into George III's kingdom, for there were plenty of Britons who felt the same about their monarch as the revolutionaries in the New World. A year earlier, John Wesley had reported to the Earl of Darmouth that most of the people he encountered on his journeys through England "heartily despise His Majesty and hate him with a perfect hatred. They wish to [soak] their hands in his blood; they are full of the spirit of murder and rebellion. . . . It is as much as ever I can do, and sometimes more than I can do, to keep this plague from infecting my own friends."[2]

Who was this king who aroused a firestorm of resentment on both sides of the Atlantic? To begin with, consider his nationality. In a sense, George III was not a Briton at all. His family line, the House of Hanover, derived from a duchy in northern Germany that was part of the Holy Roman Empire. A bizarre reproductive failure lay behind the Hanoverians' move to England: Queen Anne, the last monarch of the House of Stuart, had endured no fewer than eighteen pregnancies, but she failed to leave the British nation a single heir when she died in 1714. So George III's great-grandfather, George I, who could speak no English, came over from the Continent to begin a new dynasty.

George III was born in London on June 4, 1738. An odd and withdrawn little boy, he felt intimidated by crowds and always liked country life better than the city. He lost his father, Prince Frederick, in 1751 and grew up knowing that the death of George II, his stern grandfather, might catapult him onto the throne at any time. Taught by idealistic tutors, he swore as a young man that "the interest of my country ever shall be my first care, my own inclinations shall ever submit to it. I am born for the happiness or misery of a great nation, and consequently must often act contrary to my passions."[3]

When he inherited the crown at the age of twenty-two in October 1760, his high tone reached even higher, and a week after his accession he signed a proclamation that encouraged "piety and virtue" and condemned "vice, profaneness, and immorality."[4] This inclination to preach to his subjects became one of the hallmarks of George III's reign. The British nation soon realized that their new monarch was a rigid moralist who believed that the world was full of wicked people—and shrewd observers foresaw that the young king would raise a host of enemies against Great Britain.

The troubles in his American colonies began shortly after he came to the throne, and George quickly accepted the Revolution's challenge. To his mind, the independence movement was nothing more than a grotesque conspiracy led by firebreathing fanatics. As hostilities impended in the 1770s, he steeled himself to oppose the Americans with military force. In November 1774 he had written his first minister, Lord North, that "the New England governments are in a state of rebellion, [and] blows must decide whether they are to be subject to this country."[5] Eight months later, he told Lord Sandwich that "once these rebels have felt a smart blow, they will submit."[6]

He never wavered in his conviction that Great Britain had treated the American colonists too leniently. What they really deserved is what they now would get: a good thrashing. The revolutionaries were to be the king's whipping boys—and the king was gratified when he learned that General Howe was prepared, in August 1776, to whip them out of New York.

On the morning of August 22, 1776, the British landed fifteen thousand troops on the southwestern shores of Long Island. Unopposed, the invaders moved up to occupy the village of Flatbush in Brooklyn. General Washington sent over reinforcements from Manhattan to support the local militia, but he failed to see what the British were up to. Most of the Americans were ensconced on the heights north of Flatbush, and they expected the British to march up as easy targets and let themselves be picked off. Instead, the main British column marched by night far out to the east, silently filed through Jamaica Pass, and, on the morning of August 27, descended on Washington's army from the rear while a large body of German mercenaries made a frontal assault.

The result was easy to predict: The American militiamen saw death coming at them from all sides and fled. Most of them were rounded up by the British infantry and cavalry, but the Germans, who believed that the Yankees had been ordered to show *them* no mercy, were too busy with their bayonets to take prisoners.

America's independence almost perished that afternoon. General Washington, overseeing the defense of Brooklyn in person, might have been killed or captured if the British advance had gone forward at full tilt. But for reasons that remain mysterious, General Howe failed to press the attack. Realizing that their best alternative was escape, the Americans assembled a motley little flotilla that carried the men of the Continental Army across the East River to temporary safety in Manhattan. Benjamin Tallmadge, an officer serving with a Connecticut regiment, concluded that, in the whole history of human warfare, there had never been "a more fortunate retreat."[7]

Back in England, George III was accustomed to receiving reports from the front after a delay of a month or six weeks. He had never been discouraged by the turn of events across the Atlantic—not even when Washington's siege of Boston had forced General Howe to evacuate the city in March 1776—and news of the Battle of Long Island, which arrived in England on October 10, convinced the king that the colonists were on the brink of collapse. His subjects seemed to share their monarch's belief that the end of the war was in sight, for when word of Washington's defeat spread through London and the English countryside, church bells were rung and bonfires lit.

It was a victory for which George III could claim much of the credit. Although General Howe had control of operations in America, the strategy that guided his actions had been approved—and sometimes refined—by the king himself. In addition, George monitored every aspect of the British expeditionary force that went out to resubjugate the colonists. He had appointed not only Howe but also the other generals and senior naval officers who were struggling to defeat the spirit of independence. For all his diligence, George III still refused to recognize himself as a foreign enemy of the newly formed United States. In his own eyes, he was more American than the Americans. For he was their sovereign, and their duty to him was more than lawful; it was sacred.

Conditions on the home front in 1776 seemed to support George III's pretensions. War spending had stimulated the English economy and recent harvests had been good. So the cost of living gave His Majesty's 7 million subjects relatively little to complain about, and the unpopularity of the king that John Wesley had noted the year before had diminished considerably. The Union Jack seemed to be flying from a flagpole at the top of the world. It was an understandably complacent king who rewarded General Howe by making him a Knight of the Bath and eagerly awaited more good news from across the ocean.

The next blow fell on Washington's army in the middle of September 1776. After his brother Adm. Richard Howe attacked Manhattan with cannon from five frigates anchored in Kips Bay, Sir William landed four thousand elite troops at a spot less than one mile east of where the Empire State Building now stands. Jumping out of the flatboats that had brought them over from Brooklyn, the king's soldiers expected to meet a murderous fire from American artillery and muskets, but nary a shot whizzed their way. So where were the stalwart souls who had been ordered to stand up to the British?

George Washington experienced one of the great shocks of his life on that September 15. Near what today is Rockefeller Center, he encountered the troops that should have been defending Kips Bay. They were streaming north—in the opposite direction of the fighting—and discarding their weapons as they went. Washington shouted at the men to get hold of themselves and take up new positions in the cornfields on either side of the road. But his fury only added to their panic, which spread to the two brigades of Connecticut troops that had come up with the commander in chief to meet the British. Washington tore off his tricornered hat, slung it into the dust, and bellowed, "Good God, have I got such troops as those?"[8] He flailed away at the fleeing militiamen with his riding crop, and then he became inert. After a few minutes, a dazed and sullen Washington allowed one of his aides to grasp the bridle of his horse and guide him toward Harlem, the direction favored by his fleeing troops.

In June 1775, when the Continental Congress had appointed him to lead the American army against the king's forces, Washington foresaw that "some unlucky event . . . unfavorable to my reputation" might happen in the course of the war, and he asked all the congressmen to bear in mind that "I do not think myself equal to the command I am honored with."[9] Now his worst apprehensions had come true. In the middle of October, he decided to abandon Manhattan altogether. The Harlem River was safely crossed, but the rest of the retreat was a botched job, with the British nipping at Washington's heels and the men, who were losing faith in their commander, melting away by night and day. The debacle seemed endless, and in late November the remnants of the Continental Army, having crossed the Hudson and headed south into New Jersey, were retreating from Newark.

Although a division of three thousand Americans under Gen. Charles Lee still meandered through New Jersey, Washington had evacuated all of his own troops across the Delaware River into Pennsylvania by the second week in December. It looked as if the Royal Army would be in Philadelphia, the capital and nerve center of the colonies, within a few weeks. Fearing the "rude disorder of arms,"[10] as one delegate put it, the Continental Congress adjourned to Baltimore, and Washington wrote his brother Augustine to express his growing sense of isolation and doom: "No man, I believe, ever had a greater choice of difficulties and less means to extricate himself from them."[11] As 1776 approached its end, American hopes were all but extinguished.

The year of independence had begun on a very different note. At its start, most Americans had believed—or wanted to believe—that their real enemies were the king's advisers in Parliament. It was their hands, *not* His Majesty's, that were red with the blood shed at Lexington and Concord and Bunker Hill. George III had already written his first minister that "every means of distressing America must meet with my concurrence,"[12] but the colonists, with no access to the king's correspondence, preferred to look upon him as their wise and loving father.

When Martha Washington attended Christ Church in Cambridge, Massachusetts, on the first day of 1776, she requested that a special prayer be read during the service. It asked God to "look down with mercy upon His Majesty George III. Open his eyes and enlighten his understanding. . . . Remove far from him all wicked, corrupt men and evil councilors, that his throne may be established in justice and righteousness."[13] This kind of exhortation was still common in the colonies at the beginning of the year, and the emotional ties to royalty that it represented were still very strong.

But the appeals that the Continental Congress had addressed to George made matters no better, and each hostile act of the mother country caused the colonists to wonder if their monarch still wanted their love. A few days after Martha Washington's prayer was read, their sense of disenchantment soared. For on January 10, 1776, the speech George had given the previous October to open Parliament was finally published in Philadelphia, and Americans flew into a rage. Instead of denouncing the men and measures that had caused the colonies to revolt, the king had told Parliament that his subjects across the sea were making a "rebellious war . . . for the purpose of establishing an independent empire,"[14] and that Great Britain had no choice but to crush their insurrection. As they chewed on these bitter words, Americans were forced to see George as a traitor to the cause of liberty. They began to review their long list of complaints against Parliament—and they concluded that much of the blame belonged to an unkind, ungenerous, and unwise king.

Just then a political pamphlet entitled *Common Sense* appeared on the scene. Its timing could hardly have been better, for Thomas Paine's work was published anonymously in Philadelphia on the same day as the text of George's harsh message to Parliament. Within three months, twenty thousand copies were circulating through the colonies, and masses of people were pondering Paine's assertion that royal governments were vicious by their very nature: "In the early ages of the world . . . there were no kings, the consequence of which was there were no wars; it is the pride of kings which throws mankind into confusion."[15] In all probability, the first king was "nothing better than the principal ruffian of some restless gang."[16] As for the present line of British monarchs, it was said to spring from William the Conqueror, described by Paine as a "French bastard" who had led an army of bandits onto the island of the Anglo-Saxons.

England, in Paine's opinion, had no business governing America, for England belonged to Europe while America lay within its own world and belonged only to itself. Once upon a time, the connection between England and America might have been useful, but everything now pointed to the colonists' need to separate themselves from the mother country—who was not a real mother at all. For "even brutes do not devour their young nor savages make war upon their families."[17] Some Americans believed that all would be well if only George III were equipped with a new cabinet, but *Common Sense* argued otherwise: "If the whole continent must take up arms . . . it is scarcely worth our while to fight against a contemptible ministry only."[18]

Full independence would be the only justification for the struggle that lay ahead. Earlier, Paine had hoped for a compromise peace with England, but the deaths of the Minutemen in the spring of 1775 had caused him to curse the "hardened, sullen-tempered Pharaoh of England forever and disdain the wretch that, with the pretended title of father of his people, can unfeelingly hear of their slaughter and composedly sleep with their blood upon his soul."[19] George III had forfeited his right to rule over his subjects across the Atlantic; America's real king was the God who "reigns above and does not make havoc of mankind like the royal brute of Britain."[20]

When Loyalists read *Common Sense*, its indignation smelled like the brimstone of treason, and they vilified Paine as an enemy of order and decency. But most colonists found the pamphlet convincing, and the movement toward independence gained ground. On June 7, 1776, Richard Henry Lee of Virginia took the floor of the Continental Congress in Philadelphia to resolve "that these United Colonies are, and of right ought to be, free and independent states; that they are absolved from all allegiance to the British crown; and that all political connection between them and the state of Great Britain is, and ought to be, totally dissolved."[21] On June 11, the Congress appointed a committee to draft a statement declaring that the British subjugation of America was at an end. The result would be called the Declaration of Independence.

The ruin of the king's reputation is writ large in the Declaration, which portrays George III as the busiest and most vigorous of tyrants. The document's chief author, Thomas Jefferson, traced all acts of British officialdom in America back to their ultimate authority, and laid the blame squarely on the crown. According to Jefferson, the king desired not just to discipline his colonies, but to set up an "absolute despotism." It was a simple matter to show his policy in action. George had sent into America "swarms of officers to harass our people, and eat out their substance." He had protected his army of occupation "from punishment for any murders which they should commit on the inhabitants of these states. . . ." Worst of all, "he has plundered our seas, ravaged our coasts, burnt our towns, and destroyed the lives of our people." His aggressions drew in "the merciless Indian savages," who were urged to attack Americans "of all ages, sexes and conditions." How bad was the king of England? So bad as to be intolerable. He was, in short, "unfit to be the ruler of a free people."

Although the Declaration of Independence was a strong statement against British rule, it was not the only statement. In the general orders that George Washington issued to his army in the summer of 1775, the message of the Declaration had been neatly anticipated: "our unnatural parent is threatening us with destruction from every quarter."[22] Washington had used "parent" to mean "parent country," but it was easier to focus on a single offender, the king. Late in July 1776, the Rhode Island assembly joined the hue and cry by making it a crime to pray for the British monarch.

To the patriots' way of thinking, there was something peculiarly unjust about George III's actions. Americans had worked hard for what they possessed. They had wrested their land and their prosperity from thick forests and hardy undergrowth, from threatening weather and hostile Indians. Now, if the king prevailed, tax collectors would divert their wealth to the greedy and undeserving aristocracy that governed Great Britain. America's vital trade with the rest of the world would be cut off. The thirteen colonies would be saddled with a permanent British military establishment—loyal only to George III—whose guns could be turned as easily against the American people as against French or Spanish invaders of British North America. Religious freedom would be forced into the narrow channel of a church that would only be a transatlantic extension of the Church of England. The colonists perceived that the king and his cabinet wanted to stifle their independent spirit, and they rebelled as naturally as they breathed the air.

The success of British arms in the summer and fall of 1776 had redoubled the Americans' hatred of George III, for a weak enemy is merely scorned, while a strong one is despised to the same degree that he is feared. In the first installment of *The American Crisis,* published in December 1776, Thomas Paine wrote that "I cannot see on what grounds the king of Britain can look up to heaven for help against us; a common murderer, a highwayman, or a housebreaker has as good a pretense as he."[23] All over the United States, patriotic men and women took what consolation they could from Paine's defiance, and General Washington had his words read to the dispirited soldiers of the Continental Army.

Hoping to revitalize the Revolution, Washington prepared to go on the offensive. On Christmas night and into the early morning hours of December 26, he crossed the ice-filled Delaware River with 2,400 tattered troops and attacked three regiments of George III's Germans in Trenton, New Jersey. Many of his men stumbled along on feet that were wrapped in rags and bleeding in the snow, but they fell on the unsuspecting Germans like tigers and took most of them prisoner.

Lord Cornwallis recaptured Trenton on the second day of 1777, and once again the fate of the nation seemed to hang by a thread. Instead of tackling the larger British force, Washington stole a march on Cornwallis by slipping away on a frozen night toward Princeton. The Americans smashed several British regiments that got in their way and occupied the town, college campus and all. Then, hearing that Cornwallis was coming up behind them, Washington and his men moved on north toward Morristown. There they set up a new base of operations and were soon sallying forth to harass the enemy. General Howe, who had flattered himself that New Jersey was completely pacified, pulled back his troops until he controlled only a fifth of state.

The king blanched when he read about Trenton and Princeton in the battle reports, but his confidence in the final triumph of the British cause remained strong. His optimism was bolstered in the summer of 1777 when he heard that an American garrison had abandoned Fort Ticonderoga on Lake Champlain. George exclaimed to his queen that he had "beat them! Beat *all* the Americans!"[24] So it must have seemed, especially that September, when General Howe pushed Washington back during a series of fierce engagements in southeastern Pennsylvania and occupied Philadelphia a week after the Continental Congress had abandoned it for the second time. Howe thought this victory would mark the end of the war, and so did many Americans. But all of them were wrong.

The turning point in the Revolution came on October 17, 1777, when the American northern army forced Maj. Gen. John Burgoyne to surrender himself, six other British generals, and six thousand effectives near Saratoga in upstate New York. Benedict Arnold, who had yet to turn traitor, distinguished himself in the fighting but was badly wounded. The victory not only foiled the Royal Army's attempt to cut New England off from the rest of the United States; it also signaled to the world at large that America stood a good chance of prevailing over its former sovereign. Soon the French would get the message and come into the conflict on the American side, while Spain and Holland would also feel compelled to take up arms against Great Britain. With a much wider war in the offing, George III was obliged to rethink his strategy.

In January 1778, he wrote to Lord North that "it might perhaps be wise to strengthen the forces in Canada, the Floridas, and Nova Scotia; withdraw the rest from North America; and without loss of time employ them in attacking New Orleans and the French and Spanish West India possessions."[25] Although the king proposed to evacuate his armies from the United States, he was not suggesting that the war be abandoned: "We must at the same time continue destroying the trade and ports of the rebellious colonies. . . ."[26] In the end, thought the king, the Americans would be satisfied by the grant of a few local liberties, and then fall back into the orbit of the British Empire.

As it happened, the Royal Army did *not* leave the United States, but it did retreat from Philadelphia across New Jersey to New York, where its new commander, Gen. Sir Henry Clinton, studied alternate plans for defeating America. Clinton eventually decided to send out a seaborne expedition against Georgia and, by the beginning of 1779, the southern state was well on its way to being conquered. The lack of military progress elsewhere had introduced a strain of defeatism into His Majesty's government, but the king still refused to recognize American independence. In June 1779, he wrote to Lord North that he would endure any *personal* sacrifice to end the war, but he could not countenance the breakup of his empire.

Beset by woes and worries, George predicted that Britain would lose all her possessions in the West Indies if she made peace with America. And that loss, according to the king, would be only the beginning: "Ireland would soon follow the same plan and be a separate state. Then this island would be a poor island indeed, for . . . merchants would retire with their wealth to climates more to their advantage, and shoals of manufacturers would leave this country for the new Empire [i.e., the United States]."[27] These visions of a new world order gave George fits. Though overblown, his words do point to a unique characteristic of America's national experience: The thirteen original states already constituted a formidable world power, even in the first years of their independence.

Many Britons, scoffing at George's domino theory, believed that the biggest danger to the British state was their own executive government. On April 6, 1780, a committee of the House of Commons passed a motion declaring that "the power of the Crown has increased, is increasing, and ought to be diminished."[28] Lord North assured George that the criticism was aimed at the cabinet rather than his royal person, but the king must have thought otherwise. At least he could look down his royal nose at Parliament when he received word that Charleston, South Carolina, had fallen on May 12. Lord Cornwallis overran the rest of South Carolina before the end of August, and then he proceeded to invade North Carolina. It was beginning to look as though the British might reconquer Virginia and take undisputed control of Chesapeake Bay.

The war stretched out, enervating both sides. "I have almost ceased to hope," recorded George Washington at the end of 1780. "The country in general is in such a state of insensibility and indifference to its interest that I dare not flatter myself with any change for the better."[29] In April 1781, he wrote that "we are at the end of our tether, and now or never our deliverance must come."[30] Across the Atlantic, George III also felt the heat. He had developed a nasty temper but could still demonstrate a stubborn patience. Early in November 1781, he wrote that "I feel the justness of our cause; I put the greatest confidence . . . in the assistance of Divine Providence."[31]

Three weeks later, His Majesty heard of a devastating reversal. Word arrived from Virginia that Washington and his French allies had forced Cornwallis to surrender at Yorktown. The deliverance that Washington had almost ceased to expect had come from Louis XVI of France, who had ordered a major increase in military aid to the United States. That aid, in the form of twenty-eight ships and over seven thousand men, brought the British to their knees. Yet George III refused to despair of Divine Providence or admit defeat. He knew that his army's American adventure was over, but he still believed that the Royal Navy would humble the United States on the seas.

The king's incorrigible optimism failed to rally his nation, and on February 27, 1782—a day that George would never remember without bitterness—the House of Commons voted to end the fighting. Early in March its members declared that any diehard supporter of the war would be considered an enemy of the realm—a resolution that undoubtedly curtailed the king's freedom of speech. Everyone could see that George had suffered a great fall; even his servants looked upon him with pity.

Lord North had to acknowledge that the battle, and with it his long ministry, was finally over. He made way for Lord Rockingham while George III drew up an instrument of abdication. In it the king expressed his regret that "he can be of no further utility to his native country, which drives him to the painful step of quitting it forever."[32] It seems that George really was on the verge of giving up his throne and retiring to his ancestral duchy in Germany. In his stead he would offer Britons the Prince of Wales, who at the age of nineteen was already a spendthrift and a scoundrel.

The historical record is unclear, but perhaps it was the prospect of his foolish son's coronation that decided the king against abdicating. Instead, he swallowed his pride and accepted ministers that he loathed. His power was reduced, and he retaliated by refusing to guide his cabinet's work on peace negotiations with America. Whenever he was closeted with his advisers, George showed a scowling face and acted out little melodramas of self-pity. He was, in short, a bad loser, but his mood is understandable. Thirty-six years old when Paul Revere took his famous ride, George had turned forty-three by the time Cornwallis surrendered at Yorktown. He had devoted what might have been the best years of his life to fighting the rebels of America, and his only reward was failure, a failure of overwhelming proportions. He never really reconciled himself to the loss of the colonies, although he did comment to Lord Shelburne that Great Britain was probably better off without America, since "knavery seems to be so much the striking feature of its inhabitants. . . ."[33]

In February 1783, the Treaty of Paris took effect, giving the United States full recognition of her status as an independent nation, and in November the last British soldiers were withdrawn from New York. John Adams, one of the commissioners who negotiated the peace treaty, nurtured a strong desire to become the first U.S. ambassador to the kingdom of George III. Adams had read plenty of denunciations of himself in the British press, where he was portrayed as a mad-dog revolutionary, and he suspected that he would have been hanged by His Majesty's government if the American cause had failed. Still, he was triumphant when his supporters in the Congress secured him the job of ambassador.

Adams arrived in London to take up his duties in May 1785. He soon noticed an editorial in an English newspaper that exclaimed, "An ambassador from America! Good heavens, what a sound!"[34] There were rumors that the furious king would never allow Adams to appear at court, but they proved to be false. Abigail Adams had come to London with her husband, and she helped him prepare to meet his erstwhile enemy. She saw that John's wig was dressed and powdered with particular care, and that his silk stockings were free from runs. When all was ready, the visibly nervous ambassador strapped on his sword and sash, gave Abigail a kiss, and entered the carriage that would take him to the Court of St. James's in the middle of London.

Alighting at the palace, he was escorted into an elegant room (the king's "closet") by Lord Carmarthen, the foreign secretary. There he confronted His Majesty. Adams recited a polite speech that he had composed for the occasion, and George III expressed his approval of the ambassador's "proper" language. Then, in a trembling voice, the king added, "I will be very frank with you. I was the last to consent to the separation. But the separation having been made, and having become inevitable, I have always said—as I say now—that I would be the first to meet the friendship of the United States as an independent power."[35] Satisfied with the reply, Adams exchanged a few more words with his former sovereign and bowed himself out of the room.

The United States no longer claimed a great share of the king's attention; his principal enemies now were the liberal politicians in the House of Commons. George stopped sulking, took back up the cudgels, and gave as good as he got in his continuing struggle with Parliament. When his Machiavellian maneuvers made William Pitt the Younger first minister in December 1783, the king found himself in a position to recover most of the power he had lost during the American disaster.

Thereafter the machinery of royal government hummed along until George fell ill in the late spring of 1788. His first symptoms appeared on June 11. Striken with violent spasms in his abdomen, the king reported that he was "forced to take to my bed, as the only tolerable posture I could find."[36] He expected the attack to pass quickly, but the pain came and went for several weeks. On October 17, his complaints returned in a far more threatening form. He was sore all over, and experienced such pain in his midsection that he found it hard to breathe. In the throes of a mysterious fever, he flushed and sweated while his heart raced; all the strength went out of his limbs.

The crisis came at Windsor Castle on November 9, when the king passed from convulsions into a coma. His pulse could scarcely be detected, and George III was about as ill as a fifty-year-old man can be without dying. By November 12, the stubborn and sober moralist who wore the British crown had become, as his two eldest sons agreed, "a compleat lunatic."[37] Arising from his stupor with a vengeance, he talked nonsense for twenty hours at a stretch. He claimed that he had seen Germany in a telescope, and that London had disappeared beneath a flood, and that all marriages, including his own, would soon be dissolved. The king assaulted one of his pages, and it was rumored around the kingdom that George and the Prince of Wales had come to blows in the sickroom. One report claimed that the prince, resplendent in his fanciest uniform, was sitting up nights, waiting in vain for his father to stop raving and breathe his last.

A "mad-doctor" named Francis Willis was brought to the royal chambers and prescribed that George be put into a straitjacket. His Majesty's government could not function indefinitely with a madman on the throne, and the great question of the day was whether the king should be declared mentally incompetent and replaced by the prince. Prime Minister Pitt stalled for three months, hoping that George would recover his health and his reason. But as the weeks passed, the king's enemies in Parliament began to clamor for the prince's elevation, and the House of Commons dissolved into a chaos of partisanship. Since Dr. Willis's straitjacket seemed to be working no miracles, Pitt was forced to agree in January 1789 that most of the monarch's powers be transferred to the Prince of Wales, who would then be called the Prince Regent.

To the surprise of one and all, February brought a striking improvement in George's mental health. On the third—the day before Washington was elected president of the United States—the convalescent king was allowed to shave himself for the first time in three months. When his ability to concentrate returned, he read Shakespeare and Pope, played the flute, and translated Cicero from the Latin. The House of Lords, which had been poised to pass the Regency Bill, was told by the Lord Chancellor that the king was once again fit to rule. It had been a close-run thing. Restored to sanity, George III declared that "no power on earth" would have persuaded him to resume the throne if a regency had been created.

The medical profession has never been able to agree on a diagnosis of George III's illness, but there is little controversy about the number of his attacks. In 1801 and 1804, he experienced the same symptoms for shorter periods. The final act was an extended period of mental derangement that stretched from 1810 to George's death. But it was not until February 6, 1811, that the Prince of Wales stood up before a multitude of Britain's most illustrious men and swore to faithfully execute the office of regent. The Lord Chancellor, the Archbishop of Canterbury, and a hundred others knelt to kiss the prince's hand. The mad old king was finally out of the way, the Regency had finally begun.

Henceforth, George III would be locked up in a room that overlooked the north terrace of Windsor Castle. He had gone blind in 1805 or 1806, but there were a few things that he could still do. He spent the endless hours stroking his long white beard and playing the harpsichord and talking with ghosts. He jabbered away with imaginary companions who ranged from Alexander the Great to Frederick the Great, but he could no longer communicate with real people—not even Queen Charlotte, his wife of over fifty years. In 1819, the poet Percy Bysshe Shelley called him "old, mad, blind, despised, and dying." That George was old and mad and blind and dying is perfectly true, but was he despised?

There is evidence that he was not. When the Regency began in 1811, Britons knew that their monarch was incapacitated, but they were spared the humiliating details, and many of them still found it natural to admire him. At a time when middle-class values were growing ever stronger, he was celebrated for being faithful to his wife and loving to his large family (thirteen of his fifteen children grew to adulthood). George's honorable ways had put the Prince Regent's racy life-style to shame.

Strange as it may seem, the king's popularity actually grew as he declined into madness and senility. The process had begun much earlier. The beheading of Louis XVI of France in 1793 had given Britons a sense of the vulnerability of their own monarchy, and because George kept recovering from life-threatening illnesses, he appeared even more human—but heroic, too. The American fiasco that he presided over seemed far away and long ago; the great thing now was for the Royal Navy and Army to protect British liberties from that godless and bloodthirsty tribe of revolutionaries across the English Channel. When Britain went to war with France in the year of Louis XVI's execution, English nationalists roared like lions, and revering His Majesty became an obvious and convincing way to show support for a beleaguered Britain.

George III died on January 29, 1820, and went to an honored rest. His remains lie in the Royal Vault beneath the floor of St. George's Chapel at Windsor Castle, the fifteenth-century church that the king used to call "the cathedral." With him are his sons George IV and William IV, as well as Queen Charlotte; nearby are Henry VIII, Charles I, Edward VII. A hundred feet away is the tomb of George VI, father to the present queen. When that lady meets her end, she will probably rest close to her direct ancestor, George III, and the other silent monarchs of St. George's Chapel.

It is assumed that Prince Charles will ascend the throne as Charles III and, when he does, he will probably meditate on his forefather George III. For the two of them share a good many traits. Since England has produced so few brainy monarchs during the last two hundred years, scholarly habits are among the more notable things that George and Charles have in common. In 1972, the Prince of Wales even ventured to write an essay in defense of George, which was published as a foreword to John Brooke's biography of the king.

Charles announced that his "interest was aroused in King George III as a result of reading a book and several pamphlets on the subject of his so-called insanity."[38] Finding much to praise and little to criticize in his ancestor, Charles concluded that George suffered from a physical disease, not a psychiatric illness. It was time, declared the Prince, "that the veil of obscurity stifling the King's true personality, known and loved by his contemporaries, should be lifted."[39] Charles then proceeded to present George as a "natural and thoroughly civilized country gentleman" whose plain manners and unpretentious ways "won him immense popularity."[40] George was also, as we learn, a selfless servant of the British political system who had looked on in contentment as the power of the prime minister increased and his own power dwindled.

Somehow the argument fails to convince. Even less compelling is Charles's assertion that George would have dazzled America with his dignified presence if he had only been able to visit the colonies. Documents like the Declaration of Independence show that revolutionary America would have been more likely to tar and feather the king than greet him on bended knee. Nor would the situation have changed in the later years of George's life. Americans and Britons remained at odds for many decades after the Revolution, and events like the British burning of the White House (then called the President's House) and the Capitol building in August 1814 did little to promote understanding.

Even as late as 1895, Americans and their former masters stared at each other across the Atlantic with fear and distrust. At that time they were entangled in a crisis over—of all things—the borders of Venezuela, and both sides buzzed with rumors of war. It was only the rise of first German and then Soviet power that pushed the two countries into each other's reluctant arms and allowed them to rejoice, at long last, in their common heritage. But neither George III nor his royal dignity has anything to do with Anglo-American friendship. Whatever Prince Charles would like to believe, Americans must remember their last king as a stubborn father whom they were destined to outgrow.

3

A Pasha and His Pirates

Despite the political and personal shortcomings of George III, the warships of the Royal Navy long protected American merchantmen on the high seas. But an independent United States had to do the job for herself, and the creation of the U.S. Navy marked the modest, uncertain beginning of America's push to create a new world order. One of the first instruments of this order, the USS *Philadelphia*, was a fearsome frigate commanded by a young captain named William Bainbridge. It left U.S. waters with a crew of over three hundred officers and men in the summer of 1803 to help suppress the Barbary pirates of North Africa. The voyage was luckless, for instead of blockading the Moslem shore, the *Philadelphia* became stranded on its shoals. This calamity occurred within four miles of Tripoli on October 31.

A capital city then as now, Tripoli in the early nineteenth century controlled much of the territory that lies within modern Libya's borders, but its real business was done in the Mediterranean. Since the Tripolitans habitually preyed on the shipping of much more powerful nations, they were always ready to defend themselves against seaborne attack, and the stranded *Philadelphia* was soon face-to-face with a small fleet of hostile gunboats that sallied forth from Tripoli's harbor. Death seemed to be staring the Americans in the face. Captain Bainbridge decided to lighten the ship, force her off the shoal, and slip back out into blue water. The crew obeyed his orders with frantic zeal.

One member, Marine Corps private William Ray of Dutchess County, New York, recorded that most of the cannon were heaved overboard—to no avail. Meanwhile, shots from the Moslem gunboats—there were nine of them now—passed through the rigging of the stranded ship, which was listing heavily to port. The worst damage was done by the Americans themselves when they cut away the foremast, yet even that sacrifice failed to free the ship. After they had labored for four back-wrenching hours, the *Philadelphia* was still stuck on the sand, and Bainbridge felt compelled to surrender. In the melodramatic words of Private Ray, "the Eagle of America fell a prey to the vultures of Barbary—the flag was struck!"[1] Steps were taken to scuttle the ship, but they proved ineffective, and the local pasha's windfall included not only a crowd of hostages but also a frigate that could soon be restored to fighting trim.

When word of the disaster got about, it excited a tremendous amount of controversy. James L. Cathcart, former U.S. consul in Tripoli, wrote that the crew had missed a perfect opportunity to immortalize themselves: "How glorious it would have been to have perish'd with the ship. . . . Humanity recoils at the idea of launching so many souls into eternity . . . [but] our national honor & pride demand[ed] the sacrifice."[2] Pondering his fate as a prisoner in Tripoli, Captain Bainbridge enunciated a very different point of view: "Some fanatics may say that blowing up the ship would have been the proper result. I thought such conduct would not stand acquitted before God or man, and I never presumed to think I had the liberty of putting to death 306 souls because they were placed under my command."[3]

The question of how captain and crew should have responded to their dilemma was complicated, but the upshot of the affair was simple enough: Captain Bainbridge and Private Ray and all of their comrades were in the hands of a hostile power. After surrendering, they were stripped nearly naked. Taken ashore, they were paraded, as Ray put it, into the "dreadful presence of his exalted majesty,"[4] the black-bearded, potbellied prince of Tripoli, Yusuf Pasha. Around this enthroned ruler seemed to swirl a riot of mosaics and marble, velvet and porcelain, silk and silver. In the midst of it all were his steady, dark, and delighted eyes. Golden highlights glittered in his long blue robe, and the white turban that sat upon his head was thick with ribbons. Yusuf's sash, sparkling with diamonds, harbored two gilded pistols that matched his gilded scimitar.

Eventually, Yusuf finished inspecting his prisoners, and the officers were taken away to comfortable quarters in a house formerly used by the American consul. The men received less courteous treatment. They were marched from the audience hall and lodged, as Ray recounted, in a "dreary, filthy apartment of the castle, where there was scarcely room for us to turn round."[5] It was the first of many dismal accommodations that Ray and his fellow enlisted men would inhabit during their long imprisonment. Soon they were visited by an old sorceress. Striking her staff on the pavement, she shrieked with joy over the intimidated sailors and pressed into the crowd, clutching first one man and then another. The sorceress looked upon their presence as a personal triumph, for she had convinced herself—and Yusuf Pasha—that her incantations had caused the *Philadelphia* to run aground.

Hardly a day of captivity had passed before the enlisted men were rounded up and put to work. Carrying sacks of grain and loads of lumber, they labored on empty stomachs until hunger, as Ray testified, "began to corrode our vitals."[6] Lacking blankets, they were forced to sleep on the cold, hard dampness of the pebbly prison floor. When food did come, it was usually in the form of small loaves of musty bread, one to a man. Their jailers treated them to frequent doses of a torture known as the bastinado. After being shoved onto his stomach, the victim would have his ankles bound tightly together. Then, while one jailer sat on his back, two others would use heavy cudgels to beat the soles of his feet until they bled.

The purpose of all this mistreatment was not to kill the crew of the *Philadelphia*, and in fact, only five of them perished during their captivity. For Yusuf was keenly aware of how valuable his hostages might turn out to be. The situation was definitely promising. In 1796, the Washington administration had responded to his demands for protection money with $56,486, and tribute worth another $24,000 arrived in 1799, while John Adams was president. These sums were not enough to secure U.S. shipping from the depredations of Yusuf's corsairs. In 1802, for instance, one of the pasha's galleys captured the American merchant brig *Franklin* off Spain. Brought back to Tripoli, the ship's master, Andrew Morris, and four of his crewmen were held for ransom. Yusuf received $1,000 for each of the captives. And now there were 306 new ones to cash in.

Yusuf's family, the Karamanlis, had held sway in Tripoli for almost a hundred years. Of Arab and Berber descent, they had begun by seizing the city from the Turks and then carved out a North African principality that extended from Tunisia to Egypt. Yusuf entered history in the third generation after the founding of the dynasty. Born five years before the outbreak of the American Revolution, he was the youngest of three sons and, in the normal course of events, would never have become pasha. However, he was determined that events *not* run a normal course. At sixteen years of age, he announced that neither of his older brothers would enjoy the succession. The rightful heir, Hassan Karamanli, had laughed at his little brother's ambitions, but four years later he discovered the enormity of his error.

The two brothers met for the last time in their mother's apartment, and Yusuf had asked for a copy of the Koran, the better (as he claimed) to swear fealty to Hassan. Before the meeting, Yusuf's attendants had been ordered to unveil something far more lethal than the holy book of Islam when he held out his hands: a brace of loaded pistols. They obeyed their orders and out the pistols came. Before Hassan could defend himself there were two explosions and the stench of gunpowder. Hit twice, Hassan looked up from the floor and asked his mother if she had supported this treachery. Before she could answer, Yusuf's attendants fell upon Hassan and stabbed him to death. The new heir apparent then strolled toward the banqueting hall.

A Turkish pirate by the name of Ali ben-Zool took advantage of the confusion to capture Tripoli in 1793, causing Yusuf's father to flee to Tunis, where he died two years later. Never one to give in without a fight, Yusuf joined forces with Hamet Karamanli, his remaining brother, and drove ben-Zool away. He then turned on Hamet, who would later describe his fate: "After the death of my father, I became the lawful [pasha] of Tripoli. I continued so only five months when one unfortunate day [Yusuf] advised me to go pleasuring in the country, but I was no sooner out of the gates of the city than he shut them against me and I was obliged to go to Tunis, where I remained seven long years."[7]

Predictably, Yusuf Pasha proved to be a suspicious ruler. He was always ready to detect a slight or imagine a plot, and his favorite form of conversation was the tirade. But his luck held, and despite Hamet's attempts to assert his own right to the throne, Yusuf enjoyed his reign. He was supposedly a vassal of the Ottoman emperor in Istanbul, but that august personage was content to share Tripoli's revenues while letting Yusuf order his own affairs. Compared to a European monarch, Yusuf Pasha was no grand eminence, but he wasn't doing that badly. With a power that was very nearly absolute, he ruled a mixed population of Arabs, Moors, Turks, Berbers, Jews, Greeks, and Maltese whose numbers have been estimated at up to one million.

In Tripoli itself lived some thirty thousand souls. With its white walls and minarets and palm trees, Yusuf's capital was situated on a small peninsula and was completely enclosed by ancient fortifications. It had three gates that were opened at first light and closed at dusk. The roofs of its houses were flat and surrounded by ledges that helped catch rainwater and channel it into cisterns. When the skies were clear, as was usually the case, the roofs blossomed with the prayer rugs of a people who prostrated themselves toward Mecca five times each day. In spite of their Islamic piety, the Tripolitans had a horror of the evil eye, which they warded off with amulets containing verses from the Koran or dollops of gunpowder.

At the northeast corner of the town stood Yusuf's castle, resting on foundations that were over a millennium old. Every morning at ten o'clock the pasha showed himself to his council, who would begin to shout hosannas as soon as they caught sight of his face. Yusuf liked to gaze out over his domain from the high, open gallery of his castle, where—as Private Ray had seen—he was "surrounded by his fawning parasites. . . . From his lofty eminence the tumid potentate looks down on the groveling multitude, like fictitious Jove from the summit of Olympus. . . ."[8] Descending through labyrinthine passages to ground level, Yusuf would pass under a portal that was inscribed in Arabic characters ("Sacred to Allah and Mohammed His Prophet") and enter the rich, gilded interior of the royal mosque. Elsewhere in his castle he could visit his main arsenal, his mint, or his harem. When the city was under attack he could take refuge in a bombproof cellar.

The life of a pirate prince, then, did have its charms. Yusuf and the other buccaneers of Barbary were the inheritors of an extremely profitable racket, for their kind had been plundering European ships and extorting money from European countries regularly since the sixteenth century. By the end of the eighteenth, Britain's Royal Navy—the largest in the world—might have annihilated the pirates, but His Majesty's government was so preoccupied with revolutionary France that it lacked the extra resources to clean up the Mediterranean. So the pirates went on about their business.

For Yusuf in Tripoli and his fellow pashas in Algiers, Tunis, and Morocco, there were two kinds of foreign nations: Islamic and infidel. Among the infidels were those who paid tribute and those who refused. The pashas' modus operandi was to demand ever higher sums from the tribute payers and to make war on the nonpayers. The problem, and its partial solution, was best summarized by Thomas Jefferson: "Their system is a war of little expense to them, which must put the great nations to a greater expense than the presents which would buy it off. Yet nothing but the warring on them at times will keep the demand of presents within bounds."[9]

In 1792, a petition addressed to all the members of Congress reached Philadelphia (then the nation's capital) from Algiers. The petitioners were a group of American sailors who had been languishing in captivity since 1785. Their words evoked a life of gloom:

> Owing to the melancholy situation to which we are reduced, one of us, James Hormet, has been deprived of his senses and confined in a dungeon; the rest remain destitute of almost all the necessities of life. . . . [W]e remain employed in the most laborious work, far distant from our friends, families and connections, without any real prospect of ever seeing them more.[10]

Congress appropriated money for their ransom, but the difficulty of negotiating with the Algerines delayed the prisoners' homecoming until 1797. In the meantime, steps had been taken in Philadelphia to develop better options for dealing with the potentates.

In fact, the desire to destroy the Barbary pirates is what brought the U.S. Navy into existence. In March 1794, President Washington had been authorized by Congress to acquire six frigates, and construction of several ships soon began. Progress on the vessels was slow, and some influential congressmen wanted it to stop altogether, since they opposed the high cost of the program and saw seapower as a British vice. James Madison, then serving in the House of Representatives, held that the money required for building a blue-water navy "would be immense, and there [is] no certainty of reaping any benefit from it."[11] Washington expressed the opposite point of view in December 1796 when he sent his annual message to Congress. The president stated that U.S. commerce on the oceans of the world would not be respected without

> a naval force, organized and ready to vindicate it from insult or aggression. This may even prevent the necessity of going to war. . . . [O]ur trade to the Mediterranean, without a protecting force, will always be insecure. . . . These considerations invite the United States to look to the means, and to set about the gradual creation of a navy.[12]

Slowly but surely, the supporters of a fighting fleet prevailed over the opposition. Benjamin Stoddert, the first secretary of the navy, joined President

John Adams' cabinet in 1798, and the pace of shipbuilding picked up. Pitted against French privateers in the Caribbean, the new navy fought well, but the first U.S. man-of-war did not enter the Mediterranean until September 1800—and its mission had nothing to do with defiance. In that month and year the frigate *George Washington* was engaged in carrying tribute from the United States to Algiers.

The same Captain Bainbridge who would lose the *Philadelphia* three years later was in command of this humiliating mission. Bainbridge turned the loot over to the Moslems and made haste to sail away, but before he could go he was told that the ruler of Algiers had a further use for his ship. The Algerine ambassador to the court of the Ottoman emperor was expected in Istanbul, and it was the Americans' job to see that he got there. Bainbridge counted his guns, compared them with the far greater number of cannons on the walls of Algiers, and decided to do as he was told. The *George Washington's* new manifest recorded the extent of his burden: "Ambassador & suite, 100; negro men, women & children, 100; 4 horses, 150 sheep, 25 horned cattle, 4 lions, 4 tigers, 4 antelopes, 12 parrots; funds & regalia amounting to nearly one million of dollars."[13] Bainbridge enjoyed a small revenge by changing course when the Moslems tried to pray toward Mecca.

By the time Thomas Jefferson took the oath of office in March 1801, the United States had paid nearly $2 million into the hands of the Barbary potentates. The drain on the national treasury—and the affront to national pride—was getting to be a very old story. What is more, the money failed to slack Yusuf Pasha's greed. In May, he decided to increase his take of America's wealth by declaring war on the United States. As was customary on such occasions, Yusuf had the flagpole in front of the U.S. consulate in Tripoli chopped down to emphasize his hostility.

The pasha apparently thought of the United States as a peaceful little federation of coastal villages that was even less powerful than his own principality of towns and oases. He liked to boast that, with three ships like the *Philadelphia*, he would throw a blockade around the United States that would make the Jefferson administration sue for peace. The reality was rather different. Although frugal with military and naval expenditures in 1803, the United States had enough resources to make life miserable for Yusuf. But there was no overwhelming sense of mission in the nation's capital, now located on the Potomac; the amount of trade being lost was just not large enough to warrant a full-scale war against the pirates.

So for months the conflict ran on in a random sort of way. The Mediterranean was a complicated theater of operations with the predatory ships of the four Barbary states in evidence as well as those of a number of European sea powers, including Great Britain, France, Spain, Portugal, Sweden, Denmark, and Holland—all of which, at one time or another, had paid ransom money or tribute to the buccaneers. Jefferson saw to it that, in the midst of all this traffic, a squadron of U.S. warships began to operate in the Mediterranean, but their activities were generally confined to convoy duty, with occasional attempts to blockade Tripoli, and they were slow to take the offensive.

In their Tripolitan captivity, the *Philadelphia*'s crew continued to suffer abuse. On December 22, 1803, as Private Ray tells it, half of them

> were sent to raise an old wreck deeply buried in the sand, near the beach, eastward from the town. It was now the coldest season of the year; we were almost naked, and were driven into the water up to our armpits. We had to shovel the sand from the bottom of the water, and carry it in basket to the banks.

From dawn until two o'clock in the afternoon, the prisoners labored in the frigid waves of the wintry Mediterranean, and the first food of the day, some bits of bread, was not given to them until the afternoon. Then, "we were driven again into the water, and kept there until sunset."[14] Worst of all, no relief was in sight. The future stretched out like an endless rack of torture.

Not all of the Americans in the sphere of Barbary power were faring so miserably. Private Ray would have been consoled had he known that on December 23—the day after his long spell of wet work—Edward Preble, captain and commodore of the U.S. Mediterranean Squadron, and Lt. Stephen Decatur, commanding the U.S. schooner *Enterprise,* had captured one of the vessels that had attacked the stranded *Philadelphia* off Tripoli. This was the *Mastico,* originally a French gunboat, which the Americans recommissioned for their own service under the name *Intrepid.*

An ingenious, energetic, irascible officer in his mid-forties, Preble had begun hatching a plan to avenge the *Philadelphia* as soon as he learned of her loss. As long as the ship remained in the possession of the pasha, she represented a potent weapon that might be turned against American shipping. The great coup would have been to recapture the ship, but Preble thought it too risky to try. What absolutely had to be avoided was another fiasco like the original one, so Preble decided to take the ship out of service altogether. The frigate was to be destroyed.

Even that mission would be dangerous, for the *Philadelphia* lay at anchor under the guns of the pasha's castle and was occupied by an alert force of his soldiery. But here the ketch *Intrepid* could be useful. Seeing it approach their harbor, the Tripolitans would probably mistake it for a friendly vessel, and it might get near the captured frigate without arousing suspicion. It was worth a try, and when Preble discussed the possibility with Lieutenant Decatur, whose father had commanded the *Philadelphia* in its better days, the young officer begged to lead the raid.

Permission was granted, and Decatur was joined by sixty-seven volunteers from his regular command, as well as five midshipmen from another vessel. On February 3, 1804, he and his crew left the U.S. base of operations in Syracuse, Sicily, and headed for Tripoli. Preble had given Decatur clear instructions: "You will provide all the necessary combustibles. . . . Be sure and set fire in the gun-room berths, cockpit, storerooms forward, and berths on the berth deck.

After the ship is well on fire, point two of the 18 pounders, shotted, down the main hatch and blow her bottom out."[15]

A gale postponed the mission for days, but finally, on February 16, while the U.S. brig *Siren* waited offshore to cover her retreat, the *Intrepid* sailed alone at nightfall into Tripoli harbor. The men on deck, including Decatur, were dressed as Maltese sailors, and they pretended to be innocent traders who had lost their anchor in the stormy seas and needed to tie up to the *Philadelphia* for the night. The guards on the frigate were momentarily fooled. By the time they understood what was happening, Decatur and his men had climbed aboard. In the hand-to-hand fighting that followed, a score of Tripolitans were killed, but most of them escaped by plunging overboard.

Decatur's men were well drilled, and within twenty minutes they had set fire to the ship, reboarded the *Intrepid*, and, under fire from the pasha's shore batteries, begun their retreat from the harbor. As they fled, they could see their work take effect. Charles Morris, one of the midshipmen with Decatur, described the conflagration in his journal: "The appearance of the ship was indeed magnificent. The flames in the interior illuminated her ports and, ascending her rigging and masts, formed columns of fire. . . . [T]he occasional discharge of her guns gave an idea of some directing spirit within her."[16] All this happened, as Decatur noted, within half a gunshot of the pasha's castle. The *Philadelphia* soon burned free of her cables and, blazing furiously, drifted onto the shore, where she blew up in a spectacular pyrotechnic display. Lord Nelson is said to have called Decatur's mission "the most bold and daring act of the age."[17]

There was to be a sequel—several sequels—for Preble believed that "those barbarians" in Tripoli would "not be disposed to make peace with us until they feel sensible of our ability and determination to distress them by every possible means."[18] Returning to action with six of his ships, Preble closed a tight blockade around Tripoli. Then he sent one of his lieutenants to offer the pasha cash for freeing the crew of the *Philadelphia*. But Preble's offer was far, far below the going rate for hostages, and Yusuf, who felt genuinely insulted, rejected it out of hand. Commodore Preble then temporarily lifted the blockade, ordering most of his squadron back to Sicily to prepare for something special.

On July 25, 1804, when he reassembled his force near Tripoli, there were three brigs, three schooners, six gunboats, two mortarboats, a storeship, and, as Preble's flagship, a frigate destined to become very famous, the USS *Constitution*. The commodore had planned to attack on July 28, but a gale blew up from the northeast, threatening to beach his entire fleet, and he ordered all ships to stand out to sea. It was August 3 before the ships were back in position and everything was again in readiness.

Tripoli's defenses made it a difficult target. According to Private Ray, the town was "surrounded by entrenchments and enclosed by a wall between 20 and 30 feet in height, thick, firm and impregnable; flanked by forts, planted with heavy artillery, and formidable hosts of savage barbarians."[19] The pasha could bring 115 cannon to bear on his attackers from the shore, and his flotilla of 19 gunboats, 2 galleys, 2 schooners, and a brig mounted many more. Nevertheless, the Tripolitans did not welcome the firepower of the U.S. fleet. Ray recounts how, on August 3, some of his comrades "who had been at work on the fortifications, came running in and informed us that the whole coast was lined with our shipping. The whole town was in an uproar, every Turk [that is, Moslem] had his musket and other weapons, and wild disorder rang through every arch."[20]

Preble's men went to work with a will. In an action that lasted for more than two hours, three Tripolitan gunboats were captured, several more were raked by cannon fire, and the town was bombarded with mortars. When Preble took his flagship in to silence the pasha's batteries, the *Constitution* was struck by nine cannon balls, and the commodore himself was nearly felled when an enemy shot smashed against a 24-pounder on the quarterdeck, disintegrating into deadly shrapnel. The captives in the town, as Ray would record, had their own problems: "During the action our men were taken out of the prison several times to carry powder and shot from the magazine in the castle to the forts, and were almost beaten to death—stoned and cudgeled by every Turk in the streets."[21]

Although Preble lacked the ships and men to take the town by storm, he hoped that repeated attacks would bring the pasha to terms. Yusuf might become so intimidated that he would free the officers and crew of the *Philadelphia* with little or no compensation; he might also undertake to stop all piratical raids on American merchantmen. Whatever could be achieved by force, Preble was determined to achieve it. He continued his assaults on Tripoli through the rest of August.

On the morning of August 28, Preble took the *Constitution* in close to the harbor. After sinking a Tripolitan gunboat he hove to and blasted the pasha's fortifications with nine broadsides. Ironically, one of the casualties that resulted was the chapfallen captive, Captain Bainbridge. A 24-pound shot from one of the *Constitution*'s guns sailed into his room and almost pulped his head. His junior officers had to extricate Bainbridge from a heap of debris, but when they did they found that his only injury was a minor one to his ankle. In the meantime, Preble's flagship was being raked by the pasha's guns, and when the frigate drew off, her hull was full of the enemy's grapeshot.

As his masterstroke against Tripoli, Preble organized a final mission for the *Intrepid*. He ordered his carpenters to build a compartment in the vessel's hold and had it filled with 5 tons of black powder; on the deck overhead were placed 150 explosive shells and a heap of scrap iron. The huge charge was connected to fuses that would burn for eleven minutes. After dark on September 3, a crew of three officers and ten seamen took the *Intrepid* in toward the harbor, towing a pair of rowboats in which they hoped to escape. The thirteen went aboard the floating bomb in the knowledge that a more perilous mission could scarcely be imagined. Their plan was to set the ship ablaze and then abandon her to wreck havoc among the Tripolitans. If all went well, the explosion would sink most of the enemy's gunboats, severely damage the castle, and terrorize Yusuf into signing a treaty of peace.

Something went amiss. The Tripolitans spotted the *Intrepid* looming out of the darkness and opened fire on her. With all hands still aboard, she blew up just as she was entering the harbor—well short of her objectives. Jonathan Cowdry, the captive surgeon's mate of the *Philadelphia*, observed the tragedy from the town and recorded its aftermath: "The effect of the explosion awed the [Tripolitan] batteries into profound silence. . . . Not a gun was afterwards fired for the night. The shrieks of the inhabitants informed us that the town was thrown into the greatest terror and consternation by the explosion of the magazine, and the bursting and falling of shells in all directions."[22] If the *Intrepid* had exploded just under the walls of his castle, it might have spelled the pasha's doom. Yusuf recognized that fact and ordered a ceremony of thanksgiving and deliverance to be held in his mosque.

On September 10, Preble turned his command over to Commodore Samuel Barron. In a report to the secretary of the navy, he expressed his regret "that it has not been in my power, consistent with the interest and expectation of our country, to liberate Captain Bainbridge and the unfortunate officers and crew of the *Philadelphia*."[23] But Preble's replacement was due to Barron's seniority; it was not a judgment on the squadron's performance under his command. That judgment would come in March 1805, when Congress voted to award Preble a gold medal. A few weeks before, President Jefferson had commended "the energy and judgment displayed by this excellent officer through the whole course of the service lately confided to him."[24]

Yet something more was needed to defeat the pasha: more mobility and more surprise. The man who sought to bring these qualities into the U.S. war against Yusuf was William Eaton, an aggressive and quick-tempered diplomat in his late thirties with a long and frustrating experience of trying to deal with the Barbary potentates. Eaton, who had soldiered against the British during the Revolution, had come back to Washington, D.C., from North Africa in the spring of 1803 with a plan. His advice to Jefferson's cabinet was to begin rolling up Yusuf's flank by sending an expeditionary force from Egypt to the pasha's cities in what is now northeastern Libya.

Eaton believed that peace would never prevail unless Yusuf were removed from the throne and replaced by Hamet Karamanli, his older brother. Hamet had already made one attempt to overthrow Yusuf, and he appeared eager to try again. The hope was that Eaton and Hamet might get an army all the way across the eastern desert to Tripoli itself, where a joint attack on Yusuf could then be launched from land and sea.

Looking on Eaton's plan with favor, Jefferson appointed him "United States Navy Agent for the Several Barbary Regencies."[25] In November 1804, Eaton traveled to Egypt in hopes of meeting with Hamet, with whom he had held discussions in Tunisia. The pretender was a hard man to track down; it wasn't until February 1805 that the two finally established contact. After complex negotiations through interpreters, they signed a treaty of alliance between the United States of America and "the legitimate sovereign of the kingdom of Tripoli" that guaranteed "a firm and perpetual peace." Hamet was promised America's "utmost exertions"[26] toward removing his brother from power, and in his turn he promised to release all the American hostages as soon as he entered Tripoli. In a secret provision, Hamet agreed to deliver up his brother to the Americans, who would hold Yusuf indefinitely as *their* hostage. In order to speed the advent of his reign, Hamlet agreed to make Eaton, who liked to wear a cocked hat with a fancy plume, the commanding general of his army.

That army was a modest affair. It consisted of 11 Americans (including 8 U.S. Marines) plus Hamet's entourage of 90 men, a crew of 25 cannoneers (to service one cannon), 38 Greeks, and a troop of mounted Arabs, as well as 107 camels and their drivers. Altogether, there were about 400 men from 12 different nations, mostly Arabs. On March 8, 1805, the expeditionary force set out from Egypt along the parched Mediterranean coast toward the walled town of Derne in eastern Libya. Five hundred miles of grim going lay ahead, and although the season was early, the blazing sun and hot winds of the desert took their toll.

Thirst was the little army's constant companion. Haunted by mirages, the men advanced uncertainly, the glare singeing their eyes. Eaton's face, always on the ruddy side, turned bright red. Distrustful of their infidel general, the Arabs were soon staging little mutinies, and it took all of Eaton's threats to keep them moving ahead. Hamet himself, hearing reports that his brother had sent an army out from Tripoli to intercept them, seemed eager to retrace his steps toward the safety of Egypt; and even he was lashed by Eaton's tongue.

On March 20, Eaton wrote in his journal that "we have marched a distance of 200 miles, through an inhospitable waste. . . . [We Americans are like] pilgrims, bound across this gloomy desert on pursuits vastly different from those which lead to Mecca: the liberation of 300 Americans from the Chains of Barbarism, & a manly peace."[27] On March 29, he issued a proclamation to the people of Tripoli that offered to instruct them in the wickedness of Yusuf Pasha. Eaton insisted that the man was a "bloodthirsty scoundrel" who broke "the law of God which forbids us to be the first in aggression."[28]

America's response to his piratical ways had been to turn the other cheek. Yusuf was sent "messengers of peace with fair words" and fairer gifts, including gold, silver, and jewels. But no sooner had the pasha clutched these treasures to his breast than he returned to his villainies. Again the leaders of the United States met his outrages with patience. But they could no longer dismiss the evidence that Yusuf was a liar, a murderer, and the most of tyrannical of rulers. Eaton waxed ever more biblical:

> Know you not, you inhabitants of Tripoli and of all the neighboring countries, that it is through the just retribution of the Lord for the bloody crimes of the said traitor that you are obliged to suffer the scourges of famine and of war? You will

again be visited by pestilence if you fail to avenge yourselves on this brazen usurper![29]

Eaton was always his own best audience, and there is no evidence that his proclamation ever reached Tripolitan ears or, if it did, that it made any converts. He may not have expected it to do so. What he did expect was that the Tripolitans would be visited by war in his own person, in spite of the reluctance of the Arabs on whom he relied for his cavalry. For their part, the Arabs had their own reservations about Eaton. At one point they "examined the lace of my hat, epaulets, buttons, spurs and mounting of my arms. These they took to be all gold and silver. They were astonished that God should permit people to possess such riches who followed the religion of the devil!"[30]

Despite endless quarrels and recriminations, Eaton harried his outlandish little army on through the desert with the power of a man possessed. By April 25, he had succeeded in bringing them to a height that looked down on Yusuf's coastal town of Derne. Two days later, he ordered an attack on its garrison of eight hundred men. Supported by cannon fire from three U.S. warships in the town's harbor, Eaton—ever the swashbuckler—was soon leading a charge that carried his army into the streets. He made an easy target for Derne's defenders, and one of them put a musket ball through his left wrist. But soon the American flag—then with fifteen stars and fifteen stripes—was flapping in the burning breeze over the town's white walls.

Hamet took possession of the sheik's palace while Eaton prepared Derne to withstand the assault of Yusuf Pasha's army, which was marching across the desert from Tripoli. On May 8, its vanguard arrived and a week later it attacked in full force. The first charge failed, but on the following day a passel of the enemy broke into the town and almost managed to carry off the pretender; it was only a lucky cannonade, directed by Eaton himself, that killed two of Hamet's would-be captors and sent the rest scurrying back to their own lines.

What followed was no climactic battle but a series of skirmishes. Still, Eaton expected the U.S. fleet to deliver the supplies and reinforcements that would make it possible to advance the remaining seven hundred miles to Tripoli. In the meantime, the scorching sun seemed as much a foe as the troops of the pasha. Eaton's entry in his journal for May 25 tells the tale:

> The Scirroc wind blew in a gale from the southwest all day. So piercing was the heat that the white pine boards of our folding table and book coverings in our tents warped as if before a close fire. The heated dust penetrated everything through our garments; and indeed seemed to choke the pores of the skin. It had a singular effect on my wound, giving it the painful sensations of a fresh burn.[31]

At the beginning of June, the U.S. schooner *Hornet* anchored off Derne with news that troubled Eaton greatly. He learned that Yusuf Pasha and Tobias Lear, the American consul at Algiers, were about to enter into peace negotiations. Ten days later, the frigate *Constellation*, commanded by Capt. Hugh Campbell, arrived with the orders that Eaton had been dreading. A peace treaty had indeed been concluded. It awarded $60,000 to Yusuf for freeing the officers and crew of the *Philadelphia* and renouncing any claim to future tribute. Eaton was now directed to put himself, his fellow Americans, Hamet, and the pretender's entourage aboard Captain Campbell's ship and to leave the town at once.

It was an exceedingly bitter pill for Eaton to swallow. Fearing the frigate's broadsides, Yusuf Pasha's legions had broken camp and headed home when the *Constellation* sailed up to Derne, and Eaton saw their retreat as proof that his efforts would have eventually put Hamet on the throne of Tripoli.

He may have been right. Yusuf Pasha seems to have thought it possible, which is one reason why, after the fall of Derne, he had agreed to treat with Tobias Lear. The pasha was also sick and tired of being blockaded, and he feared that a new American offensive from the sea, especially if combined with Eaton's operations by land, might overwhelm his defenses. Even at that, the pasha would have preferred to extort far more in ransom money for the men of the *Philadelphia*: his original demand had been for $3 million.

Instead, Yusuf accepted the $60,000 and secured the liberty of eighty-nine of his own subjects, who had been picked up here and there in the Mediterranean by the American squadron and held as counter-hostages. Their return represented a very minor gain for Yusuf, for he had been heard to say that he "would not give an orange apiece for them."[32] There were a few more loose ends to tie up. In order to pacify his brother, he promised to send Hamet back his wife and children—which he did, but not until October 1807.

The pasha had found a sympathetic observer in Tobias Lear. On meeting Yusuf for the first time, Lear had reported that he was "manly and dignified, and has not in his appearance so much of the tyrant as he has been represented to be."[33] Lear was also impressed by the little ceremony of ratification that the pasha held in his castle on June 1, 1805. The U.S. envoy was placed on Yusuf's right hand and, in an atmosphere of "great order and solemnity," presented the treaty. According to custom, the pasha directed that his seal be affixed to both copies, one of which he passed to Lear "with many expressions of friendship."[34]

Some of the hostages—Private Ray, for instance—would later say that Eaton should have been given a chance to complete his mission, yet at the time their every thought was for freedom, never mind whether it was bought or fought for. This is how Ray described the situation during their final stretch in captivity, when rumors of an imminent release were running wild through the prison: "I shall not pretend to describe in adequate terms our various emotions for a number of days previous to this confirmation of our hopes. Sometimes our spirits were soaring buoyant on the wings of sanguine expectation; at other times, diving into the very gulf of despair."[35]

It was on June 4, 1805, that freedom finally came, and the men were ferried from the wharves of Tripoli to the U.S. men-of-war that now advanced peacefully toward the harbor. Amid tears and laughter, the nineteen-month ordeal came to an end. William Ray returned home in safety to tell his story in a book called *The Horrors of Slavery*, published in 1808.

Was it a victory or was it defeat? In September 1805, Commodore Preble wrote the secretary of the navy to say that "it is a pleasing circumstance and must be gratifying to every American that [peace] has been established on more honorable terms than any other nation has ever been able to command [from the pasha]."[36] A few months later Preble changed his mind, writing to tell Eaton that the treaty involved a "sacrifice of national honor which has been made by an ignominious negotiation."[37]

Eaton could hardly have agreed more. Returning to the United States, he proclaimed that the treaty insulted every American, and he flew into a rage when it was ratified by Congress in April 1806. He was particularly incensed that Hamet had been abandoned, but the pretender continued to receive financial support from the United States and his own complaints about "the King [that is, president] of America" were muted. In 1809, Yusuf appointed Hamet governor of Derne, but then the brothers had another falling-out, and after two more years Hamet was driven back into Egypt, where he died in poverty.

If the ruin of his expedition left Eaton in need of consolation (and it did), plenty was available. Preble's praise would have delighted anyone: "The arduous and dangerous service you have performed has astonished not only your country but the world. . . . You have gained immortal honor and established the military reputation of your country in the East."[38] The city of Boston recognized Eaton's achievement by naming the thoroughfare behind the statehouse Derne Street, and the Massachusetts legislature responded by awarding him ten thousand acres of land in Maine, then a dependency of the Bay State. It wasn't enough. Full of rum and rage, General Eaton threatened to become a minister of the Gospel but died a drunkard in 1811 at the age of forty-seven. (Although unbeset by any particular vices, Preble had died in 1807 at the age of forty-six.)

What of the pasha and the Karamanli dynasty? At length, Yusuf's prayers to Allah seemed to go unheard. His seafarers went on with their predatory ways, but as the technology gap widened between the Barbary powers and the West, it became harder and harder for honest pirates to make a living. Yusuf's navy shrank and his revenues declined, especially after the fall of Napoleon allowed Britain's Royal Navy to do a better job of policing the Mediterranean. The burden of taxes that the pasha placed on his people grew heavier, and his grip on power became shakier.

In the 1820s, when he had aged and appeared infirm to his sons and grandsons, civil war broke out and Yusuf was forced to abdicate. In 1835 the Ottoman Turks moved in and asserted direct control of Tripoli. The pathetic old pasha was one of their lesser catches, and they forced him to live out the last few years of his life as a prisoner in his own castle.

4

Santa Anna: The Alamo and After

The Barbary pirates had challenged the growing power of the United States on the seas, but the new republic was also to meet opponents of its new expansionist order on the North American landmass. As the course of empire took its way westward, pioneers from U.S. territories encountered the inconvenient claims of the Republic of Mexico, newly free of rule from Spain. The result in Texas was an Anglo-American rebellion against the government of Antonio López de Santa Anna, president of Mexico and general in chief of the Mexican armed forces.

During late February 1836, Santa Anna might have been the antichrist himself as far as the men of the Alamo were concerned. On the twenty-fourth, their commander, Lt. Col. William Barret Travis, addressed an appeal for speedy aid "to the People of Texas and All Americans in the World." Travis announced that the defenders of the Alamo were surrounded by "a thousand or more of the Mexicans under Santa Anna" and had been subjected to

> a continual bombardment and cannonade for 24 hours. . . . The enemy has demanded surrender at discretion, otherwise, the garrison is to be put to the sword. . . . I have answered the demand with a cannon shot, and our flag still waves proudly from the wall. I shall never surrender or retreat.[1]

Within the next few weeks, Travis's message reached its intended audience. Newspapers from Louisiana to Maine printed his plea for help and backed it up with editorials that hailed the Texans' cause, denouncing Santa Anna as a son of darkness whose aim was to drown the torch of liberty in a sea of despo-

34

tism. In faraway Philadelphia, citizens cheered while the Mexican generalissimo was burned in effigy. For his part, Santa Anna returned the feelings of enmity. When he realized that the Texans had won the hearts of their American cousins and were getting material as well as moral support from the United States, he threatened to march all the way to Washington and raise the Mexican flag over the Capitol building.

In San Antonio, at least, he had matters well in hand. Although the rebels held the Alamo, Santa Anna felt sure that their resistance would be short-lived. In the meantime, his temporary quarters—the least inadequate structure in the dusty little town—were nicely in order. Here stood the portable writing desk used by his secretary, Ramón Caro, and around the rooms could be seen Santa Anna's personal effects. There were his extra uniforms (so gorgeous in their Napoleonic gaudiness), his crystal decanters full of potions to renew his vigor, the china plates on which his initials were painted in lacy italics, a well-stuffed golden snuff box, and his silver chamber pot. Yes, everything was in its place, and the president-general, forty-two years old and at the height of his powers, felt confident that Mexico's northeastern province of Texas would return to the Mexican fold and remain there for a long time to come.

Santa Anna had few worries about the home front in that winter of 1836. Most of his countrymen would approve of whatever measures he took against the defenders of the Alamo, so long as the rebellion in Texas came to an early end. Typically, the editor of the *Gazette* of Tamaulipas commented that "Don Santa Anna, feeling—as every true Mexican ought—the disgrace thus sustained by the republic, is making every preparation to wipe out the stain in the blood of those perfidious foreigners."[2]

Though hard-pressed for funds, Santa Anna had recruited an "army of operations" and, on the second day of 1836, began the march northward from the heart of Mexico to San Antonio. He had fought in Texas twenty years earlier as a lieutenant, but it was only now that he would begin to influence the history of the United States. Considering the work that his army did among the 180-odd heroes of the crudely fortified Franciscan mission called the Alamo, he was bound to appear in that history as a villain.

By their own lights, the Texans had found in the Mexican constitution of 1824 a guarantee of self-government, and they had proceeded to govern themselves. Out under the brilliant sun, they lived in a state of near anarchy, ignoring Mexican law whenever it was possible to do so. If their distant masters decreed that they become nominal Catholics, they nevertheless went on worshiping in their Protestant way. If Mexico City forbade the introduction of black slaves into Texas, they were willing to call their human property "indentured servants." If tariffs and taxes were levied, they could somehow be ignored. This was the state of affairs in the late 1820s.

But in the 1830s, Mexican garrisons were stationed throughout the territory, and their officers began cracking down at random on smugglers and slavers. Emigrants from the United States were turned away at the borders. By closing local legislatures and insisting that Texans pay duties that were levied by Mexican officials, His Excellency Gen. Antonio López de Santa Anna became the most hated man in Texas. What the Texans proceeded to demand was strongly reminiscent of what the thirteen colonies had asked of George III: the chance for their own voices to be heard before their parent government made decisions that would determine the shape of their economy and the course of their lives. And as in the experience of the original colonists, the Texans soon learned to despair of a new relationship with their distant master.

Most Americans hailed the struggle of the Texas revolutionaries as the latest chapter in democratic heroism. Others were not so sure. The editors of the *Baltimore Gazette* commented that the rebels

> cannot as yet count enough American riflemen to drive the rightful lords of the soil [that is, the Mexicans] out of their own country; and therefore they make up a pitiful face and cry oppression, and call upon individuals to shoulder their rifles and come to their aid, and inform them as an inducement to do so that they have millions of acres—of Mexican land, let it be observed—which they will bestow on those who aid them. . . .[3]

As a matter of fact, the Anglo-American leadership in Texas did use the promise of land to lure in volunteers from all over the United States, and the campaign against Mexico was largely financed by speculators on Wall Street and elsewhere who loaned money to the rebels that would eventually be repaid with millions of acres in Texas. The title to these new domains was expected to be cleared by force of arms, and as more and more volunteers streamed into Texas with their long rifles slung over their shoulders, the speculators antici-pated a quick return on their investment.

In the ranks of the Mexicans, the fervor for independence failed to impress. Santa Anna thought the Anglo-Americans would crack when push came to shove, and he laughed to scorn his opposite number at the Alamo, the little Colonel Travis, who was only twenty-six. But the two were not entirely unalike. Both were charismatic, violently emotional, and intensely self-centered. A law-yer turned soldier, William Barret Travis had done time in a Mexican stockade for supporting the Texan cause; more literate than Santa Anna, he had written his autobiography when he was twenty-three. With such comrades as Jim Bowie and Davy Crockett, he represented a defiance that Santa Anna felt com-pelled to crush.

It was Bowie, the slave trader and confidence-man, famous in his youth for wrestling alligators, who bore direct responsibility for the battle of the Alamo. In the middle of January 1836, Sam Houston had sent him to San Antonio with a letter that instructed Lt. Col. James C. Neill, then in command, to demolish the fortifications (which were weak to begin with) and retreat eastward with his men and artillery. Upon arriving with Houston's orders, Bowie looked around the Alamo and detected, as he thought, real possibilities for a successful stand against the Mexicans. He galvanized its defenders, overseeing the building of palisades and parapets. Soon he would learn that Santa Anna's legions were closing in on the place, but the approach of danger only convinced Bowie of the Alamo's overwhelming importance. He wrote Governor Henry Smith on February 2 that the "salvation of Texas depends in great measure in keeping [San Antonio] out of the hands of the enemy. . . . [I]f it were in the possession of Santa Anna, there is no stronghold from which to repel him in his march towards [eastern Texas]."[4]

Colonel Neill soon left the Alamo; at about the same time, Bowie began to suffer from a persistent fever. By then, the young, ambitious Travis had arrived in a pair of homesewn jeans to share the command with Bowie. Perhaps it was Neill who knew the better part of valor, for there was little to convince Travis or Bowie or any of the other defenders that their stand would be successful. They felt that the fortress *had* to be held, so some miracle or other was bound to make it happen. "Soon will they become aware of their folly!"[5] was Santa Anna's remark when he heard that the Texans were determined to oppose him.

Whether they chose to recognize their peril or not, the men of the Alamo—two-thirds of whom had recently come from U.S. territory—were lamentably positioned. The old fortress would have been much easier to defend if it had been smaller; as it was, 180 irregulars were just too few to protect its long walls. Santa Anna knew that their numbers were modest, and even before inspecting the place, he believed that its chances of resisting him were nil. On arriving, he raised a blood-red banner over a church tower in San Antonio, half a mile west of the Alamo. That banner announced that Santa Anna would show no mercy. The Texans could either surrender unconditionally or accept death in the ensuing battle.

According to José Enrique de la Peña, a young Mexican officer, Santa Anna believed that "the fame and honor of the army were compromised the longer the enemy lived."[6] As a taunt, he ordered his military band to advance within earshot of the Alamo and treat its defenders to a concert. But mostly it was the Mexican cannons that serenaded them. The artillerymen on the batteries atop the walls of the Alamo replied as often as they dared, but their supplies of shot and powder were limited and they were saving most of it for the full-scale battle that would soon be upon them.

At the climactic moment, Jim Bowie was driven into bed by his stubborn fever, and young Travis had to carry on alone. He was not entirely displeased, having complained earlier that Bowie "has been roaring drunk all the time."[7] A rank novice compared with Santa Anna, Travis nevertheless won the grudging confidence of his men—no easy job, given the wiles of his adversary. Santa Anna kept up the psychological warfare that had begun with the red flag of doom and the sound of cynical music, ordering his men to worry the long, chill hours of darkness with shots and shouts and bugle calls.

One hundred sixty miles to the east, in Washington-on-Brazos, the leaders of the rebellion were meeting in convention, and on March 2 they took the irrevocable step, severing all political ties with Mexico and declaring Texas a "free, sovereign, and independent republic with all the rights and attributes which properly belong to independent nations." Ignorant of this declaration, the men of the Alamo remained in mortal danger. Their salvation depended on manpower, firepower, and logistics; and the new republic lacked the resources to march on San Antonio and put Santa Anna to flight. While Travis had to be satisfied with a mere handful of reinforcements, the enemy's numbers continued to grow, as more and more units finished the northward trek. By March 3, Santa Anna had several thousand men and twenty-one cannons and howitzers on hand.

The men of the Mexican army found themselves admiring the energy of their leader, who had been soldiering since the age of sixteen. Santa Anna was here, there, and everywhere around the Alamo, directing the installation of new batteries, marking out lines where trenches should be dug, deploying men where they would be most effective, pushing his lines forward when it was possible to do so—and, in short, personally tightening the noose around the Texans. A Mexican captain named Sánchez wrote of how "Santa Anna seeks and dashes to places of danger, while General Sesma avoids even those that are safe."[8] For the most part, his other generals trailed along behind him, as though attending a workshop in military science.

Santa Anna ordered his batteries to step up the cannonading of the Alamo, and the mud-brick walls of the old fortress began to look as cratered as the moon. Davy Crockett spoke up for many of those on the receiving end of the barrage: "I think we had better march out and die in the open air. I don't like to be hemmed up."[9] Even Travis, calling the garrison to assemble, had to admit that the situation seemed hopeless. He urged his men to stay and die at his side, for by sacrificing their lives they would slow Santa Anna's advance into Texas and give their countrymen more time to prepare his defeat. All but one stayed—and watched as their besiegers constructed scaling ladders.

At five in the morning on March 6, 1836, the president-general launched his attack. Fourteen hundred of Santa Anna's troops, soon to be joined by a reserve force of four hundred more, heard the bugle call. They rose under the first streaks of dawn and ran with a roar, hailing their republic and its leader. Travis, who had been resting in the barracks, reached the northeast battery with his sword and a double-barreled shotgun just before the first wave of Mexicans arrived with their muskets and ladders. Shouting at his men to "give 'em hell," he was quickly silenced by a ball of lead in the brain.

From a battery of piled earth north of the Alamo, Santa Anna watched and listened as the air grew turbulent with gunsmoke and dust. There were screams and explosions, curses and groans, the clash of bayonets and swords, howls of triumph and agonies of death. Chaos reigned among the Mexican columns, and they had to fall back several times, but at last they breached the walls and annihilated the resistance. Within a few hours of the initial assault, the rest of Travis's men had joined him in death. Five hundred of Santa Anna's men also fell at the Alamo, many to "friendly fire." Their bodies were respectfully buried in consecrated ground, but the remains of the Anglo-Americans were cremated in three heaps without ceremony. Years later, Santa Anna paid tribute to their courage: "Not one [Texan] showed signs of desiring to surrender, and with fierceness and valor they died fighting. Their determined defense lasted for four hours, and I found it necessary to call in my reserve forces to defeat them."[10] At the time, he was less forthcoming. "It was but a small affair,"[11] is how he summed up the battle in that winter of 1836.

The Alamo was soon a very large affair as, throughout Texas and the United States, Santa Anna was denounced as a merciless blackguard. The Natchez *Courier* lamented over the fate of Davy Crockett: "To be butchered by such a wretch as Santa Anna—it is not to be borne!" The New Orleans *Commercial Bulletin* published an ode characterizing the Mexican general as "vile scum" who was "far too horrid and too base for hell."[12] Rallies were held nationwide to honor the dead of the Alamo and raise money for the cause of Texan independence.

By early April, Santa Anna was marching in pursuit of Sam Houston and his little army as it retreated steadily to the east. The Mexican general José Urrea, on Santa Anna's orders, had already destroyed the opposition near Goliad, a hundred miles to the southeast of the Alamo. Over four hundred Anglo-Americans commanded by James Fannin surrendered to Urrea and, on March 27, most of them were massacred on orders from Santa Anna. The reputation of the Mexican army was growing blacker by the day. Even some of Santa Anna's officers were appalled by the cruelty shown to Fannin's men. José Enrique de la Peña called their deaths an incident that "focused the shocked attention of the civilized world, presenting us Mexicans as Hottentots, as savages who do not know how to respect any right."[13]

Would retribution never overtake Santa Anna? He thought not as he marched on into eastern Texas, hoping to capture the chief men of the New Republic of Texas, as well as Sam Houston's army. Total victory seemed to lie within his grasp, and he pushed his men forward as quickly as he could, far outdistancing his other generals, whose combined strength was now much greater than his own. The Texans, Santa Anna believed, were men of shattered morale, their courage failing every time they remembered the Alamo and Goliad.

In the camp of the Anglo-Americans, memories of their fallen comrades aroused very different feelings. Although Sam Houston's force numbered fewer than a thousand men, they were determined to take their revenge. On April 21, at San Jacinto, they caught the Mexicans unawares—Santa Anna was actually enjoying a siesta under a spreading oak—and in the space of about twenty minutes treated them to a heady dose of defeat. Overwhelmed by the unexpected onslaught, the Mexicans dropped their weapons, fell to their knees, and desperately repeated, "Me no Alamo! Me no Alamo!" Few were spared; by the end of the day, 630 Mexicans had been killed in the berserker battle. Only nine Anglo-Americans died. Santa Anna disappeared, but the next morning Houston's scouts discovered a dark, dignified don who was wearing a blue jacket, linen trousers, and red slippers—and hiding in the grasslands not far from the battlefield. The identity of their captive became clear when they marched him past a group of begrimed Mexican officers who shouted *"El Presidente! El Presidente!"*

Indeed it was their president—in the worst pickle of his life. Hauled into the presence of Sam Houston, who had been wounded in the ankle, Santa Anna congratulated the Texan on the capture of so vaunted a general as himself, who could fairly be called the Napoleon of the Western Hemisphere. Houston's men scorned such bravado. They demanded the death of "Santy Annie"—even though there were good reasons to keep his head out of the noose. Four thousand of his soldiers still ranged within the borders of Texas, a fact that bolstered Santa Anna's usefulness as a hostage. And keeping him alive did pay off. Eager to avoid execution, he formally made peace with the Republic of Texas and succeeded in persuading his troops—now under the command of Generals Urrea and Filisola—to withdraw beyond the Rio Grande. At that juncture Texans could truly begin to celebrate their independence.

The peace treaty was greeted with dismay by the Mexican army. According to de la Peña, the president-general had never "performed a more contemptible deed . . . than in selling out his country by relinquishing Texas' delightful territory, as if he were the sole arbiter of the Republic." De la Peña ventured to add that, if Santa Anna had possessed the slightest sense of honor, he "would have blown out his brains before signing his own disgrace."[14]

At length, the Texan leaders decided to turn their compliant prisoner loose, and near Galveston he boarded the armed schooner *Invincible,* which was then ordered to take him to Veracruz. The ship was almost under way when an unruly group of armed volunteers got wind of what was happening and demanded that Santa Anna be returned to custody. Hearing their howls, the general expected to be hauled ashore and lynched. He was forced to leave the boat and return to jail, but he lived to see another dawn.

The leaders of the new republic went back into conference. One of them, Stephen F. Austin, suggested that Santa Anna appeal for help to Andrew Jackson, then president of the United States. The general, still afraid that the Texans would lead him to the gallows, had nothing to lose by writing to Jackson. Old Hickory read his letter with interest. He knew that Santa Anna had been repudiated by his own government in Mexico City, but he advised Sam Houston, the new president of Texas, that the prisoner was worth keeping alive: "He is the pride of the Mexican soldiers, and the favorite of the priesthood. While he is in your power, the difficulties of your enemy, in raising another army, will continue to be great. The soldiers of Mexico will not willingly march into Texas, when they know that their advance may cost their favorite general his life."[15]

Jackson's advice was heeded and Santa Anna remained unhung, but he was still in danger. A drunken soldier managed to fire into his cell, and other would-be assassins were threatening to take soberer aim at this scourge of the Anglos.

Fastened to a ball and chain, the general was no match for his enemies. But in the end he convinced Houston and his colleagues to let him go. His journey back to Mexico, it was agreed, would be by way of Washington, D.C., where both sides would use the good offices of the United States to discuss where the new border between Mexico and Texas should be drawn.

Off into freedom he rode, with a commission of Texans to keep him company. They arrived in Washington on January 18, 1837, and the notorious general was greeted with open arms. The dead of the Alamo and Goliad, as well as his threats to raise the Mexican flag over the Capitol building, faded into insignificance, and the city's ballrooms and drawing rooms opened wide to admit the conquered hero. Exotic caudillos in handsome uniforms didn't pass through the District of Columbia every day, and it was only Christian to be gracious to an adversary brought low—especially since his gaze was so enthralling and his manners so exquisite. And Santa Anna seemed so sincere when he voiced his regrets over the unpleasantness that had recently taken place in the vastnesses of Texas. The hosts and hostesses of the capital all agreed: It was perfectly safe to honor this extraordinary foreign gentleman. But the discussions with President Jackson and the Texans reached an impasse, and the border between Texas and Mexico remained a matter of controversy for another decade.

When Santa Anna returned to his homeland in February 1837, he traveled aboard the *Pioneer*, a corvette of the U.S. Navy. After landing in Veracruz, he retired to his hacienda. Mexicans now paid their former president little heed, for they suspected him of hatching treasonous plots with the cunning Yankees; his enemies mocked him as "the hero of San Jacinto." He protested that he had done nothing to compromise the dignity of his country, but his disclaimers were ignored and a new government under Anastasio Bustamente pursued its own negotiations with the Republic of Texas, whose government was never recognized by Mexico City. Taking the hint, Santa Anna announced that his political career was over.

For the moment, this master of intrigue cultivated his farms and gardens: "I busied myself with domestic life, which seemed, in my melancholy state, as welcome as a desert oasis to the weary traveler."[16] But his retirement was interrupted in 1838 when a French expeditionary force landed at Veracruz. With the blessings of the frightened Bustamente, Santa Anna rushed back into the fray—and suffered wounds that were almost fatal when he led a mounted charge on a French battery. His doctors were forced to amputate his left leg below the knee.

The French soon withdrew from Veracruz, but they had done him a favor of sorts: making it impossible for anyone to deny that Santa Anna had sacrificed a great deal for his country. Never before had he seemed so valiant to his people. He trumpeted his pleasure at having been "wounded and afterwards mutilated in defense of a sacred cause,"[17] and within weeks he assumed the presidency of Mexico for the second time. In 1842, he immortalized the bony remains of his shattered limb by ordering a huge procession to bear it solemnly along to an honored place of rest: a splendidly sculptured urn atop a stone column in Mexico City's Santa Paula Cemetery.

He flirted with the idea of starting a new war against Texas, and he stirred things up by sending a raiding party to San Antonio. But repeated rebellions of rival politicians kept Santa Anna busy on the home front. A third term as president of Mexico confirmed him in his vices. He was, by anyone's standards, grossly corrupt, diverting funds from the national treasury to build up his own estate. Except when met by the irresistible force of bribery, his bureaucracy was an immovable object. Tax collectors kept his people impoverished, and the army, on which he spent so liberally, served as the foundation and guarantee of his regime. When he lost his first wife, Doña Inés, in 1844, he scandalized the nation by quickly taking a teenage bride. He tended to confuse his own vainglorious desires with the good of his country, and lavished more attention on his fighting cocks than on his congress.

Before the end of 1844, a crowd of dissidents ran riot through the streets of Mexico City. Its slogans went straight to the point: "Death to Santa Anna! Death to the robbers!" The president was nowhere in evidence, so the crowd stormed the cemetery at Santa Paula and avenged themselves on the one part of him that they could reach. Over toppled the column and down fell the urn, and then the general's martyred leg was martyred all over again.

The invective that Mexican printing presses were turning out against Santa Anna surpassed any of the denunciations that American editors had flung at him after the Alamo. One pamphleteer addressed him in these terms: "You resemble a fury of hell, blind, devastating and bloody. Amid the horrors of civil war, amid lakes of blood and mountains of dead bodies, you always present yourself like a spectre, inciting all to devastation, slaughter, and revenge."[18] Santa Anna recognized moral outrage when he encountered it and decided to lie low. But he was captured in his home state of Veracruz by an alert party of militia and jailed in Jalapa, the city where he had been born in 1794. He hoped to shame his captors by telling them that he was now being treated "worse than . . . when I was a prisoner of war among the Texan adventurers."[19] But no tears were shed for the fallen general. Still, his luck held. When he asked to be sent into exile, his wish was granted. It turned out to be a comfortable interlude in Havana.

One month after Santa Anna sailed away into exile, the Lone Star Republic had finally—on July 4, 1845—joined its fortunes with those of the Union. As the twenty-eighth state, Texas assumed a new aura of menace for the Mexicans, and the government in Mexico City prepared for war. So did the Americans. Sporadic fighting had never ceased in southwest Texas, which both sides continued to claim, and now it became a head-to-head confrontation. An army of some 3,500 men under Gen. Zachary ("Old Rough 'n' Ready") Taylor marched with brass bands blaring and battle flags flying to the Rio Grande, which the Mexicans considered an invasion of their sovereign territory. On May 11, 1846,

President James Polk sent Congress a bloated lawyerly account of the "grievous wrongs perpetrated upon our citizens [by the Mexican government] throughout a long period of years,"[20] and asked for an American declaration of war.

Two days later, by an overwhelming margin (40–2 in the Senate, 173–14 in the House), Congress gave the commander in chief what he wanted. In early September, Zachary Taylor's army, now numbering well over six thousand, descended into Mexico. The people of the United States monitored their progress with hope while the people of Mexico looked on in fear. One contemporary observer noted that "the avidity of all classes [of Americans] for news from the army" kept a constant flow of information coming back from Mexico via "mails, expresses, steamboats, locomotives, magnetic telegraphs,"[21] and the newspapers were crammed full of the latest dispatches from the front.

Conditions in Mexico made for happy reading in the United States. Taylor's advance threw the Mexican government into confusion. In the initial engagements of the war its troops made a poor show against the Yankee invaders, and anyone could see that worse was to come. Desperation inspired a desperate remedy. Santa Anna, now fifty-two years old, was hailed on returning from his Cuban exile, and in the middle of September he was given a delirious welcome in Mexico City by the same populace that had desecrated his wayward limb less than two years before. In Washington, it was believed that the general would make peace with the United States on terms that would satisfy American interests; for that reason, President Polk had secretly taken a hand in conveying Santa Anna back to Mexico. Polk was much chagrined when his puppet refused to cooperate. But there it was: Before the end of the year, Santa Anna had secured his election as president for the fourth time and raised an army of national resistance.

Early in 1847, Santa Anna launched his only offensive of the war, leading a huge force northward with the aim of annihilating the "daring foreigner who profanes with his presence the sacred territory of the fatherland."[22] Taylor made up for his inferiority in numbers by ensconcing his army in rugged terrain near Buena Vista (in the state of Coahuila) and waiting for the Mexicans to come up and attack. Santa Anna had never felt more certain of victory. But it was only fair, he thought, to give the Yankees a chance to live, and he sent Taylor a message: "You are surrounded by 20,000 men and cannot, in any human probability, avoid suffering a rout and being cut to pieces. . . . I wish to save you from a catastrophe, and for that purpose give you notice, in order that you may surrender at discretion."[23] Taylor snorted, and begged to inform *el Presidente* that his offer was unacceptable.

Now was the moment for Santa Anna to secure his reputation as a second Napoleon. Brimming with overconfidence, he moved toward the thick of the fray, only to have his horse shot out from under him. On a new mount, he ordered his men to advance along a wide front. During the course of a two-day battle, the Americans slowly gave ground, until only their artillery kept the Mexicans at bay. Darkness helped to retrieve their fortunes, and during the second night, after conferring with his generals, Santa Anna became discouraged. His men were exhausted and running short of supplies; digging the Yankees out of the mountains had been more of an uphill battle than he had imagined. He decided to fall back, hoping to tempt Taylor out of the heights and onto the plain, where the Mexican superiority in numbers might prove decisive.

But Taylor was not to be tempted, and in the end both generals, because neither army advanced beyond the battlefield, claimed victory. Americans naturally found Zachary Taylor's claim more convincing. On the strength of Buena Vista and his earlier victories in the Mexican War, Taylor was to be elected president of the United States in 1848. In the meantime, Santa Anna had no trouble finding another fight, for Winfield ("Old Fuss 'n' Feathers") Scott, the commanding general of the U.S. Army, invaded southern Mexico with twelve thousand Americans on March 9, 1847. Scott and his troops had been put ashore by the U.S. Navy near the city of Veracruz, which surrendered after a ferocious bombardment from both ship and shore. So far, so good—but the goal of the expedition was nothing less than the conquest of Mexico City.

While President Polk approved of the plan to march on the capital, he was not its ultimate source. That distinction belonged to General Scott, who, at sixty, was old enough to have fought in the War of 1812. Polk had long harbored grave doubts about Scott's capabilities, and he confided to his diary in the summer of 1847 that the general was guilty of "folly and ridiculous vanity."[24] Santa Anna, finding less to criticize in Scott, warned his people that the invaders of Mexico might actually succeed in their mission: "Perhaps the American hosts may proudly tread the imperial capital of the Aztecs. I will never witness such opprobrium, for I am decided first to die fighting!"[25]

The general was not the only Mexican who was voicing such sentiments. An American correspondent with Scott's army warned his readers that Santa Anna's "people are warlike, and have an abundant supply of munitions of war. Our battles with them improve them as soldiers. Our invasion is held by them in abhorrence, and has united all classes in determined resistance against us."[26] As it happened, General Scott and his army endured many bloody days as they closed in on their prey. They routed Santa Anna several times over, beginning at the Battle of Cerro Gordo in April 1847. The dictator suffered tremendous losses, yet he was always able to rebuild his army, and to defend the capital he commanded a force that numbered at least 25,000.

In spite of the burning desire of Santa Anna's people to save their country, the year proved to be a total disaster for *el Presidente*. The crowning degradation came on September 14 when the U.S. expeditionary force overran the last holdouts in the fortifications of Mexico City, the metropolis that General Scott had described as "the object of all our dreams and hopes, toils and dangers— once the gorgeous seat of the Montezumas."[27] At Santa Anna's behest, the capital had sent its church bells to be melted down and recast as cannon, but to no avail. The Americans came shooting and slashing on.

By the time of his triumph, Scott knew his enemy well. He wrote that Santa Anna's "vigilance and energy were unquestionable," and though he was "not deficient in personal courage," he did have one fatal flaw: On the battlefield,

he "failed in quickness of perception. . . . Hence his defeats."[28] Defeats there
were in abundance, and if Santa Anna reneged on his promise to die defending
the capital, he allowed thousands of his countrymen to perish in his place,
including *Los Niños Héroes* (The Boy Heroes). These six young cadets, who
committed suicide when their position at Chapultepec Castle was overrun, became the most famous military figures in Mexican history.

Looking on as the U.S. flag was raised over Chapultepec, Santa Anna cursed
and muttered, "These damned Yankees will always capture our batteries, even
if we put them in hell."[29] According to Santa Anna's own account, his uniform
had been "tattered by the enemy's bullets"[30] during the fighting for Mexico
City. He and his generals conferred about their plight, decided that the people
who remained in the capital were defeatists, and abandoned them to the Americans. George W. Kendall, a correspondent for the New Orleans *Picayune,* was
soon reporting that "the proud capital of Mexico has fallen . . . and Santa Anna,
instead of shedding his blood as he had promised, is wandering with the remnant of his army no one knows whither."[31]

After a few months of trying to rally further resistance against the invaders,
Santa Anna accepted the fact that the war was lost and prepared to leave the
country. Not everyone was content to see him depart. The new government of
Mexico, led by interim president Manuel Peña y Peña, wanted to detain Santa
Anna and convene a court-martial to judge his conduct during the war.

A group of Texas Rangers who were serving with the U.S. Army had other
plans for the defeated general. Led by Col. Jack Hays, they received permission from General Scott to set off in hot pursuit of Santa Anna's person. He was
with his wife and children at Tehuacán, not far from Veracruz, when he heard
that several hundred ferocious Texans who still remembered the Alamo were
headed in his direction. When the Rangers arrived, they found that the general
and his family had absconded two hours earlier, so they consoled themselves
by looting his abandoned possessions, including a walking stick encrusted with
precious stones. Santa Anna referred to this episode as an "attempted assassination." And he was probably right.

The treaty of peace that ended the Mexican War was negotiated not by Santa
Anna's subordinates but by his successors. In return for a cash payment of $15
million, Mexico renounced its claims to Texas and ceded to the United States
huge tracts of land that would eventually comprise the states of California,
Nevada, and Utah, as well as parts of Arizona, New Mexico, Colorado, and
Wyoming—"an immense empire," as President Polk put it, "the value of which
20 years hence it would be difficult to calculate."[32] It is fitting that something
on a grand scale was accomplished, for the war cost fourteen thousand American lives. Untold thousands of Mexicans also died, and the loss of territory was
a terrible blow to Mexican pride. Undismayed by such considerations, Polk
announced in December 1848 that "our beloved country presents a sublime
moral spectacle to the world."[33]

Today, most American historians consider Polk's spectacle a fairly straight-
forward land grab. Mexicans discuss it in more impassioned terms. What is
certain is that the United States soon paid a price for its new territory. Ulysses S.

Grant reckoned that "the Southern rebellion was largely the outgrowth of the Mexican War"[34]—since the conflict of North and South was intensified by the struggle to decide whether the vast territory won from Santa Anna's Mexico would enter the Union in the form of free states or slave. From the Battles of Buena Vista and Chapultepec Castle to the clash of cousins in blue and gray is not so great a distance as it may seem.

Returning to exile, Santa Anna spent the next five years in Jamaica and Colombia. But Mexico seemed no happier in his absence than in his presence, and in 1853 he was recalled and made president for the fifth time. On the eve of his sixtieth birthday, Santa Anna decreed that he be addressed as "Your Most Serene Highness." He organized his own palace guard, the Lancers of the Supreme Power, and decked them out in stunning red-and-white uniforms.

In spite of his growing megalomania, Santa Anna was briefly able to consolidate his power and rule as absolute dictator. The United States became one of the few beneficiaries of his regime for, in order to finance his extravagances, he sold off the Mesilla Valley of southern Arizona and New Mexico, thereby completing the borders of what would eventually become the lower forty-eight states. A later president, Ignacio Comonfort, retaliated for this surrender of sovereign soil, known as the Gadsden Purchase, by confiscating all of Santa Anna's houses and farms.

His regime had brought temporary stability, but Mexico's people were eager to see Santa Anna take a final bow and depart the stage of public life. Their chance came in the middle of 1855, when a revolt swept through the countryside. For the third time in ten years Santa Anna was forced to leave Mexico. He beguiled the long years of exile by penning his memoirs, which demonstrate a very casual attitude toward historical fact.

Santa Anna's next attempt at a comeback occurred in 1864, when he landed in Veracruz and offered to support Maximilian, the Austrian archduke who was seeking to ascend the long-vacant Mexican throne. Maximilan preferred the backing of Napoleon III, the French ruler. And with good reason: In April 1864, an army of French soldiers led Maximilian to his coronation as emperor in Mexico City. Santa Anna might have rejoiced, but in March he had been declared untrustworthy by Maximilian's lieutenants, who sent him back into his lonely exile.

At the end of the Civil War, the United States resolved to enforce the Monroe Doctrine by evicting Maximilian from Mexico, and Santa Anna tried to repair his fortunes by declaring himself a passionate enemy of the French-backed usurper. So, in his seventy-second year, the old schemer came to New York, where he preached a crusade to reestablish the Republic of Mexico. He stayed on in the United States for a year, but Secretary of State William Seward, who had met with Santa Anna at St. Thomas in the Caribbean, now ignored him, and his plans for "liberating" his homeland went nowhere. In 1867, when he did get back to Mexico, he was shown the short way to prison. Maximilian fared even worse; he lost his grip on power and was executed by a firing squad.

Although Santa Anna had flirted with the same fate, a military tribunal found him innocent of any capital crimes and, once again, he took himself into exile. It was in fact his final exile, and it lasted until 1874. Then, as a drowsy old man who could no longer threaten anyone, Santa Anna was allowed to come home to die. In 1876, the year of his passing, the defenders of the Alamo had been ashes for forty years.

5

The Ordeal of Emilio Aguinaldo

For twenty-five years after the Civil War, a dusty little outfit called the U.S. Army finished up the Indian wars, the outcome of which—despite events like the Custer massacre—could easily be foreseen. Then, very late in the nineteenth century, came the war with Spain. Expansionist politicians and journalists urged the Republican administration of President William McKinley to crush Spanish imperialism, which had become a special irritant in Cuba, leading to the mysterious destruction of the USS *Maine* in Havana harbor on February 15, 1898.

The Indian wars had been the final act of a very old tragedy: the desperate resistance of the red man to his eviction by the white. The Spanish-American War pointed more to the future than the past. America had won the west. Now, as never before, it would turn its attention to the wider world. With U.S. forces engaging Spain's army and navy in both hemispheres, the international community would witness the advance of an American order that would eventually result in the creation of the first full-fledged superpower on earth.

One week after the declaration of war against Spain in the spring of 1898, the Asiatic Squadron of the U.S. Navy steamed into Manila Bay under the cover of darkness. Commodore George Dewey, who led the way in the cruiser *Olympia*, had recently left the British colony of Hong Kong, where the likelihood of his attacking Spain's Oriental possession, the Philippines, had been a favorite topic of discussion for weeks. The European officers in the colony seemed to take a perverse delight in imagining that the U.S. warships would be destroyed by Spanish mines or shore batteries, and everyone suspected that Manila, a walled city with big guns of its own, would have the added protection of a Spanish fleet. Dewey remembered the attitude of his foreign colleagues in Hong Kong very well: "The prevailing impression among even the military class in the colony was that our squadron was going to certain destruction."[1]

In the event, only one Spanish battery fired on Dewey's ships as they sailed by moonlight past the island of Corregidor and into Manila Bay, and the threat was quickly neutralized by the guns of the cruiser *Boston*, fifth in line behind the *Olympia*. When the moon went down a short time later, Dewey reduced the squadron's speed to four knots. The sun was beginning to rise on a sweltering day as the tense Americans neared the harbor of Manila. Suddenly a sailor sang out; he had sighted Spanish warships five miles to the south.

Dewey increased the squadron's speed to eight knots and bore down on his prey. The Spaniards opened fire, but their shells fell wide of the mark. It was 5:40 A.M. when the sixty-year-old Dewey turned to Charles V. Gridley, captain of the *Olympia*, and intoned, "You may fire when you are ready, Gridley."[2] The squadron closed to within five thousand yards of the enemy, and Gridley gave the order. An eight-inch gun on the cruiser's forward turret spoke, and then the other five warships in Dewey's column began to blast the Spanish armada. In all, fifty-three heavy guns joined the action on the American side.

An English expert had written in 1876 that there "never was such a hapless, broken-down, tattered, forlorn apology for a navy as that possessed by the United States."[3] In twenty-two years, things had changed. Dewey's ships were now nearly state-of-the-art, while those of his opposite number, Rear Adm. Don Patricio Montojo y Pasarón, were outgunned and outdated. A man with pessimism written all over his face, Montojo had known for weeks that Dewey's squadron was ready to descend on the Philippines. He had done what he could to prepare for the day of reckoning, but the European officers in Hong Kong had greatly overestimated the Spanish admiral's destructive power.

Despite their advantages, the gunners of Dewey's squadron did not make a brilliant showing in Manila Bay. They fired 5,859 shells during the battle but scored only 142 hits. From the navigator's platform of the *Olympia*, Lt. C. G. Calkins surveyed the scene with dismay: "It was hard to be sure of the fall of any particular shell," he noted, "but many splashed ineffectually. Yet our batteries kept hammering away, straining and jarring the ship in the shock of their recoil."[4]

Observed from the other side, the effect of Dewey's firepower was more memorable. Admiral Montojo had the unenviable fate of watching his flagship, the *Reina Cristina*, being blown to bits around him:

> A fresh shell exploded in the officers' cabin, covering the hospital with blood, destroying the wounded who were being treated there. Another exploded in the ammunition room astern, filling the quarters with smoke. . . . [W]hile the fire astern increased, fire was started forward by another shell, which went through the hull and exploded on the deck.[5]

Eight of Montojo's vessels were sunk and 161 of his sailors perished on May 1, 1898. No Americans were killed, although nine were wounded, by Spanish shells, which caused only minor damage to Dewey's six warships. The overwhelming victory of the Asiatic Squadron helped make the war America's most popular foreign adventure. As Dewey himself put it, "The dash of our squadron into an Oriental bay 7,000 miles from home had the glamour of romance."[6]

The triumphant commodore was awarded the rank of rear admiral, effective immediately; soon he would be promoted to full admiral. While keenly aware that he had dazzled the American people, Dewey took his success in stride, for he had long suspected that a hero slumbered in his breast, awaiting only the magic touch of destiny to inaugurate a new era. By Dewey's lights, the success of his squadron had done just that: It had made the United States "a world-power, with a resultant impetus to the national imagination and a new entail of national responsibilities."[7] More spontaneously, William Randolph Hearst's *New York Journal* exclaimed that "the *Maine* is avenged!"[8]

The shore batteries of Manila had taken shots at Dewey just before he engaged the Spanish fleet. As he steamed into its harbor after the battle, he sent word that the city of 300,000 souls would be annihilated if his warships were challenged again. The governor-general, Don Basilio Augustín, replied that his forts would hold their fire as long as the U.S. squadron did likewise. Satisfied, Dewey ordered his captains to drop their anchors. The people of Manila, realizing that the hand of destruction had been stayed, gathered on the city's old stone ramparts and stared out at the fleet, which, though brilliantly white in peacetime, was now wearing its dun-colored war paint. A brass band aboard the *Olympia* pointed its instruments shoreward and struck up a Spanish air called "La Paloma"; still, the atmosphere was thick with tension. The Spaniards glared at the victorious fleet from their ramparts, while the Americans glared back with all the sangfroid they could muster.

In his role of incipient U.S. viceroy, Dewey was almost as wary of the Filipinos as the Spanish. He discovered that reports of political unrest in the colony were perfectly true: The islands seethed with patriots who had been fighting their Spanish masters at intervals for several years before the advent of American power in Manila Bay. By the spring of 1898, the nationalist movement had developed a group of widely recognized leaders. Chief among them was a dignified young general with amazing organizational abilities. His full name was Emilio Aguinaldo y Famy.

The Spaniards had forced Aguinaldo into exile toward the end of 1897. While the U.S. warships were still at Hong Kong, he had sent a cable to Dewey, offering to travel from Singapore for a meeting. Dewey agreed, but war was declared and the Asiatic Squadron sailed for the Philippines before Aguinaldo arrived. Finally, he was able to obtain passage to Manila Bay on an American dispatch boat, and the khaki-clad general came aboard the *Olympia* on May 19. As Dewey later remembered him, Aguinaldo "was not yet 30, a soft-spoken, unimpressive little man, who had enormous prestige with the Filipino people."[9]

The American admiral blew hot and cold about the Filipino nationalists and their young leader. He decided to cultivate Aguinaldo without bolstering his authority in a major way: "Aside from permitting him to establish himself ashore, the only aid rendered him was a gift of some Mauser rifles and an old smooth-bore [cannon] that had been abandoned by the Spanish."[10] The arms, captured by Dewey's marines from a Spanish arsenal, were put to good use. Aguinaldo ordered his men to step up their attacks on nearby Spanish outposts, which had come under Filipino fire even as the Asiatic Squadron approached from China.

There was a garrison of thirteen thousand troops in Manila, and another fourteen thousand Spaniards were scattered throughout the archipelago. Most of them were soon besieged by Aguinaldo's volunteers, who would number over forty thousand within weeks. Although Dewey had trouble grasping how much the return of "unimpressive little" Aguinaldo had electrified the country-side, he was grateful for the protection that the Filipinos afforded the American detachment that had moved ashore.

Of native Malay (Tagalog) stock, but with Chinese blood as well, Emilio Aguinaldo was the sixth of eight children of Carlos Jamir Aguinaldo, a lawyer at Kawit near Manila, and a "solicitous and loving mother,"[11] Doña Teneng, who had labored for three very long days to give him birth. According to Aguinaldo's memoirs, the midwife had despaired of a successful delivery "when my father thought of a most extraordinary plan to save my mother. Surreptitiously, he went downstairs to light a *berso* (giant firecracker). The sudden loud explosion startled my mother and . . . I saw the light of day."[12] Grown to manhood, Aguinaldo stood five feet three inches tall—about average for a Filipino—and weighed something like 115 pounds. Although he had little formal education, he gained experience as a seaborne trader, cattle rancher, and local politician before he found his true love: the cause of his country's freedom.

During the Philippine insurrection of 1896–97, he commanded the army of a secret organization known as the Katipunan, a Malay word signifying "Society of the Sons of the People." Early in the fighting he captured a Spanish general's sword inscribed "Made in Toledo 1869"—the year of Aguinaldo's birth—and thereafter, with the weapon at his side, he assumed the title of generalissimo. At first his program demanded equal treatment of colonizers and colonized, and aimed at expelling the corrupt Spanish friars who controlled so much of the archipelago. Before long he would call for the complete independence of the Philippine people, who were 7 or 8 million strong.

Lawrence of Arabia once wrote that "freedom is enjoyed when you are so well armed, or so turbulent, or inhabit a country so thorny that the expense of . . . occupying you is greater than the profit."[13] Aguinaldo worked to make Filipinos turbulent enough to drive out their European masters. But the Spanish were loathe to leave; they had, after all, been exploiting the country for over three hundred years. The history of their presence went back to the globe-girdling expedition of Ferdinand Magellan, who had been killed by Filipinos shortly after claiming the islands for the Spanish king in 1521. So the Spaniards had learned to anticipate resistance from the very beginning. They had seen scores of Filipino rebels before Aguinaldo, and expected to see scores more before they were forced to quit the archipelago.

When Dewey sailed into Manila Bay, the American war with Spain became entangled with the Philippine revolution. Aguinaldo embraced the Americans—a nation without a notable history of overseas expansion—as the harbingers of his country's liberation. But Dewey and Aguinaldo had misread each other from the beginning. After their first meeting aboard the *Olympia*, Aguinaldo believed that the admiral had recognized his authority and promised him independence for the Philippines. Dewey later denied Aguinaldo's claims and treated them as a kind of slander. Whatever was said, Aguinaldo should have realized that the word of a naval commander was no guarantee of home rule. His insistence that Dewey had officially recognized the anticolonial government was useful as propaganda but worth little as diplomacy.

Testifying before a congressional committee in 1902, Dewey drew an analogy between his experience in the Philippines and his earlier role as an officer in the Union navy: "I was in the South in the Civil War, and the only friends we had in the South were the negroes, and we made use of them."[14] Dewey saw in the Filipino insurgents another people who would "help us just exactly as the negroes helped us in the Civil War." The admiral was also emphatic about the nature of his relations with Aguinaldo: "He and I were always on the most friendly terms; we never had any differences. He considered me as his liberator, as his friend."[15]

Aguinaldo did perceive Dewey as a friend—temporarily. On May 24, 1898, when he put himself at the head of a military junta, he declared that the United States believed Filipinos to be "sufficiently civilized and capable of governing for ourselves our unfortunate country."[16] Then, on the afternoon of June 12, three weeks after the meeting aboard the *Olympia*, Aguinaldo proclaimed the Philippines a free republic "under the protection of the Mighty and Humane North American Nation."[17] The climax of the independence ceremony came when Aguinaldo unfurled a national flag of his own design. He issued a decree on June 23 that gave the new republic a provisional government with himself as president. His rationale for rebellion was hard to refute: "A people which has given proofs of valor and long-suffering in time of trouble and danger, and of industry and diligence in time of peace, is not intended for slavery."[18]

Striving to broaden the appeal of his personal rule, Aguinaldo formed a three-member cabinet on July 15. Dewey was more impressed by the Filipinos' military prowess than their political achievements:

The insurgents had been at work only two months with an organization of the flimsiest character, yet by means of guerrilla warfare, developed from years of experience in their resistance to Spanish domination, had not only advanced their lines along the beach almost to the fortifications [of Manila], but had invested the city on the inland side as well.[19]

Obviously, Aguinaldo's organization was not so flimsy as the admiral believed.

Two months after Dewey destroyed the Spanish fleet, contingents of the U.S. army began to arrive in the Philippines. The first American troops ever to cross the Pacific, Brig. Gen. Thomas M. Anderson's force of 2,500 arrived on June 30. Along the way they had paused to dispossess the Spaniards of the island of Guam, which, except for a period of Japanese occupation during World War II, has been an American possession ever since. The dark woolen uniforms worn by Anderson's men would have been more suitable for wintering in Wyoming than summering in the tropics, but Admiral Dewey was no less relieved to see them. On July 17, when an additional 3,600 men of the U.S. Army reached Manila, they were able to establish themselves close to the city without opposition, taking over trenches that had been dug by Aguinaldo's nationalists.

The U.S. command was designated the Eighth Army Corps. In charge was Maj. Gen. Wesley Merritt, the army's second-ranking officer, whose steely eyes made him look almost Prussian. Merritt arrived in the Philippines toward the end of July with the five thousand troops of Brig. Gen. Arthur MacArthur, the father of Douglas MacArthur. American soldiers in Manila, who now numbered eleven thousand, found little glory in their foreign expedition, for incessant monsoon rains kept them soaked to the skin. Wanting his own men to turn the Spaniards out of Manila, Aguinaldo treated the foreigners with suspicion. He had felt that U.S. warships posed little threat to—and might even guarantee—Philippine independence, but a horde of American troops looked like the vanguard of a new colonialism. Eventually, he would attempt to negotiate their return to the United States; for the time being, he tried to cooperate with the generals of this large and increasingly unwelcome presence.

With the Eighth Army Corps on hand, Admiral Dewey prepared to assault Manila. Suffering the familiar fate of the besieged, the people of the city had grown short on food and water but long on garbage and disease. Manila's new governor-general, Fermín Jáudenes, whose Filipino troops had deserted to Aguinaldo, saw that resistance was futile, but he refused to surrender Manila before being fired upon. Accordingly, on August 13, Dewey's flagship led the Asiatic Squadron away from its anchorage and blasted one of the city's dilapidated forts. At the same time, the American troops ashore advanced on the walled city. Jáudenes surrendered within two hours.

General Merritt reported that "after the battle the insurgent forces gathered outside the American lines endeavoring to gain admission to the town, but strong guards were posted and General Aguinaldo was given to understand that no insurgent would be allowed to enter with arms."[20] Clearly, the Filipinos had missed their opportunity. If Aguinaldo had ordered his troops to attack the city before the U.S. infantry arrived, the battle with the Spaniards would have been bloody, but he would have become sole master of Manila, and the fait accompli might have impressed the McKinley administration enough to secure Philippine independence. Aguinaldo, who did not have the advantage of hindsight, had failed to strike while the iron was hot.

On August 16, word reached Dewey that a protocol ending the 113-day Spanish-American War had been signed in Washington on August 12 by representatives of the two belligerent powers, so the fall of Manila actually followed the formal cessation of hostilities. The Asiatic Squadron and the Eighth Army Corps rejoiced, thinking the Philippine campaign over. In fact, it had barely begun.

Dewey's long months in the tropical climate had left him exhausted. Now that the U.S. Army was the major force in the Philippines, he mainly looked forward to his daily carriage ride along Manila's coastal roads. His decline into relative inactivity did nothing to hurt his reputation, and in March 1899, when Congress authorized McKinley to revive the title of Admiral of the Navy, the honor was given to Dewey. He was also allowed to use the *Olympia* as his personal transportation for returning to the United States.

In late August, General Merritt was replaced by another veteran of the Civil War and the Indian wars, Maj. Gen. Elwell S. Otis, who was plump, bald, bewhiskered, fussy, and sixty-one years old. Arthur MacArthur called him "a locomotive bottomside up on the track, with its wheels revolving at full speed."[21] Otis tried to make the Filipinos behave "like good Indians," but his major achievement was to embitter relations between himself and Aguinaldo, whom he refused to meet. When he wrote to the Filipino president, he adopted an imperious tone: "Bear in mind that the United States has swept the Spanish flag from the seas, kept Spanish troops from being sent to the Philippines . . . and has had Manila at its mercy since May 1st."[22]

When General Otis ordered the insurgents to evacuate the city's suburbs, Aguinaldo complied—and felt bitterly betrayed. By now the course of events had convinced him that the United States would try to hold the Philippines as a colony of its own, and he was determined to resist the American presence, no matter what the cost. In September, he and his cabinet established a temporary capital in the town of Malolos, twenty miles to the northwest, and convened a congress of Filipino dignitaries. But he kept most of his troops in an arc around Manila.

It was as though the Americans had passed through Aguinaldo's original siege lines only to be besieged in their turn. Back in Washington, Thomas B. Reed, the Speaker of the House, had foreseen complications if the United States occupied the islands. He remarked that "we have about ten million [Filipinos] at two dollars a head unpicked, and nobody knows what it will cost to pick them."[23] General Otis was about to find out.

President McKinley need not have pressed for American possession of the islands. The casus belli that had led to war with Spain was in the Caribbean, not the western Pacific: The United States wanted the Spaniards out of Cuba, whose people were more than eager to see them go. But McKinley felt that the electorate had gradually come to favor the annexation of the Philippines. Misreading the nation's mood when the *Maine* exploded, he had been slow to declare war on Spain and had, he knew, almost lost the public's confidence by hesitating. Now he sensed that taking over the Philippines—as well as Puerto Rico and Guam—would cement America's military triumph and promote his personal popularity. After all, the American people had approved when the Hawaiian Islands were annexed in July 1898.

The protocol ending the fighting settled all the major issues but one: the future of the archipelago. At the Paris peace conference, the Spanish made it clear that they had reconciled themselves to the loss of Cuba, but they were intent on keeping the Philippines. In a sense, Aguinaldo's insurrection served the American negotiators very well. They could claim that Spain lacked the resources to defeat the Filipino freedom fighters even if the United States *did* withdraw from the islands. On November 21, the Spanish were presented with a U.S. ultimatum demanding that they accept $20 million as compensation for the loss of their facilities in the Philippines. Fearing that the United States would resume hostilities if they refused, the Spanish accepted.

McKinley claimed that he had pondered and prayed for a long time before deciding to keep the Philippines. Ignoring the fact that most Filipinos had converted to Catholicism under Spanish rule, the president announced that America's mission was "to educate the Filipinos, and uplift and civilize and Christianize them. . . . I sent for the chief engineer of the War Department (our mapmaker), and I told him to put the Philippines on the map of the United States."[24] Instead of listening to Emilio Aguinaldo, Americans like McKinley attuned themselves to the sentiments of Rudyard Kipling, the British author of an occasional poem addressed to the new masters of the archipelago. Kipling encouraged the United States to

> Take up the White Man's burden—
>   Send forth the best ye breed . . .
> To wait in heavy harness
>   On fluttered folk and wild—
> Your new-caught, sullen peoples,
>   Half devil and half child.[25]

Caught in the coils of what they considered U.S. perfidy, Aguinaldo and his followers were sullen indeed. It seemed astonishing to them that McKinley had promised independence to Cuba—a nearby island in which Americans had been interested for decades and where they had already invested millions of dollars—yet would deny freedom to the Philippines, a distant country of whose existence they had scarcely been aware. In fact, Cuba's independence was strictly limited and subject to the prerogatives of a U.S. protectorate, but Aguinaldo's case seems strengthened in retrospect by comments that Dewey included in his autobiography of 1913:

At that time [just before the outbreak of the Spanish-American War] the Philippines were to us a *terra incognita*. No ship of our service had been there for
years. When, after my appointment as commander of the Asiatic Squadron, I
sought information on the subject in Washington, I found that the latest official
report relative to the Philippines on file in the office of naval intelligence bore
the date of 1876.[26]

A military strategist himself, Aguinaldo understood that Dewey had attacked
the Philippines in order to divert the attention of the Spanish from Cuba and
its surrounding waters, which constituted the main theater of the war. If the
Asian archipelago had been formidably defended, the U.S. Navy would have
taken no interest in it, and its conquest would not have been necessary for a
successful conclusion to the war. But there was good evidence that the Spanish
could be defeated in the Philippines, so the attack was ordered. The decision
was purely military; in the spring of 1898, few bureaucrats in Washington,
D.C., were thinking about the future disposition of the islands. The government was too preoccupied with the business of fighting and winning the war.

To Aguinaldo's mind, the islands had been liberated by his own forces and
were no longer Spain's to sell or cede. As he later put it, "Spain could not
convey sovereignty over the Philippines to the United States because we had
superseded the Spanish government with our own."[27] (In the end, the matter
came before the U.S. Supreme Court, which found that, notwithstanding Filipino protests, Spain's colonial title had been valid.) Aguinaldo had another
argument to advance: that it would be illegal for the United States to take
formal possession of the islands, since the U.S. Constitution did not provide
for acquiring overseas colonies. Senator George G. Vest, a Democrat from Missouri, agreed and told his illustrious colleagues that no territory could be governed by the United States unless it were being prepared for statehood.

Senator George F. Hoar, a Republican from Massachusetts, was less interested in the legal niceties than the moral implications of the controversy. After
describing Aguinaldo as the "Patrick Henry, Nathan Hale, and George Washington of the Philippines,"[28] Hoar said that annexing the archipelago would
make the United States "a cheapjack country, raking after the cart for the leav-
ings of European tyranny."[29] But the treaty with Spain that transferred possession of the Philippines to the United States did receive a bare two-thirds
majority in the Senate. It was ratified by a vote of 57–27 on February 6, 1899.

Not every member of McKinley's cabinet was delighted with the outcome.
Secretary of the Navy John D. Long was unhappy about, but resigned to, the
new American order. He wrote to his wife that "if I could have had my way, I
wouldn't have had the war, and I wouldn't have been burdened with Puerto
Rico or Cuba or the Philippines. They are an elephant, just as everything else
is an elephant that disturbs the even tenor of our national way, but there they
are, and my shoulder goes to the wheel."[30] Many Americans found it harder to
conform. The grand old men of New York and Boston who had spoken out
against Southern slavery in their youth saw a new John Brown in Aguinaldo
and believed that America was terribly wrong to subjugate the people of the

archipelago. They delighted in a riposte to Kipling by the president of the New York Anti-Imperialist League, Ernest H. Crosby:

> Take up the White Man's burden;
>   Send forth your sturdy sons,
> And load them down with whiskey
>   And Testaments and guns. . . .
> In a world of canting hypocrites
>   This kind of business pays.[31]

The expansionists countered the rhetoric of the anti-imperialists with a strain of their own, announcing that the Philippines had been emancipated, not conquered. McKinley said that the real conquest would come only if the United States shirked her duty and stepped aside, for then either Japan or Germany or France would establish itself as master of the islands.

Humbug, answered the anti-imperialists: like greedy Europeans, you are only creating a base for commercial expansion in east Asia, especially in China. Hoping to turn Manila into a second Hong Kong, you have sold out the freedom of the Filipinos in the name of Mammon.

Not at all, the administration replied. We will train the Filipinos in the art of self-government, and in the fullness of time their own leaders will take control of their national destiny.

In the House of Representatives, John Sharp Williams of Mississippi asked, "Who made us God's globe-trotting vice-regents to forestall mismanagement everywhere?"[32] Ignoring Williams's sarcasm, McKinley and his spokesmen continued to recite their catechism. We are the true champions of the Philippine people, they said. Rather than leave the dusky islanders in a chaos of premature independence, we are guiding them toward the day of their true liberation.

The administration's arguments sounded convincing to most Americans, but its vision needed the cooperation of the Filipinos above all else, and the Filipinos did not cooperate. Within a few months of Manila's fall, Aguinaldo's troops and their American occupiers spoiled McKinley's plans by leveling their rifles at each other. The first shots were fired in the city's eastern suburbs, at a place where the U.S. perimeter was separated from Filipino territory by the murky waters of the little San Juan River. On Saturday evening, February 4, 1899, a rambunctious young private from Beatrice, Nebraska, by the name of William Walter Grayson started out on a routine patrol. With him, suffering from the same mosquitoes and the same humid heat, was Priv. Orville Miller.

As they approached the banks of the San Juan, darkness was coming on apace. Suddenly someone whistled, and a lantern with a red glass appeared in the old Spanish blockhouse that lay just ahead. Private Grayson understood that an alarm had been given. He would later recount that "something rose slowly up not 20 feet in front of us. It was a Filipino. I yelled 'Halt!' . . . he immediately shouted 'Halto!' at me. Well, I thought the best thing to do was to shoot him."[33]

Grayson raised his .45 Springfield rifle and pulled the trigger. The Filipino fell, but two of his comrades sprang out of the shadows. Miller wounded one of them and Grayson reloaded in time to shoot at the other. The two Americans then escaped. Roaring into camp, Grayson yelled out a warning and exposed the rampant racism of the time in one and the same breath, "Line up, fellows, the niggers are in here all through these yards!"[34]

General Otis had anticipated just such an incident, and orders to launch a general offensive were transmitted to each of his units. As Aguinaldo interpreted the situation, "the Americans had a well-coordinated plan of aggression and they now put it into immediate execution."[35] After rifle fire broke out all around Manila, American artillery and Dewey's naval guns joined in the action. At the end of twenty-four hours, about three thousand Filipinos had been killed, while U.S. fatalities amounted to sixty. One American soldier wrote his parents that the fighting was more fun than a turkey shoot, and a British observer in Manila said the same thing from a different point of view, denouncing the U.S. offensive as "simple massacre and murderous butchery."[36]

The Republic of the Philippines and the United States of America were at war, and the hatred that the Filipinos had felt for the friars and soldiers of Spain was now transferred to the U.S. Eighth Army Corps. Although Aguinaldo issued a decree from Malolos that legally recognized the state of hostilities, he entered the conflict with neither rancor nor gusto, saying that "no one can deplore more than I this rupture. . . . I have a clear conscience that I endeavored to avoid it at all costs, using all my utmost efforts to preserve friendship with the army of occupation, despite frequent humiliation and many sacrificed rights."[37] The historical record bears out Aguinaldo's statement, though he was widely denounced in the American press as a despot leading a band of brigands.

Wearing khaki newly imported from Hong Kong, the U.S. troops geared up to annihilate Aguinaldo's nationalist warriors. But if General Otis had pushed them too far into the interior, he would have lacked the manpower necessary to protect Manila and secure the archipelago's other strategic islands. So Otis requested more troops—and again more troops. On the eve of the Philippine-American War there had been only 28,000 officers and men in the entire U.S. Army. By the first summer of the twentieth century, 70,000 American soldiers were serving at over 400 posts in the archipelago. The McKinley administration had decided to use a very big stick to beat a very young republic.

During the early months of the war, Aguinaldo attempted to meet the Americans on their own terms, pitting his regiments against the massed weight of the U.S. Army. When he realized that the pains of this approach outweighed the gains, he reverted to the guerrilla tactics that had been effective against the Spanish. His success was only partial. At a time when Aguinaldo needed all of his countrymen to be ardent nationalists, the political vision of too many Filipino peasants extended only as far as the next valley. Aguinaldo might have inspired their loyalty by dispossessing their landlords and giving them fields of their own to till, but he was not an agrarian reformer. The peasants knew him as more of a tax collector than a defender of their rights.

In the autumn of 1899, General Otis launched a new offensive that aimed above all at capturing Aguinaldo. The Filipino president had already experienced his share of setbacks, including the loss of Malolos, his capital, on March 1. As Otis's troops closed in on his retreating army of twelve hundred, Aguinaldo's infant daughter, Flora, perished of a fever; soon, the Americans snared the stragglers in his column, who included his mother and four-year-old son Miguel. His wife was also with him, but she became ill and had to surrender to their pursuers.

As they climbed into the rain-drenched highlands of central Luzon, Aguinaldo and his army ran out of food. His steps were dogged by three tenacious U.S. detachments, and he needed all of his cunning and luck to avoid capture. His men became exhausted and ill; Aguinaldo himself suffered from malaria and bronchitis. Finally, after ten months of harrowing adventures, the pathetic remnant of his personal command staggered into Palanan, a village near the remote and inhospitable northeast coast of Luzon, where he established a new headquarters. No longer in a position to control the daily operations of the resistance, he delegated authority to his guerrilla commanders.

When General Otis, who had not been popular with his troops, left the Philippines in May 1900, his place as theater commander and military governor was taken by Arthur MacArthur. In June, General MacArthur freed a number of political prisoners and issued a general amnesty to all of Aguinaldo's men, who were promised "complete immunity as to the past and absolute liberty of action as to the future."[38] In order to benefit from the amnesty, they were required to lay down their arms and take an oath of allegiance to the American flag. The islands were growing weary of war, but the offer attracted few Filipinos despite the thirty pesos MacArthur paid for each gun surrendered to U.S. authorities. From his fastness in Palanan, Aguinaldo countered MacArthur's offer with fresh words of defiance.

Among the U.S. troops to enter the Philippines were two black regiments who joked that they had "come to take up the white man's burden."[39] That burden grew heavier by the month. As casualties mounted, a brutal policy was instituted: Whenever advancing Americans ran into an ambush, every Filipino home for miles around was put to the torch. Aguinaldo denounced MacArthur's men for their "shameless violations of the most elementary laws."[40] Each side blamed the other for the spread of terrorism.

Both armies engaged in criminal conduct. In November 1900, the *Philadelphia Ledger* reported some revolting details of what had become a very harrowing war: "Our men have been relentless; have killed to exterminate men, women, children, prisoners and captives, active insurgents and suspected people, from lads of ten and up. . . . Our soldiers have pumped salt water into men to 'make them talk,' have taken prisoner people who held up their hands and peacefully surrendered, and an hour later, without an atom of evidence to show that they were even *insurrectos,* stood them on a bridge and shot them down."[41] Filipinos committed similar acts, inspiring U.S. forces to try and execute seventy-nine captured guerrillas for war crimes.

*   *   *

As assistant secretary of the navy in 1897, Theodore Roosevelt had written that war with Spain would be good for the moral fiber of the United States, since it would give Americans "something to think of which isn't material gain."[42] When his rough-riding days in Cuba came to an end, the Philippines seemed to call Roosevelt's name. In 1900, he lobbied the White House to become the first civil governor of the islands, but the president had already chosen Judge William Howard Taft for the job; and Roosevelt, though he had little admiration for either McKinley or the vice presidency, was forced to content himself with the second spot on the Republican ticket.

Aguinaldo knew Roosevelt by reputation, and he recognized that the rise of such a man boded ill for the Filipino cause. He therefore pinned his hopes on the Democratic candidate for president, William Jennings Bryan, whose election in 1900 might reasonably be expected to bring the Philippines peace and freedom. Shortly after his nomination, Bryan seemed to be obliging Aguinaldo, for he denounced McKinley's foreign policy as flagrant imperialism in the European or Japanese mode. As U.S. causalities from fighting the Filipinos mounted, Bryan expected the American people to revolt. When they did not, he downplayed the issue.

Roosevelt was more consistent. Out on the campaign trail, he kept repeating that the United States was coming of age in the Philippines. The nation was expanding before the eyes of the entire world, and although the process might at first be painful for Filipino and American alike, history had decreed that the United States show its great heart and courage by subjugating the people of those tropical climes. As the killing went on, Roosevelt's visions of glory began to seem unreal. Nevertheless, he helped McKinley beat Bryan by a wide margin. Aguinaldo responded to the election results with deep disappointment, but he apparently experienced no forebodings of disaster.

He should have. Unknown to anyone at the time, he was on a collision course with Frederick Funston, whom Roosevelt would one day fête as a genuine American hero. Although a brigadier general of American volunteers and winner of the Congressional Medal of Honor, Funston had the mindset of a soldier of fortune. Intercepting a set of messages from Aguinaldo, he discovered the location of the rebel headquarters at Palanan and immediately decided to descend on the place with some of his Filipino collaborators, who would be dressed like Aguinaldo's own men. Funston set about refining the details of the operation with his aide, Lazaro Segovia.

On March 23, 1901, Segovia led eighty collaborators into the square of Palanan, where sixty of Aguinaldo's guerrillas stood in formation. Convinced that they were being reinforced, the guerrillas greeted the newcomers with comradely smiles. Suddenly guns started to go off. Thinking that his own troops had fired a welcoming salute, Aguinaldo strode to the window of his headquarters and shouted, "Stop that foolishness. Don't waste ammunition!"[43] Then he realized that something very bizarre was happening: His troops were being slaughtered by the new arrivals! Horrified, he turned to face the men in the room with him. One of them was Segovia, who now shouted, "We are not insurgents, we are Americans! Surrender or be killed!" As two of his lieutenants resisted and were shot, Aguinaldo tried to draw his pistol from its holster; but his doctor, Santiago Barcelona, saved his life by staying his hand. In another moment Funston entered the village and heard Segovia shout in Spanish, "We have him!"

"You are a prisoner of war of the Army of the United States of America," Funston announced as he strode into the room. Identifying himself, Funston told Aguinaldo, who had tears in his eyes, that he would be "sent to Manila at the first opportunity in a steamer, which is coming to take us on board in the bay of this village." Aguinaldo asked in Spanish, "Is this a joke?" The next day, when Funston was describing the details of the successful operation, Aguinaldo threw up his hands and said, "Is there no limit to what you Americans can do?"[44] Much later, he would call his capture the result of "an ungentlemanly and unsportsmanlike ruse."[45]

Although Admiral Dewey suggested that Aguinaldo be shot, cooler heads in Washington understood that their worst move would be to make him a martyr. Admitting defeat, Aguinaldo helped matters along by becoming an apostate to his own cause. After twenty-three days of detention in Manila, he swore that he would henceforth owe his allegiance to the United States and urged his people to lay down their arms. This act did wonders for Aguinaldo's reputation in America. The New York Times had characterized him a liar and a looter, but now it detected in the Filipino leader a "warm, friendly, intelligent, trustworthy, and reasonable person—a man of honor with the best interests of his countrymen at heart."[46]

Later, Aguinaldo would describe his response to the sudden ruin of his fortunes: "My capture, together with the treachery and betrayal that accompanied it, left me deeply angered, then distressed, then almost completely numbed."[47] Yet he also retained hope for the future: "I could not bring myself to believe that the United States as a nation could be as bad a master as Spain. A sixth sense somehow assured me that America would sooner or later redress the sins of her individual sons."[48] It was a convenient belief, and it earned Aguinaldo more than the gratitude of the American press. It also convinced General MacArthur to make his captivity a good deal more comfortable.

Taft, the future U.S. president, who on July 4, 1901, would become the first civil governor of the Philippines, disagreed with MacArthur's decision to treat Aguinaldo leniently. Thinking him an incorrigible, Taft pressed for his banishment to Guam, which the Spaniards had used as a dumping-ground for political prisoners before the Americans began to fill it with their own set of unreconstructed Filipino nationalists. However, MacArthur, who left Manila on the same day Taft became governor, won the argument.

There was an undeniable element of opportunism in Aguinaldo's defection. Yet like so many of his countrymen, he wanted to give the United States a chance to show what it had to offer the Philippines. And the U.S. program did create basic institutions—including a network of schools, a functional judiciary, a civil service system, and a public works administration—that were far superior to the colonial apparatus of the Spaniards. But on the whole, the American attempt at social engineering in a foreign land was not a great success. The plight of the peasants, sunk in their ageless poverty, continued under the Americans, who were no more successful than Aguinaldo in instituting land reform.

On July 4, 1902, Theodore Roosevelt—who had become president when McKinley was assassinated in the fall of 1901—declared the Philippine War over and ordered Aguinaldo released. This presidential public relations effort reflected Roosevelt's perception that Americans had become sick and tired of hearing about all that death on all those godforsaken islands away off in the Pacific. But his announcement was distinctly premature, for pockets of resistance existed in the Philippines for a dozen or more years.

Still, in 1902, the war's statistical profile could be compiled without fear of great change in the future. Over a period of three years, more than 120,000 American troops had served in the Philippines. The death toll for U.S. forces topped 4,200, while more than 2,800 had been wounded; tropical diseases killed thousands more. Some 20,000 of Aguinaldo's soldiers had also died, as did over 200,000 Filipino civilians, mostly from such indirect effects of the fighting as malnutrition and epidemic disease.

The length and bitterness of the Philippine insurrection caused Americans to lose much of their appetite for foreign adventures. Their disillusionment was reinforced by the fact that the Philippines did not become a commercial godsend for the United States; its resources were not as cheap nor its markets as profitable as they were projected to be. The archipelago turned out to be a bad investment in many ways. Annexing the Philippines was a major turning point in U.S. history and opened new vistas to U.S. foreign policy—most of them unhappy. Morally, the war was a disaster; politically, it identified the new American order as hardly more noble than colonialism in the European mode.

Taken altogether, the Spanish-American and Philippine-American Wars left the United States with a legacy of dread. Cuba has remained a thorn in America's side, while the Philippine adventure created a long series of complications for both Washington and Manila. Obviously, we had been possessed by our new possessions and ensnared by our own snares, leaving ourselves overextended and exposed to attack—and to the temptation of further Asian misadventures. Even Roosevelt finally realized that the violent destruction of Aguinaldo's republic had been an aberration, and in time he feared that the Philippines would become "our heel of Achilles" in the event of war with Japan. For strategic reasons he decided to base America's Pacific might at Pearl Harbor rather than Manila and Subic Bay, and he came to favor independence for the archipelago at an early date.

For Aguinaldo, the years when most men are at the height of their influence were strangely anticlimactic. He had been a generalissimo in his late twenties, a president at the age of thirty, and a spent force at thirty-three—when he still had more than sixty years of life in him. But he did not become embittered.

After his release by the Americans, he founded the Association of the Veterans of the Revolution and worked tirelessly until he won small pensions for his old comrades. Once, in the 1930s, he stood for national office and was resoundingly defeated. He made little impression on Filipino politics from 1902 until the Japanese conquered the Philippines in 1942, when he publicly declared that his homeland should be proud of joining Japan's Greater East Asia Co-Prosperity Sphere, and served on the puppet government's council of state.

In March 1945, after Douglas MacArthur had fulfilled his famous promise to return, Aguinaldo was once again imprisoned by U.S. authorities, who considered prosecuting him for his dealings with the Japanese. Aguinaldo found a convincing way to justify his actions: "I was already in my seventies and I no longer possessed the hardiness and strength to run up [into] the mountains."[49] He was exonerated, and when the Filipinos finally gained their independence on July 4, 1946, his countrymen overlooked the several layers of tarnish on their old hero and honored him as one of the authors of their sovereignty. They were generous to do so. But it was that kind of day—a long overdue triumph for Filipino and American alike.

6

Kaiser Billy and the War to End War

There was one class of Europeans for whom the American people felt antagonism from the beginning, and for a long time thereafter: royalty. The United States grew up in the faith that the future belonged to democracy, while the monarchs of Europe were dwindling survivors of an antidemocratic age whose hour had struck. The errors of the past were understandable enough; before the birth of the United States, there had never been a modern democracy to serve as an example for the rest of the world. Now there was. And it would only be a matter of time before that example proved contagious.

Everyone in the United States knew what to expect from crowned heads. Since their vanity was infamous, their quarrels endless, and their abuse of power incessant, a world of kings would never know peace. Only the triumph of U.S.-style republics would usher in an age of human rights and the brotherhood of man. The fact that Spain was headed by the Bourbon dynasty had made it easier to initiate hostilities in 1898, but America's culminating crusade against royalty did not develop until 1917, when it went to war with George III's great-great-grandson, Kaiser Wilhelm II.

The destiny of Wilhelm, who reigned as king of Prussia and German emperor from 1888 to 1918, was to enter the world buttocks first. But the complications of his difficult birth were no laughing matter, for a clumsy use of the forceps by the royal doctors crippled his left arm for life. Despite his handicap, he developed the normal boyhood fascination with war, and learned to rest his strengthless left hand on the hilt of his little swords. Wilhelm I, his beloved grandfather, shored up his boyish confidence by making him a member of the First Foot Guards regiment—and awarding him the Black Eagle, Prussia's highest decoration—on his tenth birthday.

His English mother, Vicky, who was Princess Royal of Great Britain by birth as well as Crown Princess of Prussia by marriage, feared that Wilhelm would be corrupted by the militarism that lay over Germany like a fog. To Queen Victoria, her own mother, Vicky reported that "poor Willy in his uniform looks like some unfortunate little monkey dressed up, standing on the top of an organ."[1] But his mother's British skepticism did nothing to moderate the Prussian strain in the kaiser-to-be. By the time he reached his teens, Wilhelm was walking with the stiff stride of a young man determined to overcome his handicap and be every inch a warrior in the grand tradition of Frederick the Great and the Hohenzollern dynasty. His uniforms (he owned more than two hundred) were among the gaudiest in gaudy old Europe. The motto of this enfant terrible was "Full Steam Ahead."

Unfortunately, Wilhelm's intellectual prowess was no match for the undeniable power of his will. A chatterbox who turned a deaf ear to every tongue but his own, he hated to be left alone and needed the constant attention of servants and yes-men. He was too restless to relish paperwork; he rarely read government reports and found that even newspapers demanded an uncomfortable amount of concentration. What he did enjoy was maneuvering with his army or cruising on his yacht. Unalterably vain, he loved flattery more than riches—and almost as much as weaponry.

The members of the First Foot Guards regiment provided him with his happiest moments. He preferred their company to his wife's, and though he never danced with women, he would waltz with his officers at formal dinners. Among his comrades-in-arms, as he confessed, "I found my family, my friends, my interests, everything that I had previously missed."[2] Such sentiments did not bode well for the peace of the world, but, ironically, Wilhelm would have no direct experience of war until August 1914—and by then he was hardly in a position to risk his life on the battlefield.

Wilhelm remained with his regiment until promoted to major general and given the command of a Berlin-based infantry brigade in 1888. In June of that year, at the age of twenty-nine, he ascended the throne. His first public proclamation was addressed not to his subjects but to the officers and men of his army: "We belong to each other. . . . we were born for each other and will cleave indissolubly to each other, whether it be the will of God to send us calm or storm."[3] As the young kaiser, Wilhelm surrounded himself with an entourage of aristocratic, reactionary officers who isolated him from the civilian world as much as they dared. And they dared greatly. Wilhelm himself was, after all, their willing co-conspirator.

Two months into his reign, he staged his first large-scale review and recorded his reaction for posterity: "The great day has come and gone! My entire guards, 30,000 strong, stood under my command for the first time. And what

a magnificent parade! . . . What a feeling it is to call these troops *my own*."[4]
The conspiracy went on. During the annual war games of the Prussian army,
his generals saw to it that the kaiser's side always won the laurels. In time,
Wilhelm convinced himself that he was a naval as well as a military genius,
telling a group of his admirals that "all of you know nothing; I alone know
something, I alone decide."[5]

A manic-depressive edge marred Wilhelm's personality, and an ineradicable
element of grandiosity distorted his worldview. He longed to astound the nations, to make himself remembered in history as a king among kings. He was
always confusing Germany's military might with the strong right arm of God
and, as a sworn enemy of democracy, always thinking of himself as an instrument of the Divine Will. "We Hohenzollerns," he once claimed, "derive our
crowns from Heaven alone and are answerable only to Heaven for the responsibilities which they imply."[6]

If he never understood the meaning of humility, he nevertheless considered
himself a devout Christian of the Calvinist kind, worshiping as a member of the
established Evangelical Church of Prussia. But his faith was swallowed up by
his ego; his religious beliefs only reinforced his manias and his obsessions. On
a pilgrimage to the Holy Land in the fall of 1898, Wilhelm demonstrated his
piety by entering Jerusalem in a dazzlingly white uniform and a Prussian hel-
met that featured a glittering gold eagle. His mount, a stunning black charger,
was one of the finest warhorses ever seen in Palestine.

World War I, which almost everyone expected to be short, broke out in the
twenty-sixth year of his reign and the fifty-fifth of his life. A month after the
assassination of Franz Ferdinand, heir to the throne of the Austro-Hungarian
Empire, an editorial in *The New York Times* noted that "In this time of passion
and of peril the eyes of the world turn to the German emperor as the chief man
of Europe, the man who more than any other has the power to provoke or to
avert a great war."[7]

According to his memoirs, the kaiser opted for peace. Later, as proof of his
benevolent intentions, he pointed out that he was cruising the fiords of Norway
aboard his yacht while the European crisis was heating up. Such an itinerary,
he noted, would not have been adopted by a warmonger planning to launch a
general offensive—"a task requiring lengthy and secret preparations for mobilization and concentration of troops."[8]

The blame for the outbreak of the fighting, in Wilhelm's view, lay not in
Berlin but east and west of it: "As early as the spring and summer of 1914 . . .
war was prepared for in Russia, France, Belgium and England."[9] The kaiser
believed that his case could be cinched by a look at historical record:

> Had we ever had warlike intentions we should have struck the blow in 1900, when
> England's hands were tied by the Boer War, Russia's by the Japanese War [which
> actually did not begin until 1904], at which time almost certain victory beckoned
> us. In any event, we assuredly would not have singled out the year 1914, when
> we were confronted by a compact, overwhelmingly superior foe.[10]

What should be made of the kaiser's pleas of innocence? Given his belligerent personality and his obsession with military matters, it is impossible not to see him as the guiltiest party of 1914. Over three decades, his strutting and fretting had made the world a more forbidding place, and the massive amounts of capital that he had lavished on his generals and admirals helped to accelerate the European arms race. In the summer of 1914 he had egged on his Austrian allies, whose declaration of war against Serbia in the Balkans caused the Russians to mobilize and led to the other European mobilizations that made bloodshed inevitable. When push came to shove, Wilhelm tried to limit the extent of the conflagration, but the main thrust of his reign was to make hostilities more likely. And he was justly punished, for the crisis brought with it the German high command's worst nightmare: a two-front war.

During his more pessimistic moments, the kaiser suspected that such a contest would be long and drawn-out and ultimately unsuccessful. When, on August 4, the people of Berlin spontaneously converged on the royal residence, he came out on a balcony in a field-gray uniform and bade them "go into the churches, kneel down, and pray for help for our soldiers!"[11] Although he tried to reassure his troops by saying that they would be "home before the leaves have fallen from the trees,"[12] he waited for the outcome of the first battles with fear and trembling.

But the kaiser also savored his possibilities. If Germany prevailed, he would cast a long shadow across the postwar world. It was safe to assume that Russia, Poland, and the Baltic states would lose masses of territory to Germany, while a few more slices of strategic real estate would be cut away from France. Luxembourg might be annexed wholesale; Belgium and Holland, though probably allowed to remain independent in name, would serve Berlin as well. The huge chunks of central Africa that belonged to other European powers in 1914 would be transferred to German control, and the kaiser's sphere of influence in the Middle East and Asia would expand dramatically. Germany would, in short, become the mightiest nation on earth. It was not a scenario that could be relished in Washington, D.C.

Wilhelm's senior generals insisted on retaining operational control over the Wehrmacht, but the kaiser was the Supreme War Lord of the armed forces and there were plenty of areas where he could make his word final. It was Wilhelm's choice of commanders that determined the strategy of the German army on the western front until 1916, and it was on his orders that the surface ships of the German navy avoided engagements with the British fleet. But he left no doubt that his heart was in the battle, that he could face the cruelties of modern warfare without flinching. "Kill as many of the swine as you can,"[13] was a phrase that came easily to his lips.

On May 7, 1915, the *Lusitania*, the largest luxury liner in the north Atlantic, was torpedoed and sunk in the Irish Sea while en route from New York to Liverpool. Walter Schweiger, who captained U-20, the offending German submarine, described the British ship's death in his war diary: "An unusually heavy explosion takes place with a very strong explosion cloud. . . . The superstructure right above the point of impact and the bridge are torn asunder, fire breaks out, and smoke envelops the high bridge." Coming to an immediate halt, the *Lusitania* heeled over to starboard until the bow went under. "It appears," continued Schweiger, "as if the ship were going to capsize very shortly. Great confusion ensues on board. . . . [W]e dived to a depth of 24 meters and ran out to sea. It would have been impossible for me, anyhow, to fire a second torpedo into this crowd of people struggling to save their lives."[14]

The *Lusitania's* dead totaled 1,198, including 124 Americans. Word of the mayhem—even more than the kaiser's invasion of Belgium the previous August—ran through the American people like an electrical shock. Overnight it made them susceptible to all the Allied propaganda that was branding Wilhelm a human devil. Here, it now seemed to many Americans, was a man so cruel that he would send women and their babes-in-arms to agonizing deaths in the noxious, oil-laden waters of a frigid sea. Wilhelm was no longer just a distasteful warlord; he had become a malignant murderer.

News of the *Lusitania* hit President Woodrow Wilson hard. Needing to walk and think, he had left the White House and headed north through Lafayette Park before the Secret Service realized he was gone. He did succeed in remaining calm—almost too calm. Although he labeled the sinking of the great ship a catastrophe "unparalleled in modern warfare,"[15] the three notes of protest that he sent to Berlin were much milder than they might have been. Still, Wilhelm was more sensitive to Wilson's criticism than his restraint. When the kaiser received the third note, he filled the margins with angry notations like "Immeasurably impertinent!" and "You don't say so!" After the final paragraph he wrote: "In tone and bearing this is about the most impudent note which I have ever read. . . . It ends with a direct threat!"[16]

It ended with nothing of the sort. Outraged as he was, Wilson could not afford to provoke the kaiser. He dreamed of healing a wounded world, and if his dreams were to be fulfilled, the Germany hierarchy, every bit as much as the British and the French, would have to be full partners in the peace process he hoped to orchestrate. At any rate, the kaiser did make the seas safer for civilians. Although he kept the specific order secret from the world at large, on June 6, 1915, Wilhelm banned the sinking of passenger vessels.

Woodrow Wilson was a very different man from the German emperor, and he viewed the tragedies of war from a very different perspective. As long as Europeans were killing each other, he would suffer from a terrible sense of dread. Already, in the first month of the conflict, Wilson had written to his confidential adviser, Col. Edward House, that "I feel the burden of the thing almost intolerably from day to day."[17] The president was not alone. In the autumn of 1914, Robert N. Page, a congressman from North Carolina, would confess that "the horror of it all kept me awake for weeks, nor has the awfulness of it all deserted me, but at first it seemed a horrid dream. Now the grim reality of it stuns you."[18] To Theodore Roosevelt's mind, the United States in the second half of 1914 had seemed "blinded, terrified by the extent of the world disaster."[19]

From the beginning, American public opinion had been inclined to favor Britain and the Allies. When Germany ground the Belgians under its heel on its way into northern France, anti-German sentiment came immediately to the fore. Dead set against taking sides, the president signed a formal proclamation of neutrality and counseled the American people to remain neutral in thought as well as deed, but he murmured to the British ambassador that a victory for Wilhelm would force the United States "to take such measures of defense here as would be fatal to our form of government and American ideals."[20] While he was not eager to advertise the fact, Wilson considered the kaiser a sort of throwback to the German barbarians that the Roman historian Tacitus had written about in the first century.

The president's efforts to negotiate an end to the slaughter found no welcome in the Reich. When Colonel House traveled there to present Wilson's proposals, Wilhelm told him that war and peace were matters to be decided by the crowned heads of Europe: himself and his royal cousins, George V in England and Nicholas II in Russia. This kind of haughtiness earned him a bad reputation among American newspaper editors, but the kaiser was not without supporters and apologists in the United States. There were over 8 million Americans who had either been born in the fatherland or raised in a household where at least one parent spoke German. Many of these folk, who were clustered in the cities of the East and Midwest, displayed a stubborn singleness of mind about the war and its origins.

For them, Czar Nicholas was the great villain of the European disaster while Wilhelm, as one of their Lutheran weeklies pronounced, acted as a bulwark against the Slavic hordes: "The downfall of the German eagle [would mean] the triumph of the Russian bear!"[21] The vast personal network formed by the German-American community revered the kaiser as the savior of civilization and peddled his picture like an icon. Their eyes welled with tears in September 1914 when they read that Wilhelm had affirmed his faith in the good sense of the people of the United States, "who will not let themselves be hoodwinked by the campaign of lies which our foes are waging against us."[22]

German-Americans believed Wilhelm when he sent a wire to President Wilson insisting that it was Belgian civilians who were committing atrocities against German soldiers—and not the other way around. The kaiser's cause was also helped by the Hearst newspapers, which claimed to be objective but preferred bashing the British to any of the other combatants.

As citizens of a neutral nation, arms manufacturers in the United States wanted to sell munitions to both the Allies and the Central Powers, but they were cut off from the German market by Britain's naval blockade and minefields. While he had a high regard for the English and their culture, President Wilson was capable of taking His Majesty's government to task over the blockade—and over the Royal Navy's occasional interference with U.S. shipping on the high seas. Still, he preferred to be realistic and allow trade to continue with the European markets, especially in Britain and France, that remained open. So the Germans cried foul.

The only way for the United States to maintain a true neutrality, Berlin decreed, was for Wilson to slap an embargo on the export of munitions to either side. When the president ignored this suggestion, newspapers all over Germany berated his policies and raised resentment against the United States to a fever pitch. By the time the *Lusitania* was sunk, an American correspondent had reported from the kaiser's realm that "The hatred against everything and everybody American has become more pronounced since the Allies are said to have commenced to use American arms and ammunition against the Germans."[23]

This hatred found expression when Germany opened a terrorist campaign against the United States. Saboteurs in the kaiser's service scored their greatest coup just opposite south Manhattan, at an installation on the New Jersey shore. There, across hardly more than a quarter mile of water from Liberty Island and the Statue of Liberty, lay the huge Black Tom munitions depot, which was conducting a brisk business with the Allies. German agents vowed to destroy this major conduit of the arms trade, and in the early morning hours of July 30, 1916, the bombs they placed at Black Tom did the job, engendering the most powerful series of blasts that a metropolitan area in the United States had ever experienced.

The Statue of Liberty was gouged by shrapnel from the first great explosion and the secondary explosions that followed, while the buildings on Ellis Island suffered major damage. Three miles from Black Tom, the Brooklyn Bridge rocked and swayed, and windows were shattered all the way to Harlem. The last rumbles of this violence could be heard in Baltimore, 175 miles to the southwest. For want of a better explanation, the disaster was blamed on human negligence. *The New York Times* reported that the "explosions cannot be charged to the account of alien plotters against the neutrality of the United States. . . ."[24] The truth of the matter would not come out until after the war.

One of the busiest German operatives, Capt. Franz von Rintelen, later described how the sale of U.S. arms to Britain and France appeared to the Central Powers. The United States, he wrote, was not an "opponent who could be faced in the open field . . . it was a spectre, an intangible phantom, against which strategy, tactics, and all the courage of the German soldier were helpless. . . . [But] America had to be attacked!"[25] And attacked it was. There were two hundred acts of sabotage in the United States during the first thirty months of the world conflict, and the responsibility for the great majority of them lay ultimately in Berlin.

Presiding over this secret war was the German ambassador to the United States and Mexico, Count Johann-Heinrich von Bernstorff. The activities of his officials and agents achieved great variety and no little success. Besides paying saboteurs to damage weapons factories and powder plants, Bernstorff's lieutenants saw to it that incendiary bombs were planted on munitions ships, and that

American horses (potentially valuable for hauling supplies on the western front) were infected with anthrax bacilli.

Evidence emerged in 1915 that the military and naval attachés assigned to the German embassy in Washington were guilty of subversive activities, and at President Wilson's insistence, the two were sent home; Austria' scheming ambassador to the United States, Constantin Dumba, was also recalled for actions unbecoming a diplomat. But the suffering that the Central Powers' saboteurs caused was minor compared to what was being experienced beyond the Rhine. By the end of 1916, the kaiser's people were in dire straits, for the British blockade had turned Germany into an empty larder. Inflation soared, and the cold months became known as "the turnip winter" after the country's one remaining staple. While Germans rioted for bread, their admirals were demanding that unrestricted submarine warfare be resumed in the Atlantic.

The call was a difficult one to make. Wilhelm himself expected that such a campaign would cause the United States to enter the war, but he believed that Germany would be able to finish off the Allies before Wilson could bring American power to bear on the battlefields of Europe. The kaiser's calculations were not so wide of the mark; at that juncture, the U.S. Army was small and, in futile pursuit of Pancho Villa, scattered across northern Mexico. Wilhelm's chancellor, Theobald von Bethmann-Hollweg, had led the struggle to keep the U-boats leashed. Now, trying to credit the admirals' assertion that the submarines would end the war within six months by cutting off Great Britain's critical supplies of imported food, he summed up the majority opinion: "If success beckons, we must follow."[26] On January 9, 1917, the kaiser put his signature to an imperial order: "I command that unlimited submarine warfare begin on February 1 with all possible vigor."[27]

When Wilson learned on January 31 that the kaiser's U-boats would start their new offensive on the morrow, he quietly listened to Secretary of State Robert Lansing's pleas to punish the Germans for their audacity. Lansing's diary shows that the president, "though deeply incensed at Germany's insolent notice," had longer-range considerations in mind: "He had been more and more impressed with the idea that 'white civilization' and its domination over the world rested largely on our ability to keep this country intact [that is, at peace], as we would have to build up the nations ravaged by the war."[28] Wilson must have surprised even himself when he finally discovered the full extent of his resistance to fighting the kaiser.

On February 3, the president went to Capitol Hill and announced to a joint session of Congress that it was time to break off diplomatic relations with Wilhelm's government, which he had previously threatened to do in response to further German aggression on the high seas. But the action was meant to suggest possibilities, not to display belligerence; by sending Count Bernstorff home, Wilson hoped to pressure the kaiser into moving at last toward peace.

While a U.S. decision to join the fighting would tilt the balance of victory to the Allies, Wilson's focus was elsewhere. He wanted the war to be fought to a draw, and the sooner the better. Wilson clung to the belief that the United

States would be able to help construct a stable postwar order only if it held its fire. The American people seemed to understand and support the president's position; at all events, they were as loathe as Wilson to enter the fray. They had reelected him in 1916 on the strength of the slogan that "He kept us out of war!"

Yet America's peacetime was running short. The fault lay in Germany, where a frazzled kaiser dismissed Wilson's continued initiatives as a form of harassment. "If the president wants to end the war," said Wilhelm, "all he need do is make good a threat of denying the English pirates any more munitions, [and] close the loan market in their face."[29] Wilhelm was fed up with the diplomatic maneuvers of this quibbling president; he wanted to live in a simpler world. On March 18, 1917, he told his foreign office to put "an *end* to negotiations with America. If Wilson wants war, let him make it."[30] He was even guilty of saying that the president "should have his throat cut."[31]

In the winter of 1917, some of Wilson's final reservations were exploded when British intelligence revealed that Berlin had urged Mexico, with promises of financial support, to attack the United States. The fact that Germany's new submarine offensive was sinking American as well as Allied merchant vessels also weakened the president's resolve to stay out of the fighting.

Finally, Wilson could bear it no longer. In his war message to Congress on April 2, 1917, he denounced the kaiser's autocratic government as the inevitable enemy of democracy. Congress obliged him by declaring war on April 6, and the kaiser would henceforth count the world's wealthiest nation in the ranks of his enemies. But Wilson was heavy-hearted, not triumphant, for he knew that war measures would roll back his proud, hard-won program of domestic reforms.

On April 13, the president signed an executive order creating the Committee on Public Information, which soon grew into a mammoth propaganda agency that mobilized the mind of America against its newest and most formidable foe. The committee enjoined all patriotic citizens to help "batter down the doors of the kaiser's castles (which are the front doors of hell), wipe out the Hohenzollern dynasty and blow the kaiser off the earth."[32] The alternative was to watch Wilhelm's soldiers "goose-step along Pennsylvania Avenue and sign the Treaty of Peace under the dome of our capitol in Washington."[33]

Keeping to the high road, Wilson was soon criticizing the committee for its inflammatory propaganda: "The object of this war being peace—not a truce, but peace—the less we have of artificial hatreds, the easier and better the road to real peace."[34] But there were plenty of Americans who aimed to singe the kaiser's mustaches. Newspaper editorials across the country portrayed Wilhelm as a new edition of Attila the Hun. He was Billy the Bully, William the Bloody, the Prussian pirate—the debauched personification of Teutonic madness and cruelty, an ultrafeudal warlord who loathed freedom and despised democracy. The American people were encouraged to buy war bonds with slogans like "If *you* don't come across, the kaiser will."[35]

Hollywood got into the act with Charlie Chaplin, among so many others, doing yeoman's service for the cause. Late in the war, audiences delighted in his *Shoulder Arms,* which records the little hero's progress from boot camp to the trenches and on toward the black heart of Germany. By the time the last reel is run, the droll little doughboy has not only won the eternal love of a French beauty but captured the kaiser and crown prince as well. Wilhelm figured more prominently in the most effective propaganda picture of the war. Called *The Kaiser, Beast of Berlin,* it showed him being socked on the jaw by the captain of his bodyguard and dramatized the (fictitious) descent into madness of the submarine commander who torpedoed the *Lusitania.* The film was greeted with loud cheers of approval and broke box-office records.

It got hard to open an American magazine without coming across a word to the wise. A typical advertisement in *The Saturday Evening Post* warned against enemy espionage:

> German agents are everywhere. . . . Report the man who spreads pessimistic stories, divulges—or seeks—confidential military information, cries for peace, or belittles our efforts to win the war. Send the names of such persons, even if they are in uniform, to the Department of Justice. . . . You are in contact with the enemy *today,* just as truly as if you faced him across No Man's Land.[36]

In the midst of the propaganda storm, German-Americans, who had been a valued part of the American scene since colonial days (the Pennsylvania "Dutch" were actually *Deutsch*), became objects of ever-increasing suspicion. The governor of Iowa sponsored legislation to punish anyone who dared to use the German language in public places or over the telephone. Dachshunds were subjected to random abuse. The words *hamburger* and *sauerkraut* suddenly sounded too Teutonic by half; for the duration they became "liberty sandwich" and "liberty cabbage."

On April 4, 1918, Collinsville in southern Illinois witnessed the violent death of a young German-American miner by the name of Robert Paul Prager. The hapless victim, whose poor health had kept him from enlisting in the U.S. Navy, was wrongly accused of stealing dynamite for the purposes of sabotage and strung up before five hundred jubilant onlookers. A local jury took only twenty-five minutes to acquit the eleven indicated leaders of the lynch mob.

Other aspects of the war were more mundane but no less unsettling. From the middle of 1917 to the end of 1918, consumer prices in the United States doubled as the production of military matériel reduced the supply of goods available to civilians; adding to inflation was the $23 billion that the federal government borrowed to cover the cost of the war. To keep the recruits sober, state after state banned the sale of alcoholic beverages. After a year of war, the government decreed that Americans were to observe wheatless Mondays and meatless Tuesdays and gasless Wednesdays and unlighted evenings. An innovation called daylight savings time was introduced in March 1918. The war seemed to be changing everything. Americans could feel the ground shifting beneath their feet.

In 1914, five years after he left the White House, Theodore Roosevelt had warned the American people to get ready for war. His aim, as he claimed, was not to involve the United States in Europe's disastrous quarrels but to give the country a margin of safety no matter how things fell out: "Preparedness usually averts war and usually prevents disaster in war; and always prevents disgrace in war."[37] In arguing for the rapid expansion of the armed forces, Roosevelt stated that the United States should "act in a spirit of warm friendship toward all of [the belligerents]. . . . We admire the heroism they have shown."[38]

When the United States entered the war, Roosevelt heaped abuse on the kaiser's empire, announcing that "there is but one way to gain the respect of the Prussianized, militarist, and autocratic Germany of the Hohenzollerns, and that is by beating her to her knees."[39] The kaiser's hordes were "brutes in uniform" guilty of "wholesale murders . . . obscene and loathsome cruelties and devastations . . . carnivals of destruction in the conquered lands."[40] Roosevelt also damned the "bleating of the peace people"[41] and repeated his assertion that the United States should have declared war two years earlier, when the sinking of the *Lusitania* showed the world what the Germans were really made of.

Though in failing health, Roosevelt petitioned Secretary of War Newton D. Baker to let him raise a division of volunteers for combat duty in Europe. Baker said no. Roosevelt, who had done months of preliminary work toward creating his outfit, was deeply disappointed, and so were the Europeans. Georges Clemenceau, the French premier, wrote to tell President Wilson that all the French foot soldiers were asking for T.R. "Send them Roosevelt," advised Clemenceau," . . . it will gladden their hearts."[42]

Wilson decided to gladden his own heart by backing Baker and keeping the self-willed Roosevelt far from the front. One of T.R.'s friends publicly lamented his fate: "The most virile nature in America, instead of accompanying his sons to war, must wait at home for news of their wounds and death."[43]

T.R. might have given his right arm to trade places with Gen. John J. Pershing, whom the gods of battle were now to bless with a far more satisfying experience than his fruitless pursuit of Pancho Villa in Mexico. Yet the general's position left much to be desired. Upon his appointment as commander of the American Expeditionary Force, he found himself "called upon to make up in a few months for the neglect of years."[44]

Pershing would later claim that an earlier buildup of U.S. forces would have spelled defeat for the kaiser by the end of 1917. As it was, the crash program of national mobilization failed to work any real wonders. "With some exceptions," Pershing noted, "practically six months [passed] before the training of our new army was under way."[45] This kind of delay meant that "the war was prolonged another year and the cost in human life tremendously increased."[46]

No illusions stood between Pershing and his understanding of the Wehrmacht. In 1914 he had recognized the kaiser's army as the most formidable in military history, and in spite of sustaining several million casualties during the first two and a half years of the war, the Germans still had a fearful amount of fight left in them. The Allies were even more impressed by the kaiser's might. Late in 1917, when Vladimir Ilyich Lenin took Russia out of the war and Germany began shifting more troops westward, Britain and France became frantic to get U.S. forces into the trenches. By then, Pershing had joined the go-slowers. He warned his Allied colleagues that Americans would enter the battle only when they were fully prepared.

Pershing had been determined that his men would fight the Germans as a separate army (as they were later to do), but in the spring of 1918 the Germans' new offensive brought the Allies to such a pass that special sacrifices were required. Pershing allowed his divisions to be dispersed. To help stem the German onslaught, they plugged the gaps in the threatened front at the discretion of the French general Ferdinand Foch, the new supreme commander of the Allied armies. U.S. troops were so arrayed when Wilhelm's generals launched their last great push at the Second Battle of the Marne in July 1918.

With a characteristic lack of irony, the kaiser's commanders called their huge offensive the *Friedenstürm* (peace storm) and attacked the Marne in full knowledge that failure now would mean losing the war. Their left wing ravaged the Allied lines to the east of the French cathedral city of Reims, but the right ran into Pershing's doughboys to the west. The backbone of these green troops was stiffened by a colonel from North Dakota who was short in the leg and long in the tooth. Born during the Civil War and named after General Grant, Ulysses McAlexander led the 38th Infantry Regiment. The 3,500 troops under McAlexander's command held the front line just south of the Marne, facing two regiments of Germans who proceeded to cross the river in pontoon boats.

Although the artillery barrage had stopped, German rifles and grenades freighted the air with deadly lead. McAlexander himself was there, eager to prove what Americans could do on the battlefield "to so impress the Germans with our fighting ability and our wish to fight them that their morale would be destroyed."[47] On the banks of the Marne, McAlexander got the opportunity he was looking for. The kaiser's regiments were thinned out in midstream by a hail of American grenades until the river thickened with bobbing corpses. McAlexander was all over the battlefield, urging his men to join in the hand-to-hand fighting among the ripe fields of wheat on the banks of the river, urging them to push the enemy back and destroy the bridgehead.

The Germans had laid down a cloud of mustard gas to stifle the Americans, and McAlexander stumbled onto low ground that was thick with the vaporous poison; his every breath burned. He ran into a medic named Thompson who looked him over and asked him why he was so keen on courting death. McAlexander admitted that he could have been "about 20 miles back with a bunch of orderlies around me and a telephone to tell you fellows what to do. But, hell, I want to see what's going on."[48] Soon promoted to brigadier general, McAlexander came out of the action with a new title: the Rock of the Marne.

The 3rd Division, to which McAlexander's regiment belonged, was not alone in the front line. Six other U.S. divisions were deployed to reinforce the Allied armies, and with their help the German offensive was defeated, opening the way for a successful counterattack. Wilhelm had expected the 1918 offensive—the masterstroke so long prepared by Field Marshal Paul von Hindenburg and Gen. Erich Ludendorff—to roll on into Paris and bring the fighting to an end, but now the initiative passed to the Allies, who would keep it for the rest of the war.

The French general Charles Mangin heaped praise on the Americans for their key contribution: "You rushed into the fight as to a fête. . . . I am grateful to you for the blood so generously spilled on the soil of my country. I am proud to have commanded you during such days and to have fought with you for the deliverance of the world."[49]

When in the fall of 1918 the Germans concluded they had lost the war, they asked the Wilson administration to help negotiate an end to the fighting on the basis of the president's Fourteen Points, which stressed the need for a new world order with a League of Nations to supervise universal disarmament and guarantee peace. Generally speaking, the Allied leaders distrusted Wilson's program and only came along because they feared the United States would make a separate peace with Germany if they did not. Their apprehensions were understandable enough, for Wilson had made it clear from the beginning that he was not a traditional ally in this "war to end war." At his insistence, the United States had styled itself an "Associated Power."

The fighting ended at the eleventh hour of the eleventh day of the eleventh month of 1918. There was one last great barrage along the western front, followed by a deathly silence. The years of mud and blood were over. On November 12, when Pershing got to Paris from his headquarters upcountry, his official car was engulfed by the riotous celebration in the Place de la Concord. To the general, "it looked as though the whole population had gone entirely out of their minds. The city was turned into pandemonium. The streets and boulevards were packed with people singing and dancing and wearing all sorts of odd costumes." The staid Pershing, who had wanted to end the war by pushing on to Berlin rather than by signing an armistice, would never remember the victory celebration without chuckling: "If all the ridiculous things done during those two or three days by dignified American and French men and women were recorded, the reader would scarcely believe the story. But this was Paris and the war was over."[50]

All across the United States people held victory parades, danced in the streets, and fed huge bonfires with effigies of the fallen kaiser. In Cedar Rapids, Iowa, a high school student named William L. Shirer, who would eventually write the story of the Third Reich, looked askance at the celebrations. But he was not appalled by the gold stars in the windows of families who had lost sons in France. Nor was he overwhelmed at the sight of the armless and legless veterans who had already returned to hobble down the streets of the town. Neither was he dwelling on the fate of the young doctor who had come home from France to wheeze out his final days through lungs ravaged by poison gas. Shirer had seen all of these things, and yet he still "found it hard to swallow the fact that I would never fight in the war to make—as President Wilson said, and I believed—the world safe for democracy."[51] From coast to coast, innocent young men were feeling the same sense of loss.

The victims of wartime experience had different griefs to assuage. The United States mobilized well over 4 million men during World War I; about half were draftees, while the rest volunteered. In all, 53,513 Americans were lost in combat and another 63,000 died from disease. The bodies of 30,000, originally consigned to hasty graves, were eventually reinterred in eight military cemeteries. All eight were in Europe; despite pleas from the soldiers' families, their remains never came home. One mother learned to accept the situation by reminding herself that "it is just as near from France to heaven as from Indiana."[52]

As Germany's hopes for victory were obliterated, the kaiser had faced a choice: He could either agree to abdicate, or he could cling to his crown and be overthrown by the violent revolution that had already begun to stir in the Rhineland, Munich, and Berlin. With the help of some persuasive pressure from Woodrow Wilson, he was made to see the advantages of abdication. Exile was to be Wilhelm's immediate fate; a new socialist government was to be Germany's. The Hohenzollern empire reached a definitive conclusion when Wilhelm crossed the border from war-ravaged Belgium into neutral Holland on November 10. The last sentry on German-controlled territory marked the occasion by hurling a curse at his retreating head. Still managing to maintain his dignity, Wilhelm surrendered his sword to the first Dutch official he met.

Refusing to come to terms with his fall, he wailed that "I am a broken man. How can I begin life again? My prospects are hopeless. I have nothing left to believe in."[53] The Dutch played reluctant hosts to the distraught and aging warlord, who now walked with a cane, but they did keep him out of the hands of his enemies.

In Holland he found plenty of time—and a profusion of motives—to write his memoirs. According to the version of events he recorded there, communism was partially responsible for the downfall of the Second Reich: Toward the end of the war, soldiers had begun to fly red flags from their troop transports, and the latest conscripts "were badly tainted by revolutionary propaganda and often took advantage of the darkness of night to sneak away from the firing-line."[54]

But, at least in the Wehrmacht, the left-wing element was the exception. By and large, wrote Wilhelm, his glorious military machine had functioned perfectly to the bitter end. Anticipating Hitler, the kaiser declared that his army "was forced to collapse by the stab in the back from the dagger of the [civilian] revolutionists, at the very moment when peace was within reach!"[55] It was to squelch this kind of claim that Pershing had wanted to fight until the Germans, in the eyes of all the world, had been decisively defeated.

With the shooting over, Wilhelm could admit that the United States had not been part of a conspiracy to drag the world into war. Nevertheless, it had known how to take advantage of the situation: "All Wilson's reasons for America's entry into the war were fictitious. . . . [I]t was far more a case of acting solely in the interest of Wall Street high finance."[56] And the kaiser held a very personal grudge against the United States, for he had abdicated in the belief that Wilson would be far more gracious to Germany once he had left the throne. Instead, as Wilhelm saw it, the victorious powers used his exit "to force upon Germany not easier but harder terms."[57]

It is certainly true that the terms of the Treaty of Versailles were harsh. Germany was compelled to accept the blame for starting the war, strip herself of military and naval defenses, turn Alsace-Lorraine back over to France, surrender all claims to her former colonies in Africa and China and the Pacific, and pay the Allies huge indemnities and reparations. Wilson himself was uncomfortable with such terms, for he recognized that a new Germany, cleansed of the kaiser and the militarism that he supported, would be needed to insure the future peace of Europe.

Looking east, the president could see trouble approaching in the form of Lenin's Russia, which made it all the more imperative that Germany become a full partner in the postwar order that he envisioned. And Wilson was keenly aware of the revolutionary potential within Germany itself. To treat the defeated kaiser's empire too severely was to risk driving her into the Bolshevik camp, which was exactly what Lenin hoped for. But in spite of everything, Wilson felt forced to give in to the Allies' thirst for revenge, agreeing to the kind of stern peace that he had spent years warning the world against. Still, he told the Germans not to despair, for the treaty's faults would eventually be set right by the League of Nations.

In the meantime, the voice of the people had called for the kaiser to hang. A speaker in Carnegie Hall in New York drew wild applause from a huge audience when he denounced the Dutch as a people who "would permit the emperor to retire to his yacht and his champagne dinners while ten million men he has murdered lie rotting in the ground."[58] That the great majority of Americans and Europeans would have approved of executing the kaiser is beyond doubt, but Wilson came to believe that the legal grounds for trying the kaiser had little merit, since no international military tribunal had ever punished a high enemy official.

Wilson's stand caused some hard feelings among statesmen like David Lloyd George of Great Britain, and he finally decided to let the Allies have their way with the vanquished kaiser. They were not, however, to be satisfied. Wilhelm never had to answer charges that he had personally started the war and issued criminal orders, for the whole question became moot when the Dutch refused to extradite him.

At the worst possible moment for his peace program, President Wilson suffered a disabling stroke. The Senate added to his miseries by rejecting the Treaty of Versailles on November 19, 1919, which meant that the United States would not be joining the League of Nations. Technically speaking, a state of war existed between Germany and the United States until both countries ratified the Treaty of Berlin in 1921.

The exiled Wilhelm lived on, nursing his grudges and cultivating visions of vengeance. In 1934, convinced that the Nazis (who had come to power the year before) would soon restore him to the throne, he was planning to take a terrible revenge on the people who had allowed him to languish in Holland: "Blood must flow, much blood, [the blood] of the officers and civil servants, above all of the nobility, of everyone who has deserted me."[59]

Wilhelm's ignoble hopes were in vain; in February 1935, when his eldest son begged Hitler to fulfill earlier promises by allowing him to return home, the answer was an unalterable no. The Third Reich would follow the lead of the Weimar Republic by extending financial aid to Wilhelm, but it would not let him come back to Germany. Perhaps the Führer recognized in the ex-kaiser a man of his own mettle—and shunned the competition. For his part, Wilhelm never gave up his belief in the divine right of kings, so subordinating himself to Hitler would have been as bitter as exile.

Although Wilhelm referred to himself as "the most misused man on earth,"[60] he was discreet enough to keep his criticisms of Hitler out of the world's press. Yet he could not feel at home in a world that belonged more and more to the Nazis. Perceiving that some of his servants were spying on him for the new masters of Germany, he began to identify with the Führer's victims. He had often indulged in anti-Semitic remarks during his own glory days, but in 1938 he reacted violently against Hitler's persecution of the Jews. "For the first time," he confessed to his intimates, "I am ashamed to be a German."[61]

He did, however, feel a surge of national pride in June 1940 when the Führer's army succeeded where his own had so signally failed: in capturing Paris. He was moved to send Hitler a telegram of congratulations quoting the words of the Lutheran hymn that had once been Germany's national anthem, *Nun danket alle Gott* (Now thank we all our God). By that time the Germans had also taken Holland, and the old kaiser's household at Doorn was being guarded by a detachment of Wehrmacht troops. They were still outside his windows when he died on June 4, 1941, at the age of eighty-two, and they looked on as he was laid to rest in a chapel on the grounds of his estate.

Like Hitler, Wilhelm II was neither quite mad nor quite sane. His wholehearted support of German militarism and his diplomatic clumsiness had combined to usher in the Great War, and his lack of military genius had helped to lose it. His mistakes led to the German debacle that created the Nazis, and thirty years of his eccentric rule made it easier for the German people to accept the psychopathic behavior of Adolf Hitler. The Führer's stormtroopers did not invent the goose step; they inherited it from the armies of Wilhelm II. Thanks largely to the kaiser, World War I was the straight path that led to World War II.

7

Comrade Lenin
Sees It Through

Unlike most of the country's foreign enemies, Vladimir Ilyich Lenin could pride himself on a substantial following within the United States. One of his American admirers, the journalist Lincoln Steffens, visited Russia and came home with a ringing endorsement for Lenin's new Soviet government: "I have been over into the future, and it works."[1] Millions of impoverished Americans, who were desperate for relief from the economic disruptions caused by World War I, hoped that Steffens was on to something. But for most people in the United States, the Russian dictator was an icon of dread.

Perceiving that Lenin had captivated Russia and might prevail in Europe, middle-class Americans began to wonder if communism would spread to their own land. They were terrified by visions of U.S. workingmen rising up like Slavic bolsheviks to burn and murder, to seize and corrupt. These fears were not entirely baseless; the American Communist movement in 1919 did possess undeniable potential. There were two main Marxist parties, the Communist Party of sixty thousand, most of whom were aliens, and the Communist Labor Party of ten thousand, most of whom were U.S. citizens. Beyond these organized sympathizers, thousands more were intrigued by socialist doctrines and considered Lenin to be the greatest man of his era. After the war, the Communist faith was propagated in the United States by several hundred radical newspapers and magazines.

When sixty thousand Seattleites left their jobs during the winter of 1919, some of them had Leninist ideas in mind, for a widely read left-wing journal, the *Union Record*, had used excerpts from Lenin's writings to raise the revolutionary consciousness of Northwest workers. Basically a demand for higher wages, the walkouts started in Seattle's shipbuilding industry and spread from union to union, from longshoremen to carpenters, from teamsters to typographers, from millworkers to hotel maids, until a general strike—the first in U.S. history—had fastened itself on the city. A committee of fifteen labor leaders was appointed by the General Strike Committee to serve as the interim government of Seattle, which then had a population of 300,000.

There were no riots during the strike, but there were plenty of rumors. It was said that the city's mayor, Ole Hanson, had been assassinated. He had not been, nor was anyone else to be. Contrary to one frightening report, the city was not in flames. No one had seized a factory, no one had bombed a police station, and no one had poisoned the water supply. When the strike ended after five days, it was difficult to gauge what labor had accomplished. True, the working people of Seattle had flexed their muscles in an impressive manner. Their actions had drawn attention to the fact that most Americans had grown sick and tired of the extended national emergency caused by the war. But the strike ended as it began, with bafflement and frustration on all sides.

The sense of anticlimax was less perceptible in the world beyond Seattle. After monitoring the crisis up the coast, the editor of the *Los Angeles Times* announced that the United States had started down the long and bloody road to Leninism. The *Cleveland Plain Dealer* agreed that the fearful hosts of bolshevism had come out of hiding in the Pacific Northwest. The *Chicago Tribune* told its readers that "it is only a middling step from Petrograd to Seattle."[2]

Nervous Americans believed the distance was even shorter than that, and events were to heighten their apprehensions. On June 2, 1919, a bomb exploded in Washington, D.C., on the doorstep of 2132 R Street N.W., which happened to be the home of the attorney general of the United States, A. Mitchell Palmer; a distinguished neighbor, Franklin D. Roosevelt, then assistant secretary of the navy, called the police. Before the night was over, prominent men in seven other American cities had been subjected to similar attacks. Upon investigating the explosion on R Street, the authorities discovered that the culprit had been blown up by his own bomb. Among his grisly remains was a pamphlet that minced no words: "There will have to be bloodshed . . . there will have to be murder. . . . We are ready to do anything and everything to suppress the capitalist class."[3]

Right across the country, instances of impending anarchy kept America on edge. After its underpaid police force went on strike in the late summer of 1919, Boston's street toughs broke store windows, overturned fruit stands, and—horror of horrors—openly shot craps on Boston Common. Overreacting to such events, the city fathers blamed the strike and resultant disorders on Leninist agents. A British journalist assigned to the United States wrote that the entire country was "hag-ridden by the specter of bolshevism."[4] The *Philadelphia Public Ledger* was even more impressed: "Bolshevism in the United States is no longer a specter. Boston in chaos reveals its sinister substance."[5]

The government agreed, and Attorney General Palmer, whose presidential ambitions were imperfectly concealed, launched a nationwide series of raids against left-wing organizations, which resulted in the arrest of over ten thousand alleged Communists. Palmer's crusade, which was largely coordinated by a young federal agent named J. Edgar Hoover, featured a mass deportation in December 1919, when 249 alien radicals were forced to board the *Buford*, an army transport ship, which then carried them to Finland where they were put on a train for Russia. They arrived safely. When a German journalist asked Lenin about them in the winter of 1920, he confirmed that the Soviets had "accepted them. We are not afraid of revolutionaries here in this country. . . . if America is afraid of a few more hundred or thousand of its citizens, we are ready to begin negotiations with a view to receiving any citizens whom America thinks dangerous—with the exception of criminals, of course."[6]

It was not only deportees that Lenin's new Soviet republic embraced. Carl W. Ackerman, a special correspondent for *The New York Times*, reported in 1919 that the Marxist experiment had proved to be a magnet for Russian émigrés in America:

> Men and women who were residents of New York, Seattle, Chicago, and Newark have flocked to the land of their birth. . . . One of the bolshevist commissars of Khabarovsk, the capital of the Amur [in eastern Siberia], was a Chicago lawyer. Petrograd and Moscow were filled with political agitators from New York and New Jersey. In nearly every Siberian city were refugees from cities on our western coast.[7]

The homeward flight of America's Russian-born radicals did little to guarantee peace on the labor front in the United States. Early in the autumn of 1919, over a third of a million steelworkers nationwide walked off their jobs, and a strike in the coal industry created an energy crisis that closed factories and kept trains from running. By the end of the year, 3,600 U.S. companies had experienced strikes, and 20 percent of all American workers—4 million of them—had been on the picket lines at some point.

Everywhere the defiance of working people was blamed on the bad influence of Communist infiltrators; leaders of the labor movement were said to be radicals whose "principles stand on all-fours with those of Lenin and Trotsky."[8] But the real culprits were economic and psychological forces, not Marxists in the workplace. It was inflation, coupled with the unrest that inevitably follows the unremitting discipline of wartime, that caused the American laborer to rebel in 1919.

Regardless of the facts, red-bashers had a field day. Billy Sunday, then the most influential American evangelist, instructed the press in how to spot a bolshevik: he was "a guy with a face like a porcupine and a breath that would scare a pole cat."[9] Almost daily, big-city and local newspapers carried denunciations that were less colorful but just as heartfelt. By and large, the American people followed suit. Carl Ackerman observed that "anyone who says anything against the existing order is called a bolshevik. . . . In a drugstore in New York I heard the proprietor shout to the boy behind the soda-water counter, 'You are a bolshevik!' because the boy had burned the bottom out of the hot chocolate cooking utensil."[10]

The fear of Leninist influence continued to inspire odd instances of repression. In Waterbury, Connecticut, a clothing salesman drew a sentence of six months in jail for praising Lenin's intelligence. The good citizens of Cambridge, Massachusetts, made it a crime for the city's libraries to acquire any book that mentioned Lenin.

During his western tour in the fall of 1919, President Wilson added to the hue and cry after bolshevism: "The men who are now measurably in control of the affairs of Russia represent nobody but themselves. They have again and again been challenged to call a constitutional convention . . . and they dare not attempt it." According to Wilson, the Russian people had learned to their sorrow what the Leninists really were: rulers "more cruel than the czar himself."[11] Wilson told an audience in Des Moines that bolshevism, a thoroughly anti-American concoction, was spreading around the whole world, "until it may be that even this beloved land of ours will be distracted and distorted by it."[12] No one on the planet threatened Wilson's program for a new international order like Lenin.

Who was this man and what was this movement that so bedeviled the American imagination? Lenin was born in the city of Simbirsk (Ulyanovsk), which lies five hundred miles east of Moscow on the Volga River. The year was 1870—the same year that John D. Rockefeller founded the Standard Oil Company. Lenin's father, Ilya Nikolayevich Ulyanov, was a minor nobleman and an estimable superintendent of public schools who brought up his children in comfortable middle-class circumstances. Little if any of the blood that flowed in Lenin's veins was Russian. His ancestry was largely German and Scandinavian, but he also had Mongolian forebears, a fact that accounts for the Asiatic cast of his eyes and cheekbones. "Lenin" is how Vladimir Ilyich Ulyanov renamed himself at the age of thirty, without ever bothering to explain the meaning of his pseudonym.

Revolutionary activity was à la mode in late nineteenth-century Russia. Given the stubbornly conservative nature of the czar's government, most intellectuals sought radical solutions to the social and political backwardness of the Russian empire. Lenin's older brother Sasha, a student of zoology, decided to put his beliefs into action. Though gentle in his person, Sasha joined in a plot to assassinate Alexander III, whose father, Alexander II, had been blown up by terrorists in 1881. In March 1887, Sasha was arrested for manufacturing bombs, and his judges decreed that he should die on the gallows in May. Right up to the moment of Sasha's execution, the seventeen-year-old Lenin had shown little interest in politics, but he now felt compelled to read the socialist tracts that his brother left behind—and he read them like he had never read anything before. Lenin's wife, Nadezhda Krupskaya, later recorded that "the fate of his brother gave his mind a keener edge, developed in him an extraordinary soberness of thought."[13]

With Sasha's ghostly footsteps to guide him, Lenin gained a reputation as a student radical while studying law at the University of Kazan. Expelled for protesting against the school's administration, he was jailed for a few days and then turned loose upon the world. For the next four years he pursued a rigorous course of political and economic studies under his own direction, a course from which he emerged as one of Russia's most thoughtful young revolutionaries. The works of Karl Marx swept him off his feet; as his sister Anna remembered, "[H]e would tell me with burning enthusiasm about the principles of Marxist theory and the new horizons it was opening to him."[14] In his spare time he was also studying German, French, and English—and learning law with ridiculous ease. When the Ministry of Education granted him permission to take the bar examination, he breezed through, finishing first in a group of 124. He even practiced law for a time, though with nothing resembling the brilliance that he had displayed on the exam.

Moving from the provinces to the czar's capital of St. Petersburg in 1893, Lenin joined a left-wing circle and began preaching Marx to the nascent Russian proletariat. Because of his activities, he was constantly shadowed by police spies. In December 1895 he again found himself in custody, on a charge of publishing a subversive newspaper. This time his stay behind bars was far lengthier, running to a full year, after which he was obliged to spend three years in central Siberia. Back in Russia at the beginning of the new century, he returned to his old ways, which soon resulted in his rearrest and another spell of detention in St. Petersburg. Weary of struggling with such watchful reactionaries, he left Russia in the summer of 1900 and spent almost all of the next seventeen years in western and eastern Europe.

Lenin was far more of a battler than a compromiser. His comrades knew him as an intense, tormented man who insisted on having his own way despite his frequent nervous crises. In London during the summer of 1903, he split the Marxists of the tiny Russian Social Democratic Labor Party, which had been founded while Lenin was still a boy, into two factions, and took control of the majority (bol'sheviki), an inauspicious beginning for a name that would shortly discomfit capitalists around the world. He paid for his victory by losing his place on the editorial board of the influential underground newspaper called *Iskra (The Spark)*, which he himself had launched; so he developed other publications that, smuggled into Russia, would help sway the politics of the masses. One of them was called *Pravda (Truth)*.

From the beginning of 1905, as the czar's army and navy were suffering defeat in the Far East at the hands of the Japanese, Russia experienced a rash of civil disorders and revolutionary agitations. Living in Switzerland at the time, Lenin was seized by grandiose fantasies about getting the sailors of the Imperial navy to turn their big guns against the czarist establishment. In November he went back to St. Petersburg, where he spread his vitriolic brand of propaganda under the name of Karpov. Not fooled for a minute by his nom de guerre, the police dogged his every step. Lenin's choice was obvious: He could either stay in Russia and go back to prison, or he could resign himself to another long bout of European exile. Europe won hands down, and Lenin took his way westward.

In the summer of 1912, he moved with his wife to the part of Poland that was then controlled by Austria-Hungary, and he remained there until the world war broke out. A confused group of Austrian policemen arrested him as a czarist spy, but influential socialists in Vienna secured permission for his return to Switzerland. From his perch in the mountains, Lenin deplored the clash of armies in the lands below. He called World War I "the war to decide whether the British or the German vultures are to rule the world."[15] In Lenin's eyes, the slaughter exposed capitalism as a bloodthirsty monster that was far more eager to boost the profits of munitions dealers than to save the lives of its proletarian sons.

Although he scorned the patriotic loyalties that fueled the fighting, Lenin was determined to use the war for his own purposes. As the killing went on, he came to see the world calamity as a way to prepare himself and his comrades for the general crisis of international capitalism. "The experience of the war," he wrote, "like the experience of every crisis in history . . . stuns and shatters some, but it enlightens and hardens others."[16] While he had to endure periods of self-doubt and despair before the events of 1917 thrust him onto the stage of history, he never stopped hoping that the war would make Russia ripe for revolution.

Which is precisely what happened. The shattering defeats suffered by the czar's army and the widespread hunger that afflicted his empire seemed to present the Russian people with proof of what Lenin had been preaching for years: that Nicholas and his ministers had feet of clay. Strikes became endemic. As the corrupt, inefficient Romanov dynasty entered its final days, a spontaneous and bloody revolt broke out in St. Petersburg—then called Petrograd. The flummoxed czar, whose soldiers were deserting in droves, abdicated on March 15, 1917. In Marxist-Leninist terms, the monarchy had been overthrown by a bourgeois revolution that would have to be followed by a proletarian revolution. Lenin saw his chance to direct the second, more decisive upheaval—and feared that his moment would slip away before he could return to Russia.

Desperate to seize the day, he calculated that the fastest route from Switzerland to Petrograd would be by train through Germany and then by boat to Sweden and Finland. Happily for Lenin, the Germans were willing to accommodate him. The kaiser's foreign ministry had compiled a thick file on Lenin, and it was realized in Berlin that he might be just the man to convince the Russian people to end the fighting on the eastern front. The Germans would dictate, however, that Lenin and his comrades stay sealed inside their train as it passed through the Reich. Lenin agreed; for his part, he wanted to keep his distance from the servants of Teutonic imperialism.

All through his long exile Lenin had continued to publish works that were read in Russia, and his growing reputation as a socialist philosopher gave him the chance to demonstrate his brilliance as a political strategist. But the path to power was not easy. Once back in Petrograd (he arrived on April 16, 1917), he made no secret of his extremist tendencies, which encompassed plans to nationalize all privately owned land and to replace Russia's beleaguered army with a people's militia that would be instructed to shoot Russian conservatives, not German soldiers. Most of Petrograd's socialists thought he was half crazy. One left-wing publication analyzed Lenin as "a man of great capacities, but the abnormal conditions of underground life have dwarfed and stunted them most gruesomely. . . . Lenin's socialism is a blunt socialism; he uses a big ax where a scalpel is needed."[17]

He was also pilloried as a German agent, and a warrant for his arrest on a charge of high treason was issued by Russia's provisional government. Although he was forced to retreat to Finland in the summer of 1917, Lenin's fortune was slowly being made as Alexander Kerensky, a moderate socialist who had taken over the provisional government at the end of July, staggered from weakness to weakness—and the Russian armies continued to be beaten by the technologically superior Germans at the front. Watching Kerensky's debacle from his Finnish hiding place, Lenin developed plans for a coup d'état that would insure the triumph of himself and his bolshevik comrades in Petrograd. He returned to Russia in October 1917 and the trap was sprung on November 7. With Lenin at his side, Leon Trotsky directed operations against Kerensky from the Smolny, a three-story building on the Neva River that had once housed a school for the daughters of the aristocracy.

Bit by bit Petrograd and its public buildings fell into the hands of bolshevik troops until, by the early morning of November 8, even the Winter Palace was flying the red flag. Those members of Kerensky's government who had not fled were thrown into prison, but very little blood was shed. A joyous Lenin composed the proclamation that announced the revolution to the masses. He wrote, in part, that "the cause for which the people have fought—namely, the immediate offer of a democratic peace, the abolition of landed proprietorship, workers' control over production, and the establishment of Soviet power—this cause has been secured."[18] He had another comment to make that was not for public consumption: "From being a fugitive to supreme power! It's just too much!"[19]

Lenin went on to rule Russia with a dictator's rod of iron, yet he was never the country's president or prime minister. His highest official position, which he held beginning in 1917, was chairman of the Council of People's Commissars. The Western press, falling back on more familiar categories, usually identified him as "the bolshevik premier."[20] Whatever he was called, Lenin's charisma had made him the unquestioned leader of the most radical political movement in modern history. Nations looked on in awe as his government arrogated unprecedented power to itself, nationalizing Russia's businesses and banks, factories and railroads, farms and churches.

Not since the era of Napoleon had the world encountered such a bold spirit, and people who knew history realized that Lenin's program for a globe-girdling order of socialist utopias dwarfed even Bonaparte's wildest schemes. The capitalists had reason to be concerned.

When Nicholas II abdicated in March 1917, Woodrow Wilson had prayed that democracy would instantaneously spring up to replace czarist autocracy. During his April 2 address to Congress, Wilson said that Russia was considered "by those who knew it best to have been always in fact democratic at heart. . . . [N]ow [czarism] has been shaken off and the great, generous Russian people have been added in all their naïve majesty and might to the forces that are fighting for freedom." Wilson finished the job of gilding the lily by describing Russias as "a fit partner for a league of honor."[21]

Given the 6 million casualties—far more than any other belligerent—that their country had already sustained, the Russian people were bound to look askance at Wilson's honorable league of warring nations. What did attract them was Lenin's offer of relief from the horrors and privations of the world conflict, and the Allies only speeded the triumph of Marxism by insisting that Kerensky keep up the fight.

Two weeks after the success of the Communist coup, Lenin and Trotsky, who now served as commissar for foreign affairs, repeated that Russia would lay down her arms and formally proposed "an immediate armistice on all fronts and the immediate opening of peace negotiations."[22] Kaiser Wilhelm and his Austrian allies responded to the bolsheviks' peace overtures favorably, and the guns fell silent on the eastern front in the middle of December. President Wilson decided not to respond at all, since Lenin's regime "was established by force and not recognized by the Russian people."[23] But as the weeks passed and the bolsheviks made progress toward concluding a permanent peace with the Germans, Wilson decided to send a message to the All-Russian Soviet Congress.

The assembled Marxists learned from the president that the American people felt a "sincere sympathy" for the plight of the Russian people, beset as they were by the legions of Germany. Wilson admitted that the United States was "unhappily not in a position to render the direct and effective aid it would wish to render," but he pledged that his administration would "avail itself of every opportunity to secure for Russia once more complete sovereignty and independence in her own affairs."[24] The president should have saved his breath to cool his soup. The bolshevik response to his friendly message was yet another rendition of the oft-repeated Marxist prophecy that "the laboring masses of all countries will throw off the yoke of capitalism."[25] One of Lenin's colleagues, Grigori Zinoviev, said that his comrades' defiance had "slapped the president of the United States in the face."[26]

In spite of their bad manners, the bolsheviks *did* constitute the working government of their country, which they chose to control not from the coastal city of Petrograd but from a more secure refuge in the old inland capital of Moscow. Beginning in March 1918, Lenin could usually be found in a famous old building in the Kremlin that had housed the High Court of Chancery. "There now sits Lenin," in the words of one American visitor, "short-built and staunch-built, gray-eyed and bald-headed, and tranquil. He wears a woolen shirt and a suit of clothes bought, one would think, many years ago, and last pressed shortly afterwards. The room is quite still."[27]

The room was also quite small. No hypocrite, Lenin lived like a good socialist. When he needed a haircut he went to a barbershop and waited his turn, and he was careful to get library books back on time. His working day usually lasted seventeen or eighteen hours. He and his wife made do on a modest salary, and he complained bitterly when a Party bureaucrat raised his pay by 60 percent without asking his permission. Not everyone was charmed by his outward humility. The world-renowned Russian writer Maxim Gorky upbraided Lenin in these terms: "He does not know the masses of the people. He has never lived among them. Only from books he learned how to raise this mass onto its haunches, and how most effectively to rouse its instincts to a fury. . . . [Lenin] is leading the revolution to disaster."[28]

What really got Lenin hated in the United States was the Treaty of Brest-Litovsk, signed by the bolsheviks and Germans in March 1918. By its provisions, Russia irrevocably left the war on terms that were very advantageous to the kaiser. This peace so aided Germany that Americans were tempted to think of the Soviet government as a puppet of Berlin: after all, hadn't it been the Germans who arranged to send Lenin back to Russia from his exile in Switzerland? And when Lenin's political instrument, the Russian Social Democratic Labor Party, began calling itself the Communist Party during the month of the Brest-Litovsk Treaty, Lenin looked even more forbidding to the average American, whose newspapers had been denouncing the evils of communism since the middle of the nineteenth century.

Full as he was of hope for the future, President Wilson had failed to realize how hard it would be for autocratic Russia to turn itself into a working (and fighting) democracy. He was also deceived about the nature of the Soviet mindset. In the first weeks after Lenin came to power, Wilson thought of bolshevism as an aberration brought on by the stresses of war and the backwardness of the Russian people. Properly handled, Lenin and his party might be wooed back into the battle against the kaiser—and Russia itself might quickly evolve toward Wilson's kind of democratic liberalism.

The president's plans envisioned a middle path between European-style colonialism on the one hand and Marxist revolution on the other. The war had shown how badly reform was needed; with America's help, Wilson expected that reform to become a reality. If the nations of the world, which had been working at cross purposes since time immemorial, would only follow Wilson's guidance, they would be gathered together in the League of Nations, where every member would be persuaded (or forced) to honor international law.

No ingenue, Wilson understood that creating his new world order would require an extraordinary feat of statesmanship. In September 1918 he confided his anxieties to Joseph Tumulty, his private secretary: "What I greatly fear . . .

is that we shall go back to the old days of alliances and competing armaments and land grabbing. We must see to it . . . that when peace finally comes, it shall be a permanent and a lasting peace. We must now serve notice on everybody that our aims and purposes are not selfish."[29]

For his part, Lenin found it impossible to believe in Wilson's good faith. By Marxist definition, any leader of a capitalist country was bound to be short-sighted, militaristic, and treacherous. This ideological bias helps to account for Lenin's harsh judgment of Wilson, whom he had called "the head of the American multimillionaires and servant of the capitalist sharks."[30] Lenin considered the president's program for leading the world into a new era as nothing more than an American ploy for replacing the blatant imperialism of Europeans with a more subtle brand that was made in the U.S.A. Only with the destruction of the liberal capitalism in which Wilson placed all his faith would the way be prepared for a millennium of peace and prosperity.

Not every Russian agreed with the bolshevik analysis of the world situation—not by any means. The land of Lenin teemed with his enemies: There were people who believed in the restoration of the monarchy, and people who believed in the institution of anarchy, and people of every persuasion in between. Wilson's allies in London and Paris were clamoring to support these anti-Communists, who, being opposed to the "Reds," were given the generic name of "Whites." Enthusiasm for the Russian opposition was also prevalent on the Potomac. There was a fear in Robert Lansing's State Department that the kaiser might co-opt the Whites; as one panicky memo stated, "[I]f Allied assistance is much longer delayed the anti-bolshevik element in Russia will certainly turn to Germany."[31] It would be a big job, but the United States and the Allies began to examine the possibility of organizing an expeditionary force to join with the Whites in fighting both Germans and bolsheviks on Russian soil.

The movement toward intervention was given a tremendous boost in the spring of 1918 by the early successes of the Germans' last great offensive in France. The United States and the Allies were facing a Reich that had transferred forty divisions from Russia to the west and now threatened to capture Paris. Desperate to divert their onslaught, the Allied generals hastily drew up plans to attack the Germans from the rear—that is, to reestablish the eastern front. The British and French were especially keen on invading Russia, but Wilson's War Department thought that such plans were impractical.

Beat Germany on the western front, was the line taken by Secretary of War Newton Baker and most of the U.S. Army's general officers. The president accepted their view—and expressed very strong reservations about Allied plans for the Japanese to invade Siberia. By American lights, Japan would use such an intervention to begin planting military colonies in the Russian Far East—a situation that no one but the Japanese were eager to see develop.

On July 8, 1918, Wilson wrote to Colonel House that "I have been sweating blood over what is right and feasible to do in Russia. It goes to pieces like quicksilver under my hand."[32] But the Allied Supreme War Council, which was sitting at Versailles in France, kept pressuring Wilson to send U.S. troops to help the Whites, and the president finally capitulated, ordering U.S. expeditions to head for both northern Russia and Siberia. But he made it clear that their purpose was *not* to tackle the bolsheviks: "[T]he only legitimate object for which American or Allied troops can be employed . . . is to guard military stores which may subsequently be needed by Russian forces [hostile to Germany]."[33]

In fact, huge accumulations of valuable supplies, originally given to the czar on credit by the Allies, lay in heaps around Archangel in the north and Vladivostok in the east, and concerns that this military wealth might fall into the wrong hands were not to be dismissed. But Wilson was thinking wistfully when he limited U.S. troops to guarding these stores. Predictably enough, both of the forces that he sent into Russia ended up skirmishing with bolshevik troops. And they were not alone. By the beginning of 1919, the White armies across Russia were being supported by 180,000 troops from Britain, France, Czechoslovakia, Japan, Italy, Greece, and Serbia—as well as the United States. To say the least, the bolsheviks were receiving an emphatic vote of no-confidence from the international community.

During August 1918, in a long message to U.S. workers, Lenin complained that "the Anglo-French and American bourgeois newspapers are . . . hypocritically justifying their predatory expedition against [Russia] on the plea that they want to 'protect' [her] from the Germans!"[34] He called his country "a besieged fortress" and told his American audience that he was "waiting for the other detachments of the world socialist revolution to come to our relief."[35] There was little that workers in the United States could do to aid the Soviet state, but some of their labor unions did protest Allied intervention in Russia, and American longshoremen tried to staunch the flow of U.S.-made weapons to Lenin's enemies.

As it happened, no one in the world could save Lenin himself from personal violence. He was shot point-blank in the neck, lung, and shoulder by a lone malcontent named Fanny Kaplan on August 30, 1918, as he was getting back into his car after making a speech at a Moscow factory. His chauffeur, Stephan Gil, roared off to the Kremlin, where Lenin was injected with morphine and examined by a group of five doctors. They discovered that one bullet had missed his aorta by a fraction of an inch. There was blood in his damaged lung and almost no pulse.

It was Trotsky who taught the Russian people to see Lenin's fight against death as a sort of cosmic drama. Hurrying back from the Kazan front of the civil war, he described Lenin as the "greatest human being of our revolutionary epoch"[36] and said that his loss would be an unparalleled disaster for communism. According to Trotsky, Lenin's struggle to recover from his wounds was a new front in the war against capitalism. The masses took the cue, waiting with a mixture of hope and doom for news from Moscow, where Lenin lay feverish and bleeding. Russians had long been accustomed to venerating the martyred saints of their Orthodox faith. The new Lenin—with two bullets still embedded in his body—seemed far more worthy of worship than the old unwounded Lenin.

Soon the medical bulletins gave his comrades ease: Lenin not only lived but was up and around within two weeks. Having had time to mull the matter over, Lenin told his critic Gorky, whom he liked to meet from time to time, that the attempted assassination was "a brawl. Nothing to be done. Everyone acts in his own way."[37] Russia seemed to be genuinely relieved by his recovery. For its part, the Communist party decreed that "the working class will respond to attempts against its leaders by rallying its forces and by a ruthless mass terror against all the enemies of the revolution."[38]

Though his secret police had initiated the "Red Terror" before Lenin was wounded, new and much more dreadful deeds were fitted to these ominous words. Starting with Fanny Kaplan, who stated that she had shot Lenin because "he has betrayed the Revolution,"[39] thousands of Russians were summarily executed. And it was now that the Soviet Republic, which on September 2 had declared itself to be in a state of siege, began its long love affair with concentration camps.

How much responsibility did Lenin share for all this cruelty? When Lincoln Steffens questioned him about the terror, Lenin said that he had resisted harsh measures for as long as he could, and had only cracked down on his enemies when the people demanded it. The explanation was absurd, but it demonstrates how Lenin had fallen into the habit of claiming that his acts had been forced upon him. Yet a strain of honesty still existed in him. "Don't deny the terror," he told Steffens in 1919. "Don't minimize any of the evils of a revolution. They occur. They must be counted on. If we have to have a revolution, we have to pay the price of revolution."[40]

Trotsky lived to achieve his own vision of what had happened after Lenin was shot. "It was in those tragic days," he later wrote, "that something snapped in the heart of the revolution."[41]

The sound of snapping could also be heard in other parts of Russia. By the spring of 1919, one contingent of American soldiers at Archangel had lost patience with its arctic tour of duty. On April 11, the *New York Tribune* reported their mutiny on its front page: "A company of infantry refused to obey the orders of their officers to prepare for movement to the front lines." The report went on to say that although they finally advanced "under the urging of their officers," the rebellious soldiers "predicted general mutiny in the American forces on the Russian front if a statement was not forthcoming from Washington regarding the withdrawal of American troops from Russia."[42]

Seven months earlier, these men and the other members of the U.S. expeditionary force, who numbered four thousand, had been in a very different mood. They had been excited at the prospect of helping to bring the war to an early end, and their going had been something of a lark. But now that the fighting in France was finished, they wondered why they were stuck in the godforsaken north. Since English officers controlled them above company level, the U.S. troops suspected that they had been hijacked and placed in the service of British imperialism.

Archangel's gloom and cold—sometimes the temperature was 80 degrees below zero—had hit the Americans hard. One of them, a young officer named John Cudahy, wrote of the dreariness of life on the arctic front: "Week follows week and . . . no word comes from the War Department. . . . [T]he soldier is left to think that he has been abandoned by his country and left to rot."[43] Cudahy and his men found that existence had become "a very stale, flat drab thing in the vast stretches of cheerless snow. . . . Strong men were made cowards by the cumulative depression of the unbroken night and its crushing influence on the spirit: for the severest battles of the campaign were fought during the cold black months of winter time."[44]

At least the U.S. soldiers in northern Russia had enough to eat, which a great many Russians did not. In January 1919, Lenin had written that

> the distress of the starving workers in Petrograd and Moscow . . . and other industrial centers is indeed great. If the workers did not understand that they are defending the cause of socialism in Russia and throughout the world they would never be able to bear the hardships, the torments of hunger to which they are doomed by the Allied military intervention.[45]

This was typical of how Lenin exploited the presence in Russia of foreign troops, whom he consistently blamed for all the sufferings of the Soviet people.

Lenin loved to tell his distressed and fearful people that the capitalists had invaded Russia for only one purpose: to enslave them. While most Russians had developed deep reservations about the new Communist regime in Moscow, there could be no doubt that Lenin and his colleagues belonged to the country and understood its people better than any foreign military force ever could. If it came to a choice between the dictatorship of alien generals and the dictatorship of Lenin, national pride demanded that the people take their chances with Lenin.

Never enthusiastic about intervention, Woodrow Wilson began to realize that the positioning of Allied soldiers on Russian soil had handed the Soviet government a propaganda windfall. The president was also aware that the Russian masses were afraid that a White victory would result in the restoration of the Romanovs, a clan that would no doubt want to inflict humiliating punishments on a population that had shown little grief over the bolsheviks' execution of the czar and his immediate family. At the same time, Wilson was becoming ever more convinced that Marxists were an odious race. In February 1919 he had finally taken the gloves off, branding Lenin's movement as "that ugly, poisonous thing called bolshevism."[46] But it did not follow that bolsheviks should be killed by American soldiers—and Americans by bolsheviks.

In March, Wilson urged that all Allied troops be pulled out of Russia, thereby allowing the Russians to "stew in their own juice until circumstances have restored them to greater sanity—and to limit ourselves to preventing bolshevism from invading other parts of Europe."[47] Thus began the policy of

containment. On Wilson's orders, the U.S. troops around Archangel, who suffered two thousand casualties, were withdrawn in June and July 1919. The
other Allied troops left not long thereafter, and north Russia belonged to the
bolsheviks by February 1920.

In the Far East the situation evolved toward the same end. In August 1918
almost nine thousand U.S. troops had joined a much larger force of Japanese
in occupying the area around Vladivostok in Siberia. But Wilson had not sent
them there to fight, and except for one clash early on, they fired no shots in
anger. Instead, they drilled and guarded the trans-Siberian railway, they
guarded the railway and drilled. To help beguile the hours, they updated the
lyrics of a familiar soldier's song:

> Take me over the sea
> Where the bolsheviks can't get at me.
> Oh my, I don't want to die,
> I want to go home.[48]

Like troops in every clime, the Americans in Siberia sought refuge from bore-
dom, and some of them required treatment for alcoholism or venereal disease
or both. Most of all, they watched the Japanese, who numbered seventy thousand. This routine went on for nineteen long months, until the president finally
ordered them home.

The American pullout did not mean that peace would come to Russia. The
civil war raged on and, as 1919 progressed, the view from the Kremlin became
ever more discouraging. A Western naval blockade and the warring chaos of
the country had brought famine, and famine had brought epidemics of typhus,
typhoid, and cholera. Still backed by Britain and France, the White armies
were harrowing this earthly hell and capturing city after city, while their allies
made gains as well. Poles were advancing toward the heart of Russia from the
west, Finns from the north, and Cossacks from the east. The bolsheviks were
engaged in hostilities on no fewer than fourteen fronts along a five-thousand-
mile battle line. With its enemies closing in from every point on the compass,
communism seemed certain to perish in the cradle. How Lenin and his comrades kept their nerve through this extended crisis is anyone's guess.

In October 1919 one White army drew close enough to Moscow to make out
the domes of the Kremlin, and another actually entered the suburbs of Petrograd. For consolation, Lenin could look for a time to central Europe, where
parts of Germany, Czechoslovakia, and Hungary had experienced revolutions
and become workers' republics during the spring and summer. As a true believer, Lenin expected every European country to overthrow capitalism soon,
but none of the leftist regimes except his own was destined to survive. Russia's
fight for Marxism looked less and less hopeful, and even Lenin had taught that
Soviet communism would fail unless supported by proletarian victories in the
rest of Europe.

Leon Trotsky's military genius proved to be the salvation of the revolution.
As commissar of the armies, he descended on the battlefronts in an armored

train that soon became a legend. Time and again he would find the Red forces
in disarray. When he got to Kazan in August 1918, he discovered that "the one
desire was for retreat. The soil itself seemed infected with panic. Fresh detachments, arriving in good spirit, were immediately trapped by the mood of
defeatism."[49] In Kazan, as he had in so many other scenes of death and confusion, Trotsky turned the situation around, inspiring the bolshevik troops to
fight with amazing ferocity. From a faltering force of 100,000, he built the Red
Army into a juggernaut numbering 5 million.

Lenin never donned a uniform and had no direct experience of military life,
but he did offer Trotsky some excellent advice on the conduct of the civil war.
The two of them worked well together, and they enjoyed a tremendous advantage over their enemies in that the antibolsheviks never coordinated their efforts, so the Red Army was able to deal with them piecemeal. By November
1920, three years after the fall of Kerensky, the Whites were defeated. But
victory was achieved at a dreadful cost. The scope of Russia's tragedy is suggested by the terrible fact that the country's population, totaling 171 million in
1914, fell to 132 million by 1921.

A new disaster overtook the Soviet state in the latter year: the most widespread famine to date. Lenin seemed astonishingly unconcerned about this
new round of suffering for his people, but he did allow the Red Cross and the
American Relief Administration, which was headed by Warren G. Harding's
secretary of commerce, Herbert Hoover, to enter Russia and do what they
could to relieve the hunger. For an entire year (into 1922), American social
workers were restricted to feeding children in their soup kitchens, since Lenin
could not bear the thought of adult Russians coming into contact with capitalist
lackeys; eventually, this limitation was quietly ignored. In one of his most cal-
lous moves, Lenin later ordered the arrest of many Russians who had worked
with U.S. relief officials.

Still, the flow of parcels from individual American families had gotten
through, and Hoover's campaign against hunger in Russia had been effective.
The people of the United States had not learned to admire Lenin, but they had
learned to overcome their Red Scare worries and pity the Russian people. Millions of Soviet citizens were saved from starvation by American charity.

Even though Lenin himself rarely missed a meal, his health disintegrated
during these tragic years. From the end of 1920 he had complained of head-
aches, fatigue, and insomnia; toward the middle of 1922, at the age of fifty-two,
he suffered his first stroke. The second came that December, and the third,
striking him in March 1923, ended his public career. The last finished him off
on January 21, 1924. Lenin's seventeen- and eighteen-hour days—and the tremendous stresses of running a massive revolution—had been too much for him.
Overestimating the strength of his constitution, he had worked himself to
death, leaving behind a Russia that was still more of a ruin than a civilization,
a Russia that would prove helpless in the face of a Stalinist terror.

Secretary of State Lansing had foreseen the country's fiery trial in the autumn of 1917, when he wrote the Wilson administration's first cogent response to Lenin's revolution. "Civil war seems certain," had been Lansing's perception. "The cities will be the prey of mobs, thieves and murderers. Factions will struggle for mastery. Russia will fairly swim in blood. . . . I can conceive of no more frightful calamity for a people than that which seems about to fall upon Russia."[50]

And so it came to pass.

8

A Führer and His Reich

When it came to the subject of Adolf Hitler, President Franklin D. Roosevelt was a complete pessimist. In 1938, as British prime minister Neville Chamberlain was getting his appeasement policy into high gear, Roosevelt thought that the best possible result would be to postpone the outbreak of hostilities for a few months or years. In the long run, the president felt sure, Hitler's ambitions could only be thwarted by force.

The riot of anti-Semitism that the Nazis inspired in Germany had complicated their relations with the United States since 1933, the year that brought both Roosevelt and Hitler to power. Continuing outrages led to the crisis of *Kristallnacht* (the Night of Broken Glass) in November 1938, when German Jews were subjected to personal violence while Jewish shops and homes and synagogues were ransacked throughout Germany and Austria. Thousands of dispossessed Jews were sent to concentration camps. President Roosevelt expressed his amazement and disgust in words that today sound rather naive: "I myself could scarcely believe that such things could occur in a twentieth-century civilization."[1]

To dramatize his rejection of Nazism, shortly after *Kristallnacht* Roosevelt recalled Hugh R. Wilson, his ambassador to the Third Reich. Wilson never went back to Berlin and was never replaced. Hitler dismissed Roosevelt's response as trivial, explaining that FDR was probably Jewish himself—and certainly surrounded by a "Jewish clique" that dictated U.S. foreign policy. As for the American people, they were a race of mongrels that would eventually be dominated by the pure Germanic type: "The inferiority and decadence of this allegedly New World," Hitler taunted, "is evident in its military inefficiency."[2]

When FDR demanded in the spring of 1939 that the German dictator explain his intentions, he replied before the Reichstag with mock humility:

"Mr. Roosevelt! I fully understand that the vastness of your nation and the immense wealth of your country allow you to feel responsible for the history of the whole world and for the history of all nations. I, sir, am placed in a much more modest and smaller sphere."[3] But the German army's invasion of Poland in September 1939 proved that the Führer had never intended to remain within his own bailiwick. From the beginning he had been a prophet of German expansion, writing in *Mein Kampf* that "only an adequate . . . space on this earth assures a nation of freedom of existence."[4] This was the central obsession of his program for the German people: to win them more *lebensraum*—more living space.

Hitler himself had not been born in Germany proper but just across the Bavarian border in what was then a part of Austria-Hungary. The future Führer was christened by a Catholic priest two days after his birth, which had taken place on Easter Saturday of 1889. He spent most of his youth in the vicinity of Linz, the capital of Upper Austria. There he was systematically spoiled by his adoring mother, Klara, and sternly disciplined by his aging father, Alois, a retired customs official who died when Adolf was thirteen. At school he was alternately a shining example of model studiousness and a miserable case of adolescent rebelliousness.

In 1907 he went to Vienna, where he intended to prove himself a great architect. Twice failing to be accepted by the Academy of Fine Arts, he set himself up as a freelance painter of city views. Though these renderings sold reasonably well, Hitler squandered his money, fell into poverty, and endured a period of loneliness and neglect; as a result, he always identified the Viennese as the source of his first great frustrations. He moved to Munich in the spring of 1913. During the winter of 1914, he won exemption from the Austrian draft—whose agents had been pursuing him for months—by claiming to be medically unfit.

Considering the Austro-Hungarian empire decadent, he preferred to serve with a Bavarian infantry regiment of the kaiser's army, in which he enlisted when the Great War broke out in the summer of 1914. The middle of October saw his arrival in France, and on the second day of December he was awarded the first of the two Iron Crosses that would come his way during the war. Now twenty-five years old, Hitler thrived at the front; rather than afflicting him with despair, the horrors of no man's land seemed to assuage his paranoid and misanthropic temperament. An undoubtedly brave soldier, he was being accurate, if immodest, when he wrote a friend that "I've risked my life every day and death has been staring me in the face."[5] All his comrades attested to the courage of Lance Corporal Hitler. A colonel of noble birth named von Tubeuf recorded that "there was no circumstance or situation that would have prevented him from volunteering for the most difficult, arduous and dangerous tasks and he was always ready to sacrifice life and tranquility for the fatherland and for others."[6]

Often detailed to perilous ground, he sustained a serious thigh wound from a shell fragment in October 1916 (during the Battle of the Somme) and was serving in Belgium when British mustard gas knocked him out of action in October 1918. The effects of the gas made him feel that his "eyes had turned into glowing coals"[7]—and left him temporarily blind. By the time the war came to an end, Hitler had regained much of his vision and was convalescing at a military hospital in northeastern Germany. Facing the sure knowledge of Germany's defeat for the first time, he felt the heavens fall: "Again everything went black before my eyes; I tottered and groped my way back to the dormitory, threw myself on my bunk, and dug my burning head into my blanket and pillow."[8]

But his experience of war was not to leave him permanently disabled—far from it. The trials of the trenches had made him grotesquely strong, and the psychological ravages of Germany's defeat were destined to finish the job of hardening his character. Soon he would discover the instrument that would let him exercise his formidable new powers. Returning to Munich while still in uniform, he was assigned to an office of military investigators and instructed to monitor the activities of extremist political parties. One of these, the ultra-nationalist German Workers' Party, recognized the makings of a true believer in Corporal Hitler and persuaded him to accept a membership card in 1919. Soon he was serving on its executive committee as chief of propaganda.

Like so many right-wing ideologues, he preached that rebelling against Germany's new central government, the Weimar Republic, was a sacred duty. Prepared to back up words with action, Hitler's movement, renamed the National Socialist German Workers' (or Nazi) Party, attempted a *putsch* at Munich in November 1923. Its failure resulted in Hitler's conviction on a charge of treason and a sentence of five years imprisonment. But the trial was a public relations triumph for the ferocious little war hero with the toothbrush mustache, and he spent only nine mild months in jail, where he wrote the first sections of *Mein Kampf.*

The mass meetings that Hitler went on to address were especially effective in spreading the Nazis' crack-brained gospel. His audiences listened all too intently as he told them that the unequal peace settlement of Versailles could only be righted by a new crusade of German militarism. Convinced that his listeners were part of an Aryan master race, he advocated the founding of an expanded Reich that would include every German in Europe.

Fear of communism was a key factor in creating support for the Nazi party and its huge corps of professional thugs, who engaged in public brawls with German leftists whenever they could get the upper hand. Their leader's speeches made them feel that violence was more than justified. In the 1920s, Hitler claimed that the Leninists had murdered 30 million people in Russia, "partly on the scaffold, partly by machine guns and similar means, partly in veritable slaughterhouses, partly, millions upon millions, by hunger; and we all know that . . . this scourge is approaching, that it is also coming upon Germany."[9]

Speaking in hypnotic rhythms that overwhelmed the rational faculty, Hitler left his audiences in a fury of righteous indignation coupled with a sense of impending disaster. Time was running out, he insisted. Either the German people would rally 'round the Nazi banner or they would be overwhelmed by the plots of the Jews, who, in Hitler's myth, controlled both capitalists and Communists as well as 75 percent of the world's financial resources.

More and more Germans were sucked into Hitler's whirlpool of paranoia. Devastated by their defeat in the Great War, daunted by the astonishing hyperinflation that destroyed their economy in 1923, and, finally, crushed by the international catastrophe of the Great Depression after 1929, many Germans found it natural to adopt Hitler's belief that they were the victims of a conspiracy. The failure of Germany's fledgling democracy during the Weimar Republic seemed no less dramatic than the failure of the kaiser's monarchy. A large minority of the population, feeling adrift without a helmsman, looked longingly to the authoritarian leadership offered by Adolf Hitler—as many Italians had looked to Benito Mussolini, Hitler's future ally.

Especially after the onset of the Great Depression, events broke Hitler's way, and he was able to use electoral processes and legal means to become chancellor of Germany on January 30, 1933. Less than nine months later he ended German participation in the League of Nations. By employing terrorist tactics like the Blood Purge of June 1934, he consolidated his dictatorship and succeeded in imposing his personal rule upon the German people. His program never really varied from the vision that he had developed in the immediate postwar years. Through the force of his will and the disciplined courage of his people, he would rewrite history in blood and steel to show that the so-called Great War had been only one battle. Treachery had caused Germany to lose that battle, but the Third Reich would now proceed to shock the world by winning the really decisive confrontations. Hitler would put right what the kaiser had gotten wrong.

After Germany invaded Poland, Franklin Roosevelt's policy was a far cry from the neutrality that Woodrow Wilson had cultivated during the first three years of World War I. The president soon found himself in a struggle with Congress over aid to Great Britain, which he hoped to save from the kind of defeat that was France's fate in the spring of 1940. One of his first forthright steps—taken without seeking congressional approval—was to transfer fifty aging destroyers from the United States to the Royal Navy in exchange for the use of eight British bases stretching from Newfoundland to the northeast coast of Latin America.

Anticipating this move, Winston Churchill enthused that "each destroyer you can spare to us is measured in rubies."[10] But the destroyers deal riled isolationists, who feared that Roosevelt would use the struggle against fascism as an excuse to become the dictator of the United States. During that same month, September 1940, FDR persuaded Congress to pass the first peacetime conscription in U.S. history. As a result, 800,000 young Americans were drafted into the armed forces—a process that caused the frenzied controversy over Roosevelt's foreign policy to reach new heights.

In Germany, the real menace was warming to his task. After the fall of France, Hitler's self-confidence had reached messianic proportions. His success in conquering so much of Europe had convinced him, as he told one of his commanders, that he was now "more godlike than human," and no longer "bound by . . . the conventions of human morality."[11] It was as fair a summary of hubris as has ever been spoken.

During the autumn of 1940, he looked at the possibility of occupying a number of Atlantic islands as a prelude to an eventual war with the United States. In particular, he hoped to take the Azores from Portugal and use them as a launching pad for the long-range bombers that were on the drawing boards at Messerschmitt—advanced machines that would be able to hit New York and the other great cities of the eastern seaboard.

Hitler was tantalized by the prospect of possessing such an offensive capability. By March 1941, when the Reich was being punished by Britain's Bomber Command, he was telling his intimates that "I only regret we still have no aircraft able to bomb Americans towns. I would dearly like to teach the Jews of America what it's like."[12] While the Azores continued to attract his attention as a base for bombers, Hitler had to accept the fact that the islands might be retaken whenever Roosevelt or Churchill chose to put forth the effort. In fact, the president had foreseen the possibility of a Nazi attack and ordered the U.S. Navy to be prepared to seize the Azores on thirty days' notice.

"War with the United States," Hitler counseled his inner circle in the early spring of 1941, "will come sooner or later."[13] Still, he hoped to defeat Churchill and Stalin before locking horns with Roosevelt, so he struggled to maintain a low profile in his relations with the United States.

Out in the Atlantic a situation had arisen that complicated Hitler's attempts to keep America out of the war. His U-boat commanders cried out that U.S. warships were playing fast and loose with the recognized laws of naval neutrality by informing the British about the location of German wolfpacks, but the Führer insisted that they nevertheless refrain from engaging the U.S. fleet. After several American merchantmen were sunk by hostile German action, Hitler berated his admirals and refused to hear their arguments for turning his submariners loose on U.S.-flagged vessels. By and large, his restraining influence worked. Isolated incidents of U-boats attacking American destroyers and vice versa would inevitably occur, but by themselves they never brought Washington and Berlin to the brink of war.

However, other factors continued to rachet up tensions between the two capitals. Prodded by Roosevelt, who was practicing an increasingly one-sided kind of neutrality, Congress passed in March 1941 a "lend-lease" bill granting the executive branch sweeping powers to provide Britain and other antifascist nations with very generous amounts of military aid. Additional means were found to help the United Kingdom stand up to the Nazis. During the first half of 1941, sixty-six Axis ships were seized in American ports on the grounds that they were likely to attract saboteurs. Instead of merely being impounded, they were delivered to the British—while Hitler fumed. In June, Roosevelt gave the Führer another reason for resentment by freezing all of Germany's American assets and closing its consulates in the United States.

Throughout this period, the battered warships of the Royal Navy were welcomed into American shipyards and restored to fighting trim, while pilots attached to the Royal Air Force were trained at U.S. airfields. On orders from the president, U.S. forces took over the occupation of Iceland from British troops and established bases in Greenland that would become important in keeping Churchill's transatlantic lifeline open.

When the U.S. destroyer *Greer* was fired upon by German submarine U-652 in September 1941, an outraged Roosevelt was ready to escalate the conflict. His ire was even greater when the U.S. destroyer *Reuben James* was torpedoed at the end of October and sank with the loss of all but 45 of its 160-man crew. Calling Hitler a rogue who meant to "create a permanent world system based on force, terror, and murder,"[14] the president ordered the navy to shoot at any German warship that dared to enter the waters of the western Atlantic. Hitler wanted neither to provoke the United States nor to seem intimidated, so he countered by instructing "German ships *not* to shoot when they sight American vessels, but to defend themselves when attacked. I will have any German officer court-martialed who fails to defend himself."[15]

On May 27, 1941, the continuing crisis had induced FDR to unveil his central concerns with unprecedented candor. In a speech broadcast from the East Room of the White House and heard by an estimated 85 million people around the globe, Roosevelt stressed how much he distrusted Hitler's intentions: "What started as a European war has developed . . . into a world war for world domination."[16] Since the speech helped to mark Pan American Day, Roosevelt dealt with the Nazi threat to South America and emphasized that the United States had begun to build up its forces to repel a fascist attack on the New World. The president explained how he viewed the Nazi's long-range aims: "They plan to treat the Latin American nations as they are now treating the Balkans [that is, subjecting them to a full-scale military attack]. They plan then to strangle the United States and the Dominion of Canada."[17] America, declared Roosevelt, had entered a state of "unlimited national emergency."[18] Henceforth it would look to its arms above all else.

Roosevelt's speech was widely criticized as speculative and premature, with an unwarranted emphasis on Hitler's desire for dominating the entire world, but there can be no doubt that he had fathomed what Nazism would ultimately be about. The other side cherished different opinions. To hear Hitler tell it, it was not Germany but the United States that possessed the grand designs. *"Ja, Herr Roosevelt—and his Jews!"* he exclaimed to a reporter named Pierre Huss in the autumn of 1941. "He wants to run the world and rob us all of a place in the sun. He says he wants to save England but he means he wants to be ruler and heir of the British Empire."[19]

Four months before Pearl Harbor, Hitler blamed all of Germany's troubles on Roosevelt, "with his freemasons, Jews, and general Jewish-bolshevism."[20] And what of Roosevelt's secret agenda? In first place, according to Nazi prop-

aganda, were plans for wiping out the German race. But the Nazis would lead
the German counteroffensive, and it would succeed beyond the wildest dreams
of the doubters. Joseph Goebbels expected all of European Jewry to perish in
the world war or be driven to foreign shores: "Their last refuge will be North
America, and there too they will one day, sooner or later, end up footing the
bill."[21] A threat to invade and occupy the continental United States, and perhaps to set up extermination camps on American soil, can easily be read into
Goebbels's false prophecy.

Japan's attack on Pearl Harbor, an event that took place when Germany was
militarily the most powerful nation in the world, gave Hitler a tremendous, if
temporary, lift. "The turning point!" he exclaimed when he heard the news. To
an official in the foreign ministry, Walter Hewel, he made a startling proclamation. "Now it is impossible for us to lose the war," Hitler said, wildly exaggerating the might of Imperial Japan. "We now have an ally who has never
been vanquished in 3,000 years."[22] He personally praised the Japanese ambassador to Berlin for his country's success in catching U.S. forces off guard: "You
gave the right declaration of war! This method is the only proper one."[23]
    The source of Hitler's confidence at the time of Pearl Harbor was simple:
He thought the Japanese would be able to tie down American resources indefinitely. His immediate plan was to finish off the Russians during 1942; then he
would march into Afghanistan, from which he would be well placed to detach
the Indian subcontinent from the British Empire. There was even the possibility that his forces would be able to link up with Japanese armies that would
soon be pushing toward India through southeast Asia. If Hitler's hopes had
been fulfilled, the old American dream of remaking the world in democracy's
image would have languished for a thousand years.
    Roosevelt would do everything in his power to stem the advance of fascism,
but the president faced some very basic problems. Immediately after the beginning of hostilities with Japan, he doubted that the American people would
tolerate a simultaneous war with Germany. During the presidential campaign
of 1940, FDR had emphatically promised to send no troops to fight abroad
unless the United States was attacked by foreign powers—and the skirmishing
with German U-boats in the Atlantic seemed too minor to qualify. Ultimately,
it was Hitler and Mussolini's declaration of war against the United States on
December 11, 1941, that overcame opposition to a crusade against the fascist
dictators.
    Nazi Germany had signed no treaty that compelled Hitler to support Japa-
nese aggression; he was committed to taking on the United States only in the
event that Roosevelt initiated the hostilities. Attempting to justify his decision
for war during a speech to the Reichstag, Hitler concentrated on goading FDR,
whom he called "the main culprit of this war."[24] He echoed a charge that had
long been used by American isolationists, saying that Roosevelt counted on
foreign adventures to divert attention from the New Deal's failure to mend the

U.S. economy. He went on to contrast his personal struggle with the president's:

> When the Great War came, Roosevelt occupied a position . . . enjoyed by those who do business while others bleed. I was only one of those who carried out orders as an ordinary soldier. . . . I shared the fate of millions, and Franklin Roosevelt only the fate of the so-called upper ten thousand.[25]

Although he kept repeating that the United States lacked martial prowess, on various occasions Hitler had voiced respect for its war-making potential, and his preference had been for the Japanese either to attack the Soviet Far East or to limit themselves to taking such Asian outposts of European colonialism as Malaya and the Dutch East Indies. He would soon reveal the full extent of his reservations about fighting the United States. "This war against America is a tragedy," he said to Martin Bormann, the Nazi party secretary. "Germany and the United States should have been able . . . to support each other without undue strain on either of them."[26]

Stalin, as Hitler realized, would be the great beneficiary of the Axis war with the United States, for the Soviet dictator could now be sure that Japanese forces would be moving out into the Pacific, not invading Siberia. And units of the Red Army that had long been tied down in the Soviet Far East could move west and fight the Germans in Russia and the Ukraine.

On the Potomac, the great debate was whether to concentrate on defeating Japan before Germany or Germany before Japan. Most Americans found it an easy question to answer. The unprecedented trauma of Pearl Harbor had convinced them that the Japanese should be the first to feel the full force of their country's wrath. Roosevelt was inclined to go all-out in both theaters at the same time. His ambitions created dissension. Henry Stimson, his secretary of war, told Roosevelt that such a strategy would be no strategy at all. With plenty of prompting from the British, a "Germany First" campaign was adopted by Roosevelt and his lieutenants—meaning that the defeat of European fascism would be the chief priority of the Allied war effort.

But in 1942, Germany was much better positioned to damage the United States than vice versa. When the Führer ordered his U-boats to sink all U.S. ships on sight, the results were nightmarish. The commander of the submarine campaign, Adm. Karl Dönitz, commented that "our U-boats are operating close inshore along the coast of the United States of America, so that bathers and sometimes entire coastal cities are witnesses to the drama of war, whose visual climaxes are constituted by the red glorioles of blazing tankers."[27]

The public was panicked by all the fires off the eastern seaboard and oppressed by rumors that German bombers would soon arrive to augment the chaos. Reading reports about the disarray, Hitler chortled over Roosevelt's apparent willingness to allow "his merchant shipping [to] ply peacefully back and forth along the American coast for us to pick off like sitting ducks."[28] Corresponding with Churchill in March 1942, Roosevelt admitted that "my Navy has been definitely slack in preparing for this submarine warfare off our coast."[29]

That was putting it mildly, for during the first half of 1942, Hitler's submarines sank almost four hundred ships in American waters. The total number of U-boats lost in the same period was six. It all added up to the most disastrous defeat in the history of U.S. naval warfare. And the U-boat, incomparably Hitler's most effective weapon against the United States, continued its predations throughout the war: By V-E day, over fifteen thousand Americans had perished at sea as a result of the action of German submarines. But the real crisis began to pass when improved antisubmarine technologies on ships and long-range aircraft allowed American sailors and airmen to send more and more U-boats to the bottom. Better organized and better escorted convoys were also crucial in blunting the U-boat attack.

The Battle of the Atlantic would have been much worse if Hitler had spent more time developing his overall strategy. Early on, he had failed to recognize the U-boat's potential. Had he allotted Admiral Dönitz's submarines a larger share of the naval budget, the result might have permanently disrupted American logistics and devastated the Allies' war-making capabilities. Instead, the determination of the U.S. Navy to come fighting back from defeat prepared the way for Allied victory. An official navy report stated that "the Battle of the Atlantic was the most important single operation in World War II, for upon its outcome rested the success or failure of the United Nations' [that is, Allied] strategy in all other theaters of operation."[30]

According to Cordell Hull, his secretary of state, Franklin Roosevelt "loved the military side of events, and liked to hold them in his own hand."[31] Daily he absorbed a tremendous amount of information about the conduct of the war, and when crucial campaigns were under way, he demanded to be briefed hourly on the course of events. During the early months of the war, he shaped American strategy like a sculptor, thereby becoming the most powerful U.S. president since Lincoln.

But he neither sought nor wanted the kind of obsessive control over every detail of the war effort that Hitler insisted upon. The president's greatest contribution was rallying the American people to the Allied cause. First and last, he aimed to make the war a people's war. Two days after Pearl Harbor, he revealed his vision to a nationwide radio audience: "We are all in it together— all the way. Every single man, woman, and child is a partner in the most tremendous undertaking of our American history."[32] Blackouts and air-raid drills and bond drives soon gave point to the president's words.

For Americans, the war changed everything. In 1933, unemployment in the United States had peaked at or very near 25 percent. A decade later, in the middle of the war, it had fallen to less than 2 percent. But meat, sugar, coffee, butter, cheese, canned goods, shoes, and many other consumer goods were strictly rationed. Black markets sprang up around every corner; fully 20 percent of all American businesses were warned at one time or another during the war to mend their ways or face prosecution for illegal practices. Gasoline was in short supply and its use was subject to strict limitations, like a 35-mph speed limit on the nation's highways. Americans who took cabs tried to share them, and more and more people relied on buses and streetcars.

A Berlin magazine stated in January 1943 that the U.S. economy "was unable under Roosevelt's presidency to solve its peacetime problems; it will be even less able to cope with the more difficult war problems."[33] In spite of what the Nazis preferred to think, the U.S. military buildup was proceeding with tremendous success. Barely a year after Pearl Harbor, American war industries had equaled the combined production of Germany, Italy, and Japan; after another year the United States had doubled the Axis gross national product. "The great arsenal of democracy,"[34] as Roosevelt called a mobilized America, was fulfilling its promise and preparing for Hitler's doom.

The economy of wartime America was largely controlled by bureaucracies like the Office of Price Administration and the Office of Production Management, which had been voted emergency powers by Congress. Tax rates went up and remained high as federal spending broke all records, throwing the budget deep into deficit. Americans groaned in 1943 as the government began to take income-tax deductions from their paychecks for the first time; to keep working people from being pauperized by this change in the bookkeeping system, the IRS forgave all taxpayers 75 percent of what they owed for 1942. Inflation was reined in by wage and price controls; so although the national debt increased by tenfold from 1939 to 1945, prices rose by only one-third.

During these years the American language filled up with soldier talk. The general population learned that Big Red One was the U.S. Army's battle-hardened 1st Infantry Division, and that Class VI supplies were alcoholic beverages. A chaplain could be called a Holy Joe. For the duration Detroit—which produced no purely civilian vehicles from mid-1942 to the war's end—received a new nickname: Jeepville. Letters from boot camp complained of "M-1 thumb," which resulted when a soldier got his first digit nipped by the M-1 rifle's spring-loaded bolt as it rammed past the clip feed. That weapon weighed 9.5 pounds empty, but "after you carried [it] a mile, the decimal point fell out."[35]

Taken altogether, the World War II home front was a quiet place. While Hitler's submarine campaign remained a palpable menace off the East Coast, there were no Axis successes in sabotage to match the Great Tom disaster of World War I. Only ten saboteurs were landed on American soil from German U-boats during the whole of the war, and all ten were caught by the FBI before they could do any damage. To the consciousness of America, Adolf Hitler was both very near and very far away.

"Early this morning we heard the bombers going out. It was the sound of a giant factory in the sky." So began Edward R. Murrow's radio broadcast from London on D-Day, June 6, 1944. The air armada "seemed to shake the old gray stone buildings in this bruised and battered city beside the Thames. The sound was heavier, more triumphant than ever before."[36] Murrow's report is suggestive of the fact that Allied air power guaranteed the invasion's success. And it was largely America's ability to produce aircraft—86,000 of them in 1943 alone—that secured this all-important command of the skies. The extent of Allied air superiority retains the power to startle: On June 6, Hitler had a mere 319 aircraft in the west to send against the Allies' 12,837.

After the Normandy beachheads were secured, it was only a matter of time before the swastika came down all over Europe. Yet Hitler kept the loyalty of millions of Germans to the end. His armies were fighting to the finish with slogans like "Death and dishonor to those who fear an honorable death!"[37] The civilian attitude could be almost as soldierly. After Hitler's escape from an assassination and coup attempt in July 1944, a desolate widow living in Vienna sent him her life savings with this message:

> Mein Führer—you are all that is left to me in this world. I had a child, but he died in action in Russia at Mayevka. He had passed his examinations and had a place waiting at technical college. I had been saving up for this, but now he'll never return, my darling child! Take my money, out of joy that nothing befell the Führer.[38]

Why did the German people remain good Nazis to the last minute? Because in their eyes, the course of events seemed to bear out Hitler's prophecies. From the beginning, he had warned Germans that they were surrounded by foes who would force them to fight for survival, and he had portrayed all of Germany's military offensives as preemptive, not aggressive; the Nazis were expanding the Reich in order to defeat evil Jewish schemes and protect the master race. When Allied bombs fell on German cities and foreign troops destroyed German armies, the world was exposed for what the Führer had always said it was: hostile in the extreme. Germany's fault, then, lay not in its warring ways, but in failing to develop its full strength.

At the beginning of 1945, in his last New Year's message to the German people, Hitler predicted that an Anglo-American victory "would mean not only the dismemberment of the German Reich, the deportation of 15 to 20 million Germans to foreign lands, the enslavement of the rest of our people, but also the mass starvation of further millions of Germans."[39] But the Führer did not preach hopelessness. Even during the last months of the war, he still thought it possible to return to the offensive, for revolutionary weapons of mass destruction—veritable miracles of German ingenuity—would soon be made operational. This kind of false expectation was nothing new. As early as February 1940, Hitler had convened a meeting of his top Nazis to tell them that breakthroughs in German military technology would bring the war to a successful conclusion within six months.

The Führer's desperate sense of hope kept him believing that, at worst, the war would be fought to a draw. Even the atomic bomb figured into his plans. On February 14, 1945, as Allied bombers were reducing the city of Dresden to rubble and ashes, he told Dr. Erwin Geising that, though Germany was being mauled, he "would get her out of it. The British and the Americans have miscalculated badly. . . . Some time ago we solved the problem of nuclear fission, and we have developed it so far that we can exploit the energy for armaments purposes." The Führer thrilled to imagine atomic fireballs descending on the Allied armies: "They won't even know what hit them! It's the weapon of the future. With it, Germany's future is assured. It was Providence that allowed me to perceive this final path to victory."[40]

In fact, Hitler had done little to encourage the Nazis' nuclear program, refusing in the late 1930s to credit claims that the "Jewish physics" of Albert Einstein could result in a fabulous breakthrough in destructive technology. Heinrich Himmler, the head of the S.S., complicated matters by arresting some of Germany's leading nuclear physicists on suspicion of disloyalty. Other factors figured in: Many Nazi scientists sincerely believed that the war would be over before any nation's program could produce a nuclear weapon. So, in 1945, the Nazis' atomic bomb project was still very small and offered no prospect of immediate success. Hitler's unwarranted optimism of February of that year was probably the result of conversations with Martin Bormann, whose specialty was telling the Führer what he wanted to hear.

While direct evidence is lacking, Hitler may have expected to mate his atom bomb to an intercontinental ballistic missile that would obliterate American cities. He undoubtedly knew that Wernher von Braun, whose V-2s terrorized England late in the war, had drawn up plans for an ICBM, designated the A-10, that was meant to strike the United States from Germany. At any rate, Hitler's fantasies failed to keep his spirit from flagging at times. Six weeks after talking with Dr. Geising, he blurted out to one of his civilian subordinates, Fritz Sauckel, that the war was probably lost—though his faith in the ability of the Reich to stage a stunning comeback remained generally unshaken until eight days before his death, when spearheads of the Red Army broke through the northern defenses of Berlin.

Sleeping only three hours a night at the close of his life, Hitler had become a physical and nervous wreck. Thanks to his quack doctor, Theodor Morell, he was a borderline drug addict. But three long years of defeat had prepared Hitler to embrace the ultimate failure. His way out would not be that of the kaiser, whom he scorned as a quitter. Well before the beginning of the war, he had promised that "we may be destroyed, but if we are, we shall drag a world with us—a world in flames."[41]

Certainly he had succeeded in devastating the Jewish population of Europe. It was his proudest achievement, one that the impending Allied victory could never undo. As early as December 1942, Edward R. Murrow had given Americans a glimpse of the hell that the Führer had created in his European fortress. "One is almost stunned into silence," Murrow professed in a broadcast for CBS news, "by some of the information reaching London." Incredible as it seemed, "millions of human beings, most of them Jews, are being gathered up with ruthless efficiency and murdered."[42] Murrow then let the chilling words fall:

"The phrase 'concentration camps' is obsolete. . . . It is now possible to speak only of extermination camps."[43] As Allied armies liberated those grim places in the spring of 1945, the world was appalled by the full extent of Hitlerian evil.

The camps showed the Nazi order at its most horrendous, but there were plenty of other appalling spectacles in Hitler's Europe. For the Führer intended that the triumphant Allies, especially the hated Russians, inherit nothing but a wasteland. Blaming his generals for losing the war and screaming that the German people were no longer worthy of him, Hitler was pleased to order the destruction of everything in Germany that could be destroyed. All public and private records were to be consumed by flames, all industrial plants to be rendered unworkable, all cultural objects from paintings to palaces to cathedrals to be ruined.

Fortunately, such orders were generally resisted. His lieutenant for industry, Albert Speer, perceived that Hitler had become "a man to whom the end of his own life meant the end of everything."[44] Sickened by the madness of his own government, Speer countermanded the directives that Hitler issued in the last days of the war.

Toward the end, Joseph Goebbels resorted to horoscopes, a practice that Hitler usually disdained. As near as Goebbels could tell, the stars would be fixed against the Führer and the Reich until the middle of April 1945, when some extraordinary breaks would come Germany's way. As it happened, President Roosevelt fell victim to a fatal stroke on April 12. Overjoyed at the news, Goebbels immediately telephoned Hitler: "My Führer, I congratulate you! Roosevelt is dead. It is written in the stars that the second half of April will be the turning point for us."[45] In spite of his earlier skepticism, Hitler was an immediate convert to this last gasp of Nazi optimism.

A proclamation to his soldiers on the eastern front was written by Goebbels and issued over the Führer's signature on April 14. It read in part: "At the moment when fate has carried off the greatest war criminal of all times [Roosevelt] from the face of this earth, the war's turning point has come."[46] Hitler took what consolation he could as the world crashed down around his ears.

His first taste of U.S. power had come on the western front during World War I, when he had fought opposite American lines and been menaced by American artillery. In his last days it was the thunder of Stalin's big guns that burst over his bunker. But it might have been the arrival of U.S. troops, not Soviet soldiers, that forced Hitler to kill himself. On April 23, 1945, Brig. Gen. Doyle O. Hickey of the U.S. Army had been prepared to cross the Elbe River and send the hundred tanks of his 3rd Armored Division rumbling across the final fifty miles to Berlin.

Shouting over a field telephone from his temporary command post, a beer hall in the central German city of Dessau, General Hickey challenged his corps commander to order him into the Nazi capital: "Why can't we go to Berlin, for God's sake? It's wide open, I tell you, wide open. We can beat the goddam Russians." His pleas fell on deaf ears. Reduced to tears as he put down the handset, Hickey turned to his staff and said, "We can't go. There's—there's some kind of agreement about the Russians taking Berlin."[47]

It was true, and the agreement had been made at the highest levels: Shortly before his death, President Roosevelt had refused to approve of any change in strategy that would interfere with the Red Army's conquest of Berlin. Considering that his end-game battles with Nazism cost Stalin over 300,000 casualties during the last three weeks of the war, and that his siege of Berlin was a particularly bloody operation, it is difficult to wish that Americans instead of Russians had fought their way to the portals of Hitler's bunker.

Although his mind was clouded by defeat and despair, Hitler could still imagine his postwar fate, whichever of the Allied armies captured him: He would be tried and executed as a war criminal. Death by his own hand would be an infinitely more acceptable alternative, for such an end would place him forever beyond the reach of his encircling enemies. During the summer of 1944, he had privately revealed his attitude to suicide: "It is only a fraction of a second; then one is released from all that and has one's rest and eternal peace."[48] Now that fraction of a second was drawing near.

He would arrange matters so that even his physical remains would escape the wrath of the Allies' judgment. Just before he and Eva Braun killed themselves, Hitler told his adjutant, Otto Günsche, to be sure that both of their corpses were burned to ashes. Probably thinking of how the Soviets had preserved Lenin's body, Hitler expressed a fear that his corpse would be "put on display in some waxworks in the future."[49] His political testament, dictated thirty-six hours before the end, told the world that "I die with a happy heart. . . . From the sacrifice of our soldiers and from my own unity with them unto death will spring up in the history of Germany the seed of a radiant renaissance of the National Socialist movement."[50] As he uttered these words Berlin was being shattered, raped, and looted over his head.

The precise details of his suicide remain mysterious, but it appears that both he and Eva Braun took poison, and that he made sure of his own death by shooting himself through the brain with a pistol. Lest they be tempted to believe that their Führer had died in a cowardly fashion, the German people were told that he had fallen in battle while defending Berlin from the Jewish-Marxist menace. The radio announcement of his death was accompanied by "Siegfried's Funeral Music" from Wagner's *Götterdämmerung*.

But in rumor the Führer lived on. Some said he had escaped from Berlin by air and from Germany by submarine. Reports from various quarters placed him on an obscure islet in the Baltic, or hidden by Gen. Francisco Franco among Spanish monks in the Sierra Morena, or roughing it with sturdy bandits in the uplands of Albania, or leading a life of austerity on the windswept plateau of Tibet—or plotting the beginnings of a Fourth Reich in a retreat on the Argentine pampas. Hitler existed in none of those places, yet even in death he retained the power to haunt the human mind in every part of the globe.

9

The Rising Sun
of Hideki Tojo

The most forbidding aspect of fascism was its power to endanger U.S. interests in the Pacific and Asia as well as in Europe. Though the machinations of Hitler and Mussolini dominated the headlines of U.S. newspapers, Japanese designs obviously belonged in the same category as those of Germany and Italy. With world tensions on the rise through the 1930s, a strategic nightmare seemed to be forming: The United States might be forced into a catastrophic two-ocean war. And in the long run, Japan, which was willing to devote 70 per-cent of its budget to military spending, might prove to be America's deadliest foe.

Franklin Roosevelt was not the first president whose lieutenants had pondered Japanese intentions. By 1933, when he moved into the White House, American planners had been worrying about the militarism of the Japanese for decades, and when they invaded Manchuria from their Korean colony in 1931, U.S. concern rose sharply. In 1937, the Japanese army used its Manchurian base to attack China proper, where it encountered an American presence based on missionary as well as commercial activity. U.S. flags were soon painted on the roofs of American schools, hospitals, and churches throughout eastern China, but the pilots of Japan's Imperial air force took few pains to avoid them. In fact, they sometimes seemed eager to bomb such buildings.

Other U.S. targets were equally appealing. The threat to American shipping on the Yangtze River was dramatized when Japanese fighters attacked the gunboat USS *Panay* and three Standard Oil tankers in December 1937, killing two American sailors. The incident created a crisis in Japanese-American relations, but the emperor's government quieted matters by apologizing and paying an indemnity of over $2 million. Imperfectly mollified, President Roosevelt stepped up aid to the Chinese Nationalists under Chiang Kai-shek. For their part, the Japanese continued to push deeper and deeper into Chinese territory. Clearly, they had slammed shut the "Open Door" that the United States had advocated for China since the turn of the century.

One of the generals who had launched the attack on the Chinese was Hideki Tojo. His superiors found his performance so commendable that, in the middle of 1938, they awarded Tojo the number two position in the war department. When Prince Konoye Fumimaro became prime minister for the second time in July 1940, he promoted Tojo to minister of war. By then the world's eyes were on Hitler, who had just defeated France. For the Japanese, the moment was pregnant with possibility. It seemed the perfect time to set the banner of the rising sun on such Southeast Asian properties as Indochina and Indonesia, which were colonies of France and Holland, respectively. Since the Führer had conquered both European powers, the Japanese eagerly cemented their already close ties with the Germans.

Hideki Tojo was a natural advocate of an alliance with the Third Reich, for he had served as a military attaché in Germany during the early 1920s and had come to admire Hitler in the 1930s. He considered it a sort of personal triumph when Japan formally joined the Axis in September 1940. Now the way would be open for his country to engage in a decisive struggle with the United States, a struggle that Tojo had been anticipating for over twenty years.

His first opportunity to study Americans at close range had come during the joint U.S.-Japanese occupation of eastern Siberia at the end of World War I. At that time, Tojo saw U.S. troops at a great disadvantage, for they had little sense of what they were supposed to achieve in the Russian Far East and their morale had not been high. In 1922, Tojo had crossed the United States by train during his journey back to Japan from Germany, and what he observed confirmed him in his anti-American prejudices. In Tojo's eyes, the general population of the United States seemed slack in appearance and outlook. These people, he thought, were too interested in material pleasures to put up much of a fight. He dreamed of the day when they would learn what the warlike Japanese could do.

It was no wonder that Tojo looked at the world through the barrel of a gun. His father had been an army general who served in victorious wars against China (1894–95) and Russia (1904–1905). Born in Tokyo at the end of 1884, Tojo received the education expected of a senior officer's son, graduating from a military academy after first attending a military prep school. It took him a long time to follow his father up through the ranks: Commissioned too late to distinguish himself during the Russo-Japanese War, he held the rank of first lieutenant for seven years.

Perseverance is what worked best for Tojo, and after almost thirty years in the army he reached the rank of major general. As head of the Japanese military and civilian police in occupied Manchuria in the mid-1930s, he gained a reputation as a sort of Asian Himmler. Personal ruthlessness served him well as he advanced to chief of staff of the Kwangtung Army, the Japanese force that he helped prepare for the invasion of China.

A taciturn man, Tojo wore horn-rimmed spectacles with round lenses. He relieved his inner tensions by chain-smoking. One Western observer remarked that his face "has a parched look, as though he had caught his head in an oven. . . . He is humorless, hardboiled, and as subtle as a piledriver."[1] His nickname was Kamisori, "the Razor." The father of seven children, Tojo reflected his own government's policy of encouraging large families—the better to justify Japanese expansionism and fill the Imperial armed forces. His wife, Katsuko, was given credit for coining the propaganda slogan "Having children is fun."[2]

In military circles, Tojo was known as an excellent tactician but a poor strategist. Japan's sun might have risen higher if the order of his talents had been reversed, for his army and navy faced strategic dilemmas on all fronts. After Hitler's invasion of Russia in June 1941, there was a temptation to renew the fighting with the Soviets in Siberia, which had gone badly for the Japanese in the late 1930s. But what Japan really needed was oil, and that resource was most abundant around the South China Sea. Accordingly, the Japanese, who had already established bases in northern Indochina (today's Vietnam, Laos, and Cambodia), engulfed southern Indochina in July 1941. Now Japan could menace Thailand, Malaya, the Dutch East Indies—and the U.S. presence in the Philippines.

The Roosevelt administration retaliated by freezing Japanese assets in the United States, tightening up trade restrictions, and embargoing the shipment of all petroleum products to Japan. Mindful of Japanese military and naval superiority in the Pacific, the War and Navy Departments proceeded to strengthen U.S. defenses in the Philippines and throughout the area. Washington's actions were not without influence in Tokyo for, prior to the embargoes, Japan had imported 90 percent of its gasoline and almost three-fourths of its scrap iron from the United States—both of which were crucial to its ability to make war. Now, in the second half of 1941, Roosevelt's secretary of state, Cordell Hull, told the Japanese that their credit and their imports would be restored as soon as their armies withdrew from China and Indochina.

But the militarists in Tokyo, who had long since silenced their civilian critics, were determined to suffer no such loss of face. As for Tojo, he only felt confirmed in his suspicions about American motives. The central purpose of U.S. foreign policy, he felt sure, was to frustrate Japan's desire to build a "Greater East Asia Co-prosperity Sphere"—that is, a large empire that would gather in all the European colonies in the Far East and Pacific. The only real alternative to kowtowing to Washington, it seemed to Tojo, was a war to achieve Japan's imperial designs. "I know it's risky," he confessed in the late summer of 1941, "but I still think it would be better than to be ground down without doing anything."[3]

Called to appear before the emperor on October 17, 1941, Tojo was startled to hear that Hirohito had chosen him prime minister and instructed him to form a new cabinet, in which, as it turned out, he would figure as his own minister for war and internal security. In Tojo's person the imperialists had carried the day. Now plans for Japan's great offensive could be finalized.

A month before Pearl Harbor, Tojo was refining his reasons for expanding the Japanese empire:

> Two years from now we will have no petroleum for military use; ships will stop moving. . . . We can talk about suffering and austerity, but can our people endure such a life for long? . . . I fear that we would become a third-class nation after two or three years if we merely sat tight.[4]

And what if Japan launched out? Tojo said that it all depended on the people. If the entire nation would unite "in iron solidarity and go forward, nothing can stop us. . . . Wars can be fought with ease."[5]

Roosevelt's State Department recognized Tojo's elevation to the premiership as a sign that Japan was tilting toward an attack on U.S. forces—probably in the Philippines—and the administration was advised to prepare the armed forces for the beginning of hostilities. Since U.S. Army cryptographers had broken one of the chief Japanese codes, the president knew in the first days of December 1941 that the Imperial fleet had put to sea in fighting trim, but its destination remained a mystery. None of the president's inner circle imagined that the Japanese were bold enough to hit Pearl Harbor, despite evidence to the contrary. During the summer of 1941, such evidence had been augmented when the U.S. Navy boarded no fewer than seventeen Japanese "fishing" boats that had violated Hawaii's territorial waters. Each was well provided with telescopes, cameras, charts, and radio transmitters.

At the last minute, the army's chief of staff, Gen. George C. Marshall, was handed the text of an intercepted Japanese message that carried tremendous consequences. The message all but proved that war was imminent in the Pacific. Galvanized, Marshall sent Lt. Gen. Walter Short, the army commander in Hawaii, an urgent warning: "Japanese are presenting at one p.m. eastern standard time today what amounts to an ultimatum. . . . [B]e on the alert accordingly. Inform naval authorities of this communication."[6] Unfortunately, Marshall's warning was delayed in transmission and did not reach General Short until after the last Japanese bomb had fallen on Pearl Harbor. Nevertheless, Hawaii should have been better prepared. Already on November 27, Marshall had warned Short that "hostile action" in the Pacific was "possible at any moment."[7]

But the failure of American watchfulness was so complete that the attack went pretty much as planned by its architect, Adm. Isoroku Yamamoto, commander of the Japanese Combined Fleet. The armada that he sent against Pearl Harbor consisted of 31 ships, including 6 aircraft carriers, 2 battleships, and 2 heavy cruisers. It carried 432 planes, of which 353 directly participated in the raid. Launched as the task force approached Oahu undetected from the north, the Japanese planes found their targets anchored neatly in pairs. At 7:55 in the morning of December 7, the first bombs began to fall on the Pacific fleet.

The *Arizona* was hit harder than any other vessel at Pearl Harbor. Torpedoes did most of the damage to her sister ships in Battleship Row, but the *Arizona* was the victim of eight gravity bombs. Although one of them apparently sailed directly down her funnel, the mortal blow was struck by an armor-piercing bomb that blew up her forward ammunition magazines. In the thick of the fray, a boatswain's mate named John Anderson helped move his injured comrades into the small rescue boats that had come to the *Arizona's* aid. "Everything was on fire," he recalled, "the ship was on fire, the water was on fire and there [were] people . . . in this fire and I thought God Almighty, how are they going to make it?"[8] The death toll was very high: No fewer than 1,177 of the *Arizona's* sailors and marines perished.

All told, the raid lasted two hours and ten minutes. The total number of U.S. dead on Oahu, including civilian fatalities, was 2,403; the Japanese lost only 129. Twenty-one vessels of the U.S. Navy's Pacific Fleet were sunk or damaged. Of that number, 5 were battleships: *Oklahoma, California, Nevada, West Virginia,* and *Arizona.* The Japanese got the surface ships of their armada away intact, but they did lose one full-size and 5 midget submarines. The raid cost the U.S. 162 aircraft to Japan's 29. When Hideki Tojo heard the early reports back in Tokyo, he "rejoiced over the miraculous success."[9]

It had been in the spring of 1940 that the Pacific Fleet was shifted from San Diego to Hawaii as, it was hoped, a deterrent against Japanese aggression. Never had a change in the deployment of U.S. naval forces proved more ill-advised, and the question of responsibility could not be avoided. A succession of military commissions and congressional committees were convened to investigate the disaster, but the job of assigning guilt reached an uncertain conclusion.

Obvious mistakes could, however, be laid bare. Repeated testimony showed that the military commanders on Hawaii had been misled about the nature of the threat they faced. Believing that the Japanese inhabitants of Oahu were prepared, on instructions from Tokyo, to open a campaign of sabotage, the Pacific command had ordered that its ships and planes be bunched together, to make them easier to guard. As a result, on December 7, the Japanese pilots were confronted with an extraordinary collection of inviting targets.

There were, to be sure, some mitigating factors. What Admiral Yamamoto really wanted was to catch the three aircraft carriers of the Pacific Fleet tied up at Pearl Harbor, yet all three were out at sea and never so much as glimpsed by the Japanese. In addition, the vital support facilities at Pearl Harbor—the fuel storage tanks, maintenance shops, submarine base, and resupply ware-houses—were left almost untouched by the Japanese pilots, who seemed mesmerized by Oahu's warships and airfields.

Ironically, it was on the U.S. home front that the attack produced its greatest results—results that would hurt the Japanese as nothing else could. For years, Roosevelt had been working tirelessly to unite the nation in the face of the fascist threat. Now Japan had finished the job for him overnight. Since Pearl Harbor had been hit without a prior declaration of war—even while Japanese diplomats were engaged in delicate negotiations with the Roosevelt administration—the revulsion experienced by the American people was very strong. There was essentially no opposition when, on December 8, the president asked Congress to "declare that since the unprovoked and dastardly attack by Japan on Sunday, December 7, a state of war has existed between the United States and the Japanese Empire."[10]

Shortly after ravaging Pearl Harbor, the Japanese hurled themselves against Wake Island, Guam, Hong Kong, the Philippines, Thailand, Burma, and Malaya—and everywhere they met with success. The empire grew by leaps and bounds as Tojo's troops overran all the major islands of the southwestern Pacific, giving Japan the mineral riches of Borneo and Sumatra, Java and New Guinea. Not even Hitler's blitzkrieg moved with such overwhelming momentum as the Japanese juggernaut. Displaying the rampant overconfidence that would later be termed *victory disease*, the *Japan Times Advertiser* let the word go forth: "Over tens of thousands of miles, from the Arctics to the Tropics . . . the land has rumbled to the tread of Japan's legions or the skies have thundered to the roar of Japan's winged knights."[11]

Horrified Americans reacted with unprecedented anger to Japanese aggression. Citizens in the nation's capital vented their outrage by urging the government to hew down the cherry trees on the Tidal Basin at the Jefferson Memorial—trees that had been a gift from the Japanese at the end of World War I; one enterprising patriot took matters into his own hands and chopped down four of them. In Yonkers, the owner of a curio shop culled his offerings with a hammer and displayed the debris in his front window with a sign that read, "This is Our Stock of Jap Goods."[12] Popular songwriters aimed at the hit parade with such new ditties as "Goodbye, Momma, I'm Off to Yokohama," "Slap the Jap Right Off the Map," and "To Be Specific, It's Our Pacific."[13] Two weeks after Pearl Harbor, *Time* magazine reported that "Japanese are hesitant, nervous in conversation, [and] laugh loudly at the wrong time."[14]

Among the first to suffer the effects of the country's indignation were Americans of Japanese ancestry. On February 19, 1942, President Roosevelt signed Executive Order 9066, which caused over 110,000 Japanese-Americans to be turned out of their homes on the West Coast and sent to ten relocation centers in high desert country farther inland, there to remain until late in the war. (It would be a very long time before the United States paid compensation to these victims of war hysteria.) As the fighting intensified and the Japanese became identified with death marches and kamikaze strikes and fanatical atrocities, American hatred of anything and everything Japanese deepened.

Eleven weeks after Pearl Harbor, as the nation was settling in to listen to one of President Roosevelt's fireside chats, the Japanese fired on the California coast near Goleta west of Santa Barbara. The attack was carried out by a large I-class submarine of the Imperial Navy, the I-17. It was late in the day on February 23, 1942, when the I-17 surfaced several hundred yards off Highway 101 and began bombarding the oil derricks of the Signal Oil and Gas Company with its 5.5-inch deck gun.

Hostile actions by the Confederate Navy aside, no warship of an enemy nation had shelled the continental United States since the War of 1812. But the historic nature of the event was no guarantee of spectacular results: The thirty-five-minute attack caused a mere $500 worth of damage, which included a crack on the gear casing of an oil well pump. There was no time for the Japanese to survey the results for themselves. Fearing that a longer stay would subject his sailors to an American counterattack, the I-17's commander, Capt. Kozu Nishino, ordered his vessel to resubmerge and slip back out to sea.

Only one casualty emerged from the incident: Capt. Barney Hagen of the U.S. Army was wounded as he tried to disarm an unexploded Japanese shell and had to be hospitalized for fifty days. But back in Japan, the press reported that the submarine had caused "heavy damage" and "unnerved the entire Pacific coast." Radio Tokyo announced that the attack "was a warning to the nation that the paradise created by George Washington is on the verge of destruction."[15]

The I-17 did leave a rattled California in its wake, and the seeds of panic that its crew had sown on American soil were soon to sprout anew. During the early morning hours of February 25, Los Angeles experienced a war scare of the first order. The 9:00 A.M. final edition of the *Los Angeles Times* tried to summarize the earthshaking news: "L.A. AREA RAIDED! Jap Planes Peril Santa Monica, Seal Beach, El Segundo, Redondo. . . . [F]oreign aircraft flying both in large formation and singly, flew over Southern California early today. . . . [T]he anti-aircraft defenses of the city roared into action and soon the entire southwestern skies of the city were ablaze with orange bursts."[16]

Such reports were subject to revision. The truth about the "Battle of Los Angeles" was that it never took place. Inexperienced antiaircraft crews, with the attack on Signal Oil and Gas fresh in their minds, had been misled by local radar operators into believing that enemy aircraft were over the city. The army gunners had then started firing at the beam spots of their own searchlights and proceeded to target their own air bursts. Before they were finished 1,440 rounds of live ammunition had been expended.

Less than two months later, the Japanese would have been delighted to discover that their fears were just as illusory. But the bombs that hit targets in Tokyo, Yokosuka, Kobe, and Nagoya on April 18, 1942, were real—as real as Col. Jimmy Doolittle's airmen and their sixteen bombers. Although the twin-engined B-25s that were used to attack Japan belonged to the army air force, their launching platform was Adm. William Halsey's aircraft carrier *Hornet*. The Doolittle raid, coming in the midst of a succession of American setbacks, inflicted little damage on the Japanese war machine, yet it created a sensation in the United States and did wonders for American morale.

Across the Pacific, the emperor's subjects were shaken. A patriotic song of 1941 had claimed that "enemy planes are only mosquitoes."[17] Now the Japanese were forced to sing a different tune. One young civilian wrote that "the bombing of Tokyo and several other cities has brought about tremendous change in the attitude of our people toward the war. . . . It does not seem anymore that there is such a great difference between the battle front and the home front."[18] Adm. Osami Nagano, the Japanese navy's chief of staff, was more succinct. "This shouldn't happen," he muttered between clenched teeth. "This simply should not happen."[19]

While the Japanese were incapable of responding to the Doolittle raid in kind, they did what they could to harass the western United States. A historical marker in extreme northwestern Oregon tells one tale: "On June 21, 1942, a 5.5-inch shell exploded here, one of 17 fired at Columbia River harbor defense installations by the Japanese submarine I-25." It was, as the plaque goes on to say, "the only hostile shelling of a military base on the U.S. mainland during World War II."[20] An even more remarkable incident occurred in southern Oregon during the second week of September, when submarine I-25 returned to American waters with a more complex task to fulfill, one that involved a seaplane that the sub carried in a small tubular hangar just forward of its conning tower.

The pilot of this improbable little aircraft was Warrant Officer Nobuo Fujita. When his mission was first described to him, Fujita was struck dumb by the potential magnificence of the thing: He was to bomb the United States itself. "My mind considered Seattle, Portland, San Francisco, Los Angeles," Fujita later recalled. "Perhaps I could hit a vital target. . . . I did not consider for a moment that my quite small reconnaissance plane could carry only two 76-kilogram [170-pound] bombs." When Fujita's briefing officer, Commander Iura, spread out the charts for the mission, he pointed to the southern coast of Oregon and said, "You will bomb these forests for us."[21] Fujita's disappointment was intense: "Any cadet could bomb a forest! A thing like that would be impossible to miss."[22] Commander Iura comforted Fujita by assuring him that his incendiary bombs would start a major conflagration among the cedars and firs of the mountainous Northwest.

I-25 left its Japanese harbor at Yokosuka on August 15, 1942. Less than three weeks later it entered American waters, and at dawn on September 9, Fujita's little airplane was catapulted off the sub's foredeck. The sequence of events that followed were etched in his memory: "Behind us the I-25 submerged to move to our rendezvous point to await our return. I flew toward Cape Blanco light, crossed the coastline, and went inland on a southeast course about 50 miles." Shortly after their first bomb fell just south of Wheeler Ridge in Oregon's Siskiyou National Forest, Fujita and his observer, Okuda, could see smoke from the fire of their heart's desire. "It gave me great satisfaction," as Fujita later put it, "to get some revenge for the bombing of my homeland by Doolittle's raiders. I felt that it partially evened the score. We flew a few more miles and dropped the second bomb."[23]

For the first time in its history the United States had been attacked by an enemy aircraft. Unhappily for Fujita, however, the bombs fell into a forest that had been moistened by several days of rain and fog. What smoke did rise from the bomb sites attracted the attention of forest rangers who quickly extinguished the smoldering fires.

Its first mission finished if not fulfilled, Fujita's little low-winged seaplane landed safely on the ocean swells beside I-25. A derrick then hoisted it aboard, where it was quickly disassembled and sealed inside its hangar. As the submarine started to dive, it was spotted by the pilot of a twin-engine Lockheed Hudson aircraft on a routine antisubmarine patrol. Although Capt. J. H. Daugherty of the army air force failed to make a positive identification of his target, he took a chance and attacked I-25 as it disappeared beneath the waves. His bombs struck close enough to flood the sub's switchboard room and briefly plunge its interior into darkness, but I-25 sustained no major damage. The incidence did not deter Fujita, the samurai firebug, from flying a second mission on September 29, when he dropped two more incendiaries on the Oregon wilderness fifty miles north of Wheeler Ridge. It was another fruitless attempt: again the bombs failed to raise fires.

The effort to burn down U.S. forests would soon be continued by the makers of Japan's balloon bombs. Typically, these "windship weapons" measured over thirty feet in diameter and carried a payload of one thirty-three-pound antipersonnel bomb plus four incendiary devices. Schoolgirls were employed to stitch the balloon's paper panels together; the finished products were filled with hydrogen gas in sumo wrestling halls and other large public buildings. A bungee cord was generally used to help secure the payload beneath the balloon.

Launched from the east coast of Japan, the balloons were carried across the Pacific in about a hundred hours on the strong winds of the jet stream. They were engineered to drop their bombs from an average altitude of thirty thousand feet and then to burn themselves to ashes in the high thin air. Faulty mechanisms often allowed the balloons to be spotted low in the sky or on the ground. Beginning in the autumn of 1944, over 350 of these potentially lethal weapons turned up in the western United States and Canada. But on only one occasion did a balloon bomb prove fatal to American citizens: At 10:20 on the morning of May 5, 1945, a Sunday school class of five children and the wife of an Alliance Church pastor discovered a downed balloon during a picnic outing near Klamath Falls in southcentral Oregon. When they prodded its payload, the antipersonnel bomb exploded, killing all six.

With this one tragic exception, Japanese attacks on the continental United States during World War II amounted to little more than shots from a popgun. In the fullness of time the American response would sound around the world like the crack of doom.

While the defeat of Germany was given priority in the American war effort, Roosevelt's careful grooming of the U.S. Navy and Marine Corps throughout his presidency meant that the United States would make a quick recovery from its losses at Pearl Harbor and begin to advance on the Japanese homeland. From the earliest months of the war, the submarines of the U.S. Pacific Fleet took a heavy toll on the Japanese ships that were striving to keep their far-flung empire supplied. In the middle of 1942, the United States scored a signal victory at the Battle of Midway, where Admiral Yamamoto lost his four best carriers. The Japanese navy had never tasted defeat in modern times, but from now on it would slowly empty the cup, until even the giant battleship *Yamato*, heart and soul of the fleet, went down—lost close to Japan in April 1945. Not even the kamikazes, deadly as they were, could retrieve the empire's cause.

When the 25,000-man Japanese garrison on the strategic island of Saipan was annihilated by determined American invaders during the summer of 1944, pressure mounted on General Tojo to resign. He resisted fiercely. "As long as the gods' rays shine upon me," he screamed at one of his subordinates, "Japan rests upon my shoulders!"[24] He tried to deflect criticism by offering to fire his chief ministers, but on July 18, Tojo and his entire cabinet were forced to submit their resignations on orders from the emperor. His place was taken by another militarist, Gen. Kuniaki Koiso.

Tojo's departure left a gaping hole in the Japanese hierarchy, for at various times he had served as his own secretary of foreign affairs, education, munitions, and commerce—as well as chief of staff of the Japanese army and minister for war. Now time lay heavy on his hands. "If only I could write a poem or something," he wailed to his wife. "I ought to have taken more of an interest in those things."[25] On May 25, 1945, U.S. firebombs provided an unwelcome break in his monotonous existence when they fell around his home in Tokyo's Setagaya suburb, burning down the cottage that he kept as a study and destroying part of his personal papers.

He was anything but alone in his misery. In November 1944, Boeing B-29 long-range bombers had begun to hit Japan from the Mariana Islands, some thirteen hundred miles south of Tokyo. At first, the army air force had tried to destroy only military targets with precision bombing, but they soon had to admit failure; the Japanese were dispersing their war production so quickly that trying to neutralize it piece by piece had become a hopeless task. So from February 1945, Gen. Curtis LeMay directed an air offensive against the home islands that aimed to burn the country into submission.

LeMay's B-29s had turned most of Japan's cities into ash heaps by the middle of 1945. Tokyo lost 16 square miles and 89,000 of its inhabitants during one of the earlier firestorms on March 9. In June 1945, Japan's official news agency announced that "Tokyo, Yokohama, Nagoya, Kobe, and Osaka have ceased to exist."[26] There was little exaggeration in this report, but still the Japanese endured, still the war went on, with a terribly bloody invasion of Japan planned for the autumn of 1945. The Supreme Council for the Direction of the War decreed that every Japanese man, woman, and child be mobilized to defend the homeland. As they awaited the final conflict, the Japanese people were instructed to "laugh and treat the present [air] attacks as a joke."[27]

The battle for the island of Okinawa from April to June 1945 demonstrated how catastrophic the remaining months of the war might be. By the time U.S. forces ended all resistance, they had sustained almost 50,000 casualties, while the Japanese suffered 117,000, including Okinawan civilians. There had to be another way, and a handful of men at the highest levels of the U.S. government knew what it was. For even as its Pacific offensive island-hopped toward Japan, the United States was in the process of acquiring the world's first atomic bomb.

It was fear of German, not Japanese, technological capabilities that had caused the international community of atomic scientists to coalesce under American guidance—and with American financing—in the intensive Allied effort known as the Manhattan Project. Their initial success came in the early hours of July 16, 1945, when the world's first nuclear device was secretly exploded in an uninhabited section of the New Mexican desert known as the Jornada del Muerto (Journey of Death).

Apocalyptic pronouncements were common in the aftermath of the test. Dr. George Kistiakowsky, who headed the team that developed the high-explosive lenses in the bomb's core, predicted that "at the end of the world, in the last millisecond of earth's existence, man will see what we have just seen."[28] After reading the classified report on the overwhelming event in the desert, Winston Churchill rumbled that "this atomic bomb is the second coming in wrath."[29]

Although the device was developed too late to knock out Germany, it could still be used to shorten the Pacific war. The means of delivery would be a B-29 named *Enola Gay* whose pilot, Col. Paul Tibbets, was chosen for the mission because of his exemplary combat record in North Africa and Europe. Taking off from the Pacific island of Tinian at 2:45 A.M. on August 6, 1945, Tibbets and his eleven-man crew headed for Japan at 200 mph, gradually climbing to an altitude of over thirty thousand feet. The weapon in their bomb bay, nicknamed "Little Boy," weighed five tons. Never before in history had statistics been so deadly.

As the B-29 approached Hiroshima, its bombadier, Maj. Thomas Ferebee, could make out the city's peninsulas and the six tributaries of the Ota River. At 8:15 A.M., as the cross hairs of his bombsite covered his aiming point, the Aioi Bridge, the *Enola Gay's* bomb-bay doors swung open and Little Boy began its plunge toward earth. Ferebee could see it drop away: "It wobbled a little until it picked up speed, and then it went right on down."[30] At an altitude of 1,890 feet, the bomb detonated with an unearthly flash.

The crew member with the best view of the explosion was the tail gunner, Staff Sgt. Bob Caron, whose description over the plane's intercom system was captured on magnetic tape. As *Enola Gay* flew on a circular course around Hiroshima, Caron talked about the column of smoke that was rising from the center of the city: "It has a fiery red core. A bubbling mass, purple-gray in color, with that red core. It's all turbulent. Fires are springing up everywhere, like flames shooting out of a huge bed of coals." He tried to count the fires: "One, two, three, four, five, six . . . fourteen, fifteen . . . it's impossible. There are too many to count. Here it comes, the mushroom shape. . . ."[31]

For the people of Hiroshima, the change had been most sudden. The flash of detonation was so searing that it burned flesh at a distance of two miles. At ground zero, human beings were not merely incinerated, they were vaporized. Farther out, bodies were strewn everywhere; for an instant, as many of them expired, the earth heaved and convulsed. Darkness fell like thunder as the air became a chaos of fiery dust.

Dr. Michihiko Hachiya, the director of the Hiroshima Communications Hospital, was at home when the bomb exploded. "I remember vividly," he would write, "how a stone lantern in the garden became brilliantly lit and I debated whether this light was caused by a magnesium fire or sparks from a passing trolley."[32] Luckily, his house was far enough from ground zero to allow his survival. But his clothing was blown off—and his flesh cut and torn and blistered by the blast. With his bloodied wife, Yaeko, staggering along at his side, he managed to traverse the fiery streets and reach the building next to his hospital, where members of his staff forced him onto a stretcher.

As he lay there in misery he suddenly realized that the flames were closing in. "Fire! Fire!" he shouted. "The hospital is on fire!"[33] Dr. Hachiya and the rest of the patients were moved into open grounds nearby. There the situation was little better:

The sky filled with black smoke and glowing sparks. . . . Updrafts became so violent that sheets of zinc roofing were hurled aloft and released, humming and twirling, in erratic flight. Pieces of flaming wood soared and fell like fiery swallows. . . . It was all I could do to keep from being burned alive.[34]

Father John A. Siemes, a Jesuit professor living on the outskirts of Hiroshima when the bomb fell, reported that "none of us in those days heard a single outburst against the Americans on the part of the Japanese, nor was there any evidence of a vengeful spirit." According to Father Siemes, "The Japanese suffered this terrible blow as part of the fortunes of war—something to be borne without complaint."[35]

Not all of the bomb victims were so restrained. On August 11, as Dr. Hachiya lay in his hospital bed mulling over the dreadful news from Nagasaki, he heard a rumor that the Japanese had attacked the west coast of the United States with new long-range bombers. A man from a town on the outskirts of Hiroshima was spreading the story that Japan also possessed the atomic bomb and had used it to destroy San Francisco, Los Angeles, and San Diego. Dr. Hachiya described the reactions of his fellow patients: "The whole atmosphere in the ward changed, and for the first time since Hiroshima was bombed, everyone became cheerful and bright. Those who had been hurt the most were the happiest."[36] Victory, it seemed to these woebegone people, was finally in sight.

What actually came about was defeat: defeat for Japan and anxiety for all the world. In Hiroshima and Nagasaki, the anxiety had descended in its most extreme form. "Aside from physical injury and damage," as the Manhattan Project's investigators determined,

> the most significant effect of the atomic bombs was the sheer terror which [they] struck into the peoples of the bombed cities. . . . [A]fter the atomic bombings the appearance of a single plane caused more terror and disruption of normal life than the appearance of many hundreds of planes had ever been able to cause before.[37]

And that is what the atomic bomb has remained: the ultimate in terror weapons.

At least 78,000 people died at Hiroshima. At Nagasaki, where a second bomb fell among hills that sheltered much of the city from the effects of the blast, another 25,000 perished. The motives behind President Harry Truman's decision to use the new weapon on Japan have been endlessly debated, but the central question will always be painfully clear: Was such vast destruction really necessary? Those who answer "no" have a credible case to make. They say that Japan was in such dire straits by the summer of 1945 that its surrender was inevitable and probably imminent. The other side is just as convinced that, without the bomb, only an invasion of the home islands would have ended Japanese resistance, and that such an invasion would have produced up to a million American—and untold Japanese—casualties.

Where one stands in this debate depends on more than one's estimation of the morality or immorality of Truman's decision to use the bomb. It is also a function of how threatened one feels by the nuclear arms race. At any rate, the atomic bomb held no terrors for Hideki Tojo. When he learned of the destruction at Hiroshima and Nagasaki, he waxed philosophical: "Our ancestors must have lived in caves at one time. So can we." Believing that radioactive contamination was harmful only when it seeped into water, Tojo decided that "if we don't take baths for seven months we aren't going to die, and if we can stand it that long, we will win."[38]

If the bomb only aroused Tojo's defiance, the arrival of U.S. occupation forces in Japan made him despair. In September 1945, when U.S. military police appeared at his home with an arrest warrant, Tojo tried to kill himself with a .32-caliber pistol. An eyewitness recorded that a stream of red spurted from his chest "like water coming out under pressure from a hole in a burst pipe."[39] There was no doubt in Tojo's mind that he was a dead man, but he remained conscious and indulged in a rambling soliloquy, promising that he would "become a god to protect our land after my death."[40]

More to the point, he apologized for taking so long to die. One war correspondent in attendance, jaded at the end of a long war, kept the death watch with rude impatience. Dragging on his cigarette, he grimaced and said, "I hope this fish dies in time for me to make my deadline."[41] Tojo struggled to breathe his last, but both he and the correspondent were disappointed. Missing his heart, the bullet had punctured a lung, creating a "sucking wound" that was serious but not fatal. A U.S. Army doctor arrived, sewed up the entry and exit points, and gave Tojo a transfusion of American blood plasma, as well as a shot of morphine. Then he was rushed to an army hospital in Yokohama, where more plasma awaited him.

A few months later, at the International Military Tribunal for the Far East, a fully recovered Tojo agreed to legal assistance from American lawyers on one condition: that his defense not attempt to implicate Hirohito. The fallen warlord drew a firm line: "I want nothing said or presented that will bring the emperor into this; I know they are going to hang me."[42] When he entered the witness stand on December 26, 1947, Tojo indulged in a gesture of contempt for Allied authority; he pulled out a handkerchief and loudly blew his nose. Joseph B. Keenan, the chief prosecutor at the trials, met contempt with contempt. "Accused Tojo," he began, "I shall not address you as general because . . . there is no longer any Japanese army."[43]

Keenan went on to insinuate that a long affidavit submitted by Tojo to the court was "a continuation of imperialistic, militaristic propaganda."[44] Tojo answered back, swearing that he and his nation were innocent. He claimed that all of Japan's military actions were undertaken in self-defense, and denounced as "an utter absurdity"[45] any suggestion that Japan had engaged in aggression between 1931 and 1945. By Tojo's reckoning, he was *responsible* for the conduct of the war but *guilty* of only one thing, which was not listed in the indictment: He was guilty of failing the emperor by leading Japan to defeat. Disagreeing, the court convicted him on seven counts out of nine, including conspiracy to wage aggressive war and cruelty to prisoners of war. He was among 720 Japanese officers and civilians sentenced to die for their crimes.

As his time ran out Tojo got religion—and found in himself the touch of the poet that he had sought in vain after his dismissal from high office. "Looking up, I hear reverently the voice of Buddha calling me from the limitless sky."[46] So went a verse that he composed when he realized that the war crimes tribunal was going to require his life. The Allies hanged him on December 23, 1948—just short of his sixty-fourth birthday. Few, if any, protests were heard from the Japanese people.

Nor had they shed many tears when Tojo attempted suicide, for their obsession was Hirohito and the future of the Imperial system. There had been reason for anxiety, since the Truman administration had left the question of the emperor's fate ambiguous. It was not the wisest of policies, for the Japanese might have given up weeks earlier if they had been assured that Hirohito could retain his throne. The emperor himself finally ordered Japan to surrender without a guarantee that he would be treated leniently; after Hiroshima and Nagasaki, his one desire was to get the killing stopped.

When he met Hirohito for the first time, Gen. Douglas MacArthur, the new military governor of occupied Japan, detected a real nobility in his erstwhile enemy: "He was an emperor by inherent birth, but in that instance I knew that I faced the First Gentleman of Japan in his own right."[47] Hirohito had done well to impress MacArthur, for the general's influence proved decisive in saving him from standing trial for war crimes. Basically a pragmatist, MacArthur had no desire to deal with the millions of angry Japanese who would have protested such a legal process. And as it happened, Hirohito turned out to be the best ally the triumphant Allies could have gained. Without his cooperation, the hard feelings caused by the war might have created immense difficulties for the occupation authorities and embittered Japanese-American relations for generations.

Since time immemorial the Japanese people had believed the emperor to be the divine son of heaven, directly descended from the sun goddess Amaterasu. Adhering to tradition, Hirohito had never spoken in public, not until his recorded voice was broadcast on August 15, 1945, telling his people that the war was lost. What did they think of their emperor then? Dr. Hachiya probably represented the majority opinion when he wrote that Hirohito "had been victimized by the military clique who, in defeat, were prepared to thrust the entire responsibility on his shoulders. Insidiously, and by degrees, the military group, professing allegiance to the Emperor, had come to dominate the entire nation."[48] Loyalty to Hirohito was all that was left to Japanese like Hachiya: "I prayed the Emperor would be spared and not taken away on a battleship. That *would* be the end!"[49]

Hirohito remained on his throne but his divinity departed. He renounced it himself, telling his people in a radio broadcast on January 1, 1946, that his ties with them "do not depend upon mere legends and myths. They are not predicated upon the false concept that the Emperor is divine and that the Japanese people are superior to other races, and fated to rule the world."[50] Now Hirohito would demonstrate his common humanity. For the first time in his reign, which had already lasted almost twenty years, he "came down from the clouds" and took to going out among his people.

Mimicking the crowned heads of Europe, he visited schools and factories and chrysanthemum exhibits, and cut ribbons when new highways were opened. He seemed ill at ease on such occasions, as he listened to polite explanations and repeated over and over, "Ah so, ah so." Some of his less reverent subjects began to call him "Ah-so-san." Things had gone too far for His Majesty when a sooty miner in northern Japan tried to shake his hand. "Let's do it the Japanese way," Hirohito quietly commanded. "You bow to me, and I'll bow to you."[51] The incident touched off a furious national debate: Should the miner be considered a hero of the new era, or whipped within an inch of his life for insulting the emperor?

In the end, the miner was merely forgotten. The memory of Hideki Tojo has not fared much better.

10

Joseph Stalin's American Dream

In America's experience of her enemies, Joseph Stalin occupies a unique position. No other foreign leader has ever evoked such contradictory reactions from the government and people of the United States. None other has been treated so coolly, and then embraced so warmly, and then rejected so totally.

The initial coolness came to an end soon after Franklin Roosevelt became president. Rather than wait for the Soviet system to adopt a less hostile view of the capitalist world, Roosevelt in 1933, his first year in the White House, extended diplomatic recognition to Stalin. The step was not taken without unusual provisos, which included a Soviet pledge to refrain from injuring "the tranquillity, prosperity, order, or security of any part of the United States," and to shun any conspiracy "which has as its aim the overthrow or the preparation for the overthrow . . . of the United States."[1] Though such language shows that Roosevelt was well aware of the Communist agenda, he hoped that a new approach to Stalin would create major opportunities for American business and help revive the depressed U.S. economy.

Unfortunately, he was disappointed. In the matter of trade, the Soviet-American relationship failed to take off because its historical baggage was so weighty. Stalin feared Japanese aggression in the Far East and wanted guaranteed loans to purchase U.S. arms and industrial exports, but the first American ambassador to the USSR, William Bullitt, insisted on a precondition: that the United States be reimbursed for Russian debts incurred during World War I—before the Communists took over. Owing to Soviet Russia's shortage of hard currency, Stalin was loath to settle the accounts of the czar and Alexander

Kerensky, and his refusal ended the possibility that warm relations would develop between Washington and Moscow during the 1930s.

Three years after exchanging ambassadors with the United States, Stalin would institute the Great Terror, quickening the pace of the terrible purges that eventually took the lives of between 20 and 30 million Soviet people. Although he was able to disguise most of the evil that he was visiting on his own country, there was no way for Stalin to hide the deal that he made with Hitler in August 1939, or the Red Army's invasion of eastern Poland twenty-six days later, or his winter war against Finland in the months just beyond. The USSR was expelled from the League of Nations for its Finnish adventure, but the West could not afford to read Russia out of the international community. As bad as Stalin's record had become, his potential for mischief at the beginning of World War II could barely compete with the actual aggressions of Adolf Hitler.

In the spring of 1941, both Franklin Roosevelt and Winston Churchill tried to warn Stalin that Germany was preparing to hurl its armies against the Soviet Union. In the grossest miscalculation of his entire career, Stalin supposed that Washington and London intended to distract and confuse him, and finally to entangle him in a war with the Nazis. So he continued to play to Berlin. Alexander Solzhenitsyn has suggested that Stalin "had trusted one person, one only, in a life filled with mistrust. . . . That man was Adolf Hitler."[2]

His tremendous lapse nearly cost Stalin everything. It also boded ill for the fate of the West. Had Russia succumbed to Hitler's first offensives, it could have forced the United States and Great Britain to recognize a Nazi empire that stretched from the Pyrenees to the Urals.

Stalin's paranoia never allowed him to believe that the United States, or any other nation, really wished him well. Recognizing the nature of his mindset, U.S. diplomats tried to put the Soviet dictator at his ease. Even before Pearl Harbor, the Roosevelt administration was encouraging a carefully filtered view of Stalin as a benign "Uncle Joe." When FDR's intimate adviser Harry Hopkins visited Moscow in the wake of the German attack, he described Stalin to the U.S. press as "an austere, rugged, determined figure in boots that shone like mirrors, stout baggy trousers and snug-fitting blouse. . . . He's built close to the ground, like a football coach's dream of a tackle."[3]

The moment of Hopkins's visit was pregnant with possibilities for Russian-American cooperation. Uncharacteristically, Stalin suggested that a large force of U.S. soldiers would be welcome on Soviet soil. But after the Nazi invasion bogged down he would change his tune, allowing only one base for American warplanes to be set up in southern Russia, and even that limited arrangement would soon be canceled.

Roosevelt expressed his basic approach to Stalin in the middle of the war. It was sympathetic to the point of absurdity: "I think if I give him everything I possibly can, and ask nothing from him in return, *noblesse oblige,* he won't try to annex anything and will work with me for a world of peace and democracy."[4] FDR would go to his grave still full of misapprehensions about the personality of Joseph Stalin. In the winter of 1945, just weeks before his fatal stroke, Roosevelt reminded his cabinet that Stalin had once studied for the priesthood, a stage in his life that had supposedly been a happy influence: "I think that something entered into his nature of the way in which a Christian gentleman should behave."[5]

During the Great Depression there were plenty of conservatives who considered Roosevelt's economic programs Communistic, so the president may have decided that there was little downside in cozying up to Stalin. As for the Soviet regime, Roosevelt apparently saw it as a sort of roughhewn, semi-Oriental welfare state that would, in time, come to resemble the America of his own New Deal. At any rate, Stalin claimed to be constructing a democratic society in which all citizens would truly be equal, and this chord FDR found particularly congenial. By contrast, the British Empire seemed to be ruled by aloof conservatives who were committed to protecting an imperialism that was no longer a progressive force in the world.

Stalin, who had actually preferred the fascist powers to the Western democracies, was acutely aware that he had won Roosevelt's friendship, and he played his advantage for all it was worth. Already in October 1941, the United States had granted $1 billion worth of credit to the Soviet Union. Sensitive to the dictator's every scowl, the president pressed Britain to do things that Churchill believed were counterproductive at best. These included sending convoys of supplies into northern Russia by a sea route that was vulnerable to Nazi submarines, surface ships, and dive bombers. To please Stalin, the president also pressed Churchill to make definite plans for invading France at an early date— not originally in 1944 but as early as 1942, long before Anglo-American forces were prepared for such an undertaking.

Of the forty-four countries that received U.S. supplies during World War II, only Great Britain was allotted more Lend-Lease aid than the Soviet Union. Acting unilaterally, Roosevelt sent thousands of American aircraft to the Soviet Union through bases in Alaska. He even allowed Ladd Field at Fairbanks to be operated jointly by the air forces of the U.S. and USSR. The bar at the officers' club there proudly displayed a smiling picture of Comrade Stalin, and the bartender delighted Soviet pilots with his bountiful supplies of bourbon, soft drinks, cigars, and chocolate bars.

The war matériel that went to Stalin included ammunition and rifles, trucks and tanks, jeeps and locomotives. Almost all of the field telephones used to coordinate Hitler's defeat on the eastern front were made in the United States, and 15 million Soviet soldiers pushed westward in American-made boots. The Red Army also consumed over 4 million tons of American foodstuffs. At one point in the war, the American public, which had grudgingly become accustomed to eating its toast with margarine, protested vehemently at the revelation that the Roosevelt administration had shipped 65,000 tons of butter to the USSR.

Roosevelt and Stalin came face-to-face for the first time at the Tehran conference with Churchill in November 1943. Whether or not he realized it at the time, the president set the tone for the entire summit when he accepted an invitation to stay in a guest house at the Soviet embassy compound. Throughout the proceedings, Roosevelt freely displayed his partiality for the Russian cause. On his return to the United States, he bragged about how he "began to tease Churchill over his Britishness. . . . Winston got red and scowled and the more he did so, the more Stalin smiled. . . . I kept it up until Stalin was laughing with me, and it was then I called him 'Uncle Joe.'"[6]

For his part, Churchill feared that Roosevelt's regard for Stalin presaged a major catastrophe. He saw a danger that the president's policies would eventually allow the Russians to occupy eastern Europe—and then to strike boldly westward toward Britain. Watching Roosevelt's performance at Tehran, the prime minister became deeply depressed. "I want to sleep for billions of years,"[7] is how Churchill described his mood to Lord Moran, his personal physician.

The U.S. media tended to encourage Roosevelt's courtship of Stalin, for many American journalists found it just as convenient as the president to avoid the truth about the Soviet regime. Walter Duranty of *The New York Times*, an enduring apologist for the USSR, explained that Stalin was not really a Communist but a socialist, and that socialism was actually "state capitalism." *Life* reported that the dictator smoked American cigarettes and pipe tobacco. Writing for the *American Mercury* in February 1944, Arthur Upham Pope predicted that Stalin's Russia would soon become more democratic than the United States. A year later, *Time* told the nation that Premier Stalin had "achieved the world's greatest economic revolution."[8]

Nevertheless, America's tolerance of Marxism worked on an obvious double standard: The only good Communist was a foreign Communist in the vanguard of the fight against fascism. Few politicians on the Potomac were comfortable with the fact that the American Communist party, which faithfully toed the Stalinist line, had increased its membership to an all-time high of almost 100,000 by 1939, and domestic radicals, who had gained considerable influence over popular culture during the depression, continued to be harshly treated by the federal government. All through the war years, the House Un-American Activities Committee went on investigating and stifling leftist dissent within the United States, and J. Edgar Hoover's FBI spent more time worrying about Communist influence in the Roosevelt administration than Axis penetration of U.S. borders.

There were even those who thought that American interests lay more with Germany than with the Soviet Union. Senator Robert Taft of Ohio said that "communism masquerades, often successfully, under the guise of democracy. . . . it is a false philosophy which appeals to many. Fascism is a false philosophy which appeals to very few indeed." Therefore, reasoned Taft, "the victory of communism would be far more dangerous to the United States than the victory of fascism."[9] This argument had one glaring flaw: It had been Hitler, not Stalin, who had ignited the world war and who fed its flames.

The son of poor parents who had started life as serfs, Stalin was born in December 1879. He was raised in a little house of crude brick on a cobblestone street in a village called Gori. His mountainous homeland, Georgia, while not a part of Russia proper, was one of the southwestern extensions of the czar's empire. Stalin's real name was more than a mouthful: Joseph Vissarionovich Dzhugashvili. His father, an alcoholic cobbler, seems to have been only rarely at home. His mother, Catherine, a seamstress, was a devout Orthodox Christian who, as a boy of the village observed, "loved [her son] to distraction."[10]

At maturity, Stalin stood only five feet four inches tall, and his face showed the scars of an early case of smallpox. There were other physical defects: His left foot was congenitally deformed and his left arm, its growth stunted by a childhood injury, remained stiff throughout his life. When he was nine years old, his mother enrolled him in a church school, where he carried off all the prizes. According to one of his classmates, he "not only performed the religious rites but also always reminded us of their meaning."[11] His reward, as Roosevelt knew, was to be allowed to prepare for the priesthood in the Georgian capital of Tbilisi, where the seminary was a dim, dreary place run by stern disciplinarians. Rebelling, Stalin began to study Marx in secret.

The inevitable expulsion came in May 1899. Almost immediately he began a new career as a Marxist agitator and propagandist. An uninspiring public speaker whose Russian was marred by an outlandish accent, he worked behind the scenes at organizing the oil workers in boom towns like Baku on the Caspian Sea. Despite his low profile, he got himself noticed by the czarist authorities and was forced to endure the first of his eight arrests and seven spells of Siberian exile. His crimes would eventually include the planning of bank robberies, and it seems likely that he also profited from informing on his political rivals.

Around 1903, he married a woman named Catherine Svanidze, who proved to be a modest and loyal wife. In 1907, he mourned her passing with some memorable words: "This creature softened my stony heart. She is dead and with her my last warm feelings for all human beings have died."[12] After shedding the name Dzhugashvili, he had been known as "Koba"; now he would call himself Stalin, "the man of steel."

The work of destroying czardom went on. Among the myriad of socialist parties in the Russia of his day, Stalin was most drawn to the far left, and by the time of his first meeting with Lenin in 1905, he was already known for espousing the Leninist line. For his part, Lenin found Stalin very useful during the great events of 1917. Assigning him duties as a personal assistant, Lenin also secured him a place on the editorial board of *Pravda*. His Georgian roots made him an obvious choice to become the People's Commissar of Nationalities, but he used the position like a old-fashioned Russian imperialist. When his homeland tried to establish its independence from the new Soviet regime, he went back to Tbilisi and ordered the Leninists there to "break the wings of this Georgia!"[13]

Other tasks awaited Stalin's powers of persuasion. He served as a member of Lenin's Politburo and as a political adviser to the Red Army during the civil war, which is when he first emerged as a rival to Leon Trotsky, whom he would ultimately drive into exile and have murdered. In 1922, Stalin assumed his most important post, the general secretaryship of the Communist party. Slowly but surely, he packed the Party bureaucracy with his own henchmen, and even before the death of Lenin in 1924, he had formed a faction that was well positioned to frustrate his ideological foes.

Above all, he advanced his fortunes by keeping his own counsel. As one of his secretaries noted, Stalin "possessed in a high degree the gift for silence, and in this respect he was unique in a country where everybody talks far too much."[14] It finally began to dawn on Lenin that Stalin had to be stopped: "This cook's dishes," he determined, "will be too peppery."[15] In January 1923, Lenin had described Stalin in a postscript to his political testament as "too rude" for the high offices that he occupied. Stalin's power, as Lenin put it, should pass to a comrade who would prove to be "more tolerant, more loyal, kinder, less capricious."[16]

It was advice that would never be acted upon. By the time the contents of the testament became widely known, Stalin's position was already unassailable, and the voice of Lenin, sounding from beyond the grave, could no longer threaten him. Comrade Stalin claimed to be Lenin's devoted pupil and heir, the only man worthy of his legacy—and no one was in a position to contradict him. He hid the fact that he had insulted Lenin's wife, Nadezhda Krupskaya, drawing a rebuke from Lenin himself that asked "whether you are agreeable to retracting your words and apologizing or whether you prefer the severance of relations between us."[17] Stalin apparently offered an apology. But after Lenin's death, when Krupskaya tried to curb his abuses, Stalin apparently told her to keep quiet or he'd get someone else to play Lenin's widow.

Forsaking the pursuit of world revolution, which had held such attractions for Lenin and Trotsky, Stalin announced that his goal would be "socialism in one country." No one's fool, he recognized that his autocratic plans for restructuring Soviet society would arouse intense opposition, and he aimed to brutalize his opponents into submission. He took the offensive by conducting campaigns against literally millions of his own people, who were accused, almost at random, of espionage and sabotage and terrorism. Stalin had developed a taste for political murder early on: "To choose one's victims, to prepare one's plans minutely, to slake an implacable vengeance, and then to go to bed—there is nothing sweeter in the world."[18] Now he would kill to his heart's content, devastating the peasants for their resistance to the collectivization of agriculture (which resulted in widespread famine), the intellectuals for independent thinking, the veteran bolsheviks for understanding that he had betrayed the revolution, and the Red Army for its old associations with Leon Trotsky.

Stalin's Russia was full of informers and rotten with secret police; no one could trust anyone else. Much like Hitler, Stalin infected his entire empire with the paranoia that was central to his own psyche. The final justification for all of his programs, including his notorious five-year plans, was his repeated assertion that time was running out for the Soviet experiment. Either the people would accept Stalin's leadership and work together to develop enough heavy industries to support a modern military machine, or foreign powers would invade Russia again, reducing the Marxist experiment to ashes.

Solzhenitsyn has vividly portrayed how the "Father of the Peoples" terrified his subordinates: "[O]ne mistake in his presence could be that one mistake in life which set off an explosion. . . . [H]e did not listen to excuses, made no accusations; his yellow tiger eyes simply brightened balefully, his lower lids closed up a bit—and there, inside him, sentence had been passed." Thinking himself safe, the victim "left in peace, was arrested at night, and shot by morning."[19]

A product of Stalin's second marriage, Svetlana Alliluyeva, captured the essence of the Russian people's danger: "It was as though my father were at the center of a black circle and anyone who ventured inside vanished or perished or was destroyed in one way or another."[20] Fearing assassination, he kept his public appearances to a minimum, yet he became the absolute master of one-sixth of the world's landmass, and of the 180 million people of 170 nationalities who inhabited it. In fact, Stalin in Russia exercised power across a much wider spectrum than Hitler in Germany. And the larger his figure loomed over the ramshackle Soviet empire, the more terrifying became the excesses of his regime.

According to Svetlana, in 1953, Stalin died

> a difficult and terrible death. . . . His face altered and became dark. His lips turned black and the features grew unrecognizable. The last hours were nothing but a slow strangulation. . . . He literally choked to death as we watched. At what seemed like the very last moment he suddenly opened his eyes and cast a glance over everyone in the room.

Then Stalin performed his last act: "He suddenly lifted his left hand as though he were pointing to something above and bringing down a curse on us all."[21]

The curse had been brought down well before Stalin's death. An American journalist named Eugene Lyons observed that Stalin's policies acted on the USSR with all the benevolence of molten lava. Lyons's voice was heard in the West, but so were the voices of many others who had a very different story to tell. With the capitalist world sunk in depression, it seemed natural to suppose that Marx's day had come, and that Stalin's Russia was the place where the grass grew greener. Soviet propaganda inspired naive trust when it claimed that Russia was advancing in nine-league boots toward the socialist paradise. In fact, the Soviet Union in the 1930s was a place of famine and despair, of repression and enslavement. As bad as capitalist reality could be after the Great Crash of 1929, it held no horrors to compare with the nightmare regime of Joseph Stalin.

Having never been ruled by an enlightened or popular regime, most Russians mistook Stalin for a great man. Even their dismal standard of living failed to deter the Soviet people from adulating him. Thanks to *Pravda* and scores of other official propaganda organs, he remained an illustrious figure for those who had learned to keep their mouths shut and survive within his system. And more than an illustrious figure, for he was presented as a sort of god in human dress, all-wise and all-just and yet very human into the bargain. An official biography of 1940 stated that "everyone knows his modesty, his simpleness, his delicacy toward people, and his lack of mercy vis-à-vis the enemies of the people."[22]

As his personality cult expanded, it seemed that half of the cities in the Soviet Union would end up bearing his name. There were sixty-two Stalinskis, seven Stalinos, and two Stalinsks, as well as at least one each of the following: Stalinabad, Stalinissi, Staliniri, Stalin-Aul, Stalinogorsk, and Stalingrad. During World War II (known in Russia as "the Great Patriotic War"), Stalin would serve as head of the Soviet government and the Red Army as well as master of the Communist party; with victory over Hitler would come his decision to promote himself from field marshal to generalissimo of the Soviet Union. As Russia moved into the postwar era, worship of Stalin grew until Lenin was almost a forgotten man.

The record of Soviet suffering in World War II is painful to scan. It included the deaths of at least 20 million people—about equivalent to the population of Canada in 1965. Over seventeen hundred towns had been destroyed, as well as some seventy thousand villages. Twenty-five million Russians were left without adequate housing. In a country that relied heavily on trains for transportation, more than forty thousand miles of railroad tracks had to be replaced. The figures were staggering, the country on its knees. It might have been completely prostrate without the $10 billion in supplies that the United States had sent during the course of the war.

There was rejoicing at Torgau in Germany on April 25, 1945, when victorious units of the U.S. Army and the Red Army advanced to join forces in the heart of Europe, but the future lay hidden in a thick and threatening cloud. Although the war had been won, the peace could easily be lost. President Roosevelt had died on April 12, and with him perished moderation's chief voice. Ever the optimist, FDR had hoped for the best, expecting "Four Policemen"— the United States, the Soviet Union, Britain, and China—to control the new United Nations organization and reorder the postwar world. There could be no doubt that Roosevelt meant the U.S. and the USSR to become the major pillars of international stability, but even before the fall of the Third Reich, a new scramble for dominance had begun. The postwar ground rules were clear to Stalin and, he thought, should have been clear to all: The future of each European country would depend upon the Allied power or powers most responsible for its liberation. Countries occupied by the Red Army would adopt socialism. The Russian dictator would obviously *not* fulfill his promise, made to Roosevelt and Churchill at Yalta, to hold free elections throughout eastern Europe.

While Harry Truman was a relative novice in foreign affairs, he soon understood the role that Stalin would play in the postwar world. "Victory," he determined, "had turned a difficult ally in war into an even more troublesome peacetime partner."[23] President Truman felt that the United States was at a disadvantage against the Soviet dictator's unscrupulousness and mastery of intrigue, and he hoped to be propped up by the power of the atom bomb. Sole possession of the weapon, coupled with the belief that the Stalinists would be unable to explode their first atomic device for a decade or more, suggested to Truman that, if necessary, the United States could create a new world order without Soviet cooperation.

The president was in Germany at the Potsdam summit meeting with Stalin and Churchill when word of the first successful A-bomb test reached him in July 1945. Upon reading the initial reports, Truman felt "tremendously pepped up" and experienced "an entirely new feeling of confidence,"[24] as Secretary of War Henry Stimson put it. After Truman was assured that the bomb would be ready for use against Japan within days, he "was a changed man," according to the observation of Churchill. "He told the Russians just where they got on and off and," Churchill wrote, "generally bossed the whole meeting."[25] The day of *pax atomica* had begun.

The shift in Truman's outlook would prove to be lasting, with enduring consequences for Soviet-American relations. It immediately revolutionized the way in which the United States looked at its military alliance with the USSR, especially in regard to the end of World War II in the Far East. In February 1945 at the Yalta Conference, Stalin had promised to engage Japanese forces in Manchuria and north China. At the time, his commitment had been welcomed by Roosevelt as a means of speeding the defeat of Japan and greatly reducing the number of American casualties in the Pacific. Before the successful A-bomb test, Truman had also been eager for Stalin to attack the Japanese from his bases in eastern Siberia. Now, with the bomb in the arsenal, it seemed likely that the United States could compel Japan to make an early peace without help from Russia.

As he anticipated the first atomic bombardment of Japan, Truman feared that Stalin would use his Yalta promise to strike a weakened enemy at small cost and lay claim to a share in the postwar occupation of the Japanese home islands. In any event, the Red Army invaded Japanese-occupied Manchuria six days before Hirohito called on his people to lay down their arms. But owing to U.S. pressure, this extension of Russian power was temporary. After stripping the region of its industrial plant, the Soviets withdrew from Manchuria during the next spring and never did set foot on the Japanese home islands.

Another early test of President Truman's resolve would come in Iran, which in 1941 had been saved from falling into the German sphere by the coordinated arrival of both Soviet and British troops. The terms of the joint occupation had been well defined. There had been a clear understanding that all foreign forces would leave the country early in the postwar period, and the British had departed on schedule. Not so the Soviets. "There is a very dangerous situation developing in Iran," was Truman's judgment in March 1946. "The Russians are refusing to take their troops out . . . and this may lead to war."[26] Truman's concern was only natural. The Soviet army of occupation—thirty thousand strong in the northern part of Iran—was well positioned to threaten Turkey, Iraq, and Syria as well as the young shah's government in Tehran.

Keenly aware of the need to safeguard the region's oil resources, Truman prepared to drive Stalin back. At the beginning of 1946, the president had said that he was "tired of babying the Soviets" and would henceforth treat them to "an iron fist and strong language."[27] For the nonce the president would keep the fist in reserve, but the strong language was soon forthcoming, especially when he began to publicize his displeasure with Russia's continuing presence in Iran. In this case, words and warnings sufficed: Stalin responded by removing his troops within days. The Iranian crisis took its place among the many confrontations that would punctuate Soviet-American relations in the postwar period.

From his position high up in the State Department, Dean Acheson surveyed the troubled scene in June 1946 and perceived that "all our lives the danger, the uncertainty, the need for alertness . . . will be upon us. This is new to us. It will be hard for us."[28] Acheson was right. A grim future awaited American diplomats and the American people, for Stalin would not be as easy to discourage in eastern Europe as in Manchuria and Iran.

Almost thirty years after the 1917 revolution, there was only one other Communist country in the world besides the Soviet Union. That country was Outer Mongolia. Now things would change—and radically. As Stalin maneuvered to create a belt of Communist governments in eastern Europe, he aroused intense American suspicions about the extent of his ambitions. The U.S. ambassador in Moscow, Averell Harriman, told the president that Soviet actions amounted to a "barbarian invasion of Europe."[29] There were few voices in the West that cared to contradict such a perception, which was reenforced by Winston Churchill's famous "Iron Curtain" speech at Fulton, Missouri, in the winter of 1946.

The year 1947 was decisive, its events dictating the shape of things to come. In March, the president announced what came to be called the Truman Doctrine, a solemn pledge that the United States would do everything within its power to stop Stalinist expansion, beginning, if Congress voted its assent, with $300 million in aid for Greece, which was threatened by a Marxist insurgency, and $100 million for Turkey, which shared a rugged, militarized frontier with Russia and controlled access to the Black Sea. Congress did vote in favor of the aid package, and Truman signed the program into law on May 22. In June, Secretary of State George C. Marshall told the graduating class of Harvard University that the administration had developed a plan for reconstructing the war-shattered economies of Europe, which were threatening to collapse completely; even Russia was invited to share in the large influx of American capital. Inevitably, Stalin would see the Marshall Plan as a direct challenge to his sphere of influence, and responded by tightening the Soviet screws on eastern Europe.

As 1947 went on, the non-Communist government of Hungary fell in a coup d'état that was engineered by the Kremlin, and relations between Truman and Stalin became increasingly bitter. Antidemocratic clampdowns continued in

Poland, Bulgaria, and East Germany, while Romanian Marxists forced the abdication of King Michael. The West's smiling image of Uncle Joe was gone, never to return. Daunted by this consolidation of Soviet power in eastern Europe, Secretary Marshall warned that western Europe was also in danger from Communist subversion. Far more frightening was the possibility that Stalin would follow his subjugation of eastern Europe by sending the Red Army west.

Between 1945 and 1947, the United States had reduced the numbers of its servicemen from 12 million to a mere 1.4 million. Now it began to rearm, with Congress passing a national security act that established a separate air force but unified the overall command structure of the military, combining the Department of War (that is, the army) and the Department of the Navy into the new Department of Defense; the Central Intelligence Agency (CIA) and National Security Council (NSC) were created by the same act. Soon Congress answered Truman's call to reinstitute the military draft. Such preparations were obviously meant to impress one man far more than any other: Joseph Stalin.

The results were disappointing. In February 1948, pressure from the Russian dictator reduced Czechoslovakia to a satellite, completing the Soviet conquest of eastern Europe. At about the same time, the CIA informed President Truman that it did not foresee a world war breaking out within the next sixty days; beyond that time frame, all bets were off. The nations of western Europe were even more pessimistic, expecting an invasion by the Red Army at any moment. Disaster seemed imminent in June, when West Berlin was blockaded by Soviet ground forces. The Allied response, orchestrated from the White House, was a strenuous and costly airlift that went on for almost a full year.

This effort was supplemented by a higher state of readiness in America's strategic bombing force. In July 1948, sixty U.S. Air Force B-29s, thought to be capable of devastating the Soviet Union with atomic bombs, were stationed at forward bases in England. Plans were drawn up to threaten Stalin with over three hundred nuclear weapons and twenty thousand tons of conventional explosives. There was a general fear around the world that a terrible new war was in the offing—a war that would plunge the planet into a new dark age. Circling their wagons under U.S. leadership, the western Europeans sat down with members of the Truman administration and planned a closeknit military alliance called the North Atlantic Treaty Organization (NATO), which would be formally established in 1949—the year of Stalin's seventieth birthday.

The United States considered this step to be purely defensive, but the ever-suspicious Stalin read the situation otherwise. He seemed to think that Washington was not only after his new satellites but would stop at nothing less than the eradication of communism in Russia—the formation of NATO could be for no other purpose. Soviet fears were further heightened when West Germany began to rearm and moved toward full membership in the North Atlantic alliance.

Stalin's answer would be to lay the foundations for the Warsaw Pact, which would be officially established in 1955. To his mind, eastern Europe was now a Soviet fiefdom that had to be protected from U.S. threat and interference.

The traditional invasion route into Russia—used by Napoleon as well as Hitler—lay through Poland, and Stalin believed that no one had the right to keep him from sealing it off.

In retrospect, the cold war would have set in even if the Soviet Union had been controlled by a far less paranoid personality. Russia's traditional enemies had been Japan and Germany, and thanks to its victorious campaigns in World War II, the United States now occupied the territory of both. Such a geopolitical situation all but guaranteed the rise of severe Soviet-American tensions. In addition, the recent experience of Hitler had made everyone wary of any compromise that might be interpreted as appeasement. It would be a long time before the foreign policy of either the United States or the Soviet Union would lose the impress of the events that catapulted them into World War II: Germany's surprise attack on western Russia, and Japan's surprise attack on Pearl Harbor.

There was a certain psychological advantage in the Soviet camp. As the U.S. chargé d'affaires in Moscow, George F. Kennan, put it in March 1946:

> [A] hostile international environment is the breath of life for [the] prevailing internal system in this country. Without it there would be no justification for that tremendous and crushing bureaucracy of party, policy and army which now lives off the labor and idealism of Russian people.[30]

Stalin was far more at home than Truman in an atmosphere of distrust, for he was a ruler who needed enemies in order to thrive.

If the cold war proved congenial for Stalin's domestic politics, it wrecked havoc within the borders of the world's greatest democracy. On the home front, Americans fell victim to a red scare, a scare mimicking the worst aspects of the anti-Communist hysteria that descended on the United States after World War I. The atmosphere of unrest was exploited by conservatives in Congress. They had plenty of old scores to settle with the New Deal Democrats who had directed the government for so long, and the hour of reckoning had come around at last. The air over Washington grew ever thicker with paranoia as unsettling news of Communist successes continued to flow in from abroad. In 1949 alone, the United States had to stand by and watch as Mao Zedong finished his conquest of power in China and Russia successfully tested the atomic bomb.

At the same time, the Soviet air force acquired the TU-4, a long-range bomber based on the design of the B-29 that was capable of delivering nuclear weapons to the continental United States. To many, the U.S. seemed well on the way to losing the cold war. The outlook was grim as America girded up its loins and began to rearm in earnest.

The entire situation was a nightmare come true. Americans were now facing an adversary who would soon have the ability to do what Hitler could only dream of: bring terrible devastation to the American heartland. It seemed that history, so replete with wars and slaughters, had finally caught up with the

United States. The kaiser's agents could blow up a few American factories, and the Führer's submarines could decimate U.S. shipping, but it was only now, in the dead center of the twentieth century, that the American people would experience how it felt to live in a state of continuing insecurity—a state of fear.

The power of the dreadful new reality could be seen in the fate of the nation's first secretary of defense. James V. Forrestal had come to Washington in 1940 from the Wall Street investment banking firm of Dillon, Read, where he had served as company president, and taken up the duties of assistant secretary of the navy. When his boss, Frank Knox, died of a heart attack in the spring of 1944, Forrestal was invited to step in and fill his shoes. Soon the new navy secretary was voicing his major complaint. In a letter of September 2, 1944, Forrestal wrote that

> whenever any American suggests that we act in accordance with the needs of our own security he is apt to be called a god-damned fascist or imperialist, while if Uncle Joe suggests that he needs the Baltic provinces, half of Poland . . . and access to the Mediterranean, all hands agree that he is a fine, frank, candid and generally delightful fellow.[31]

Forrestal's hatred of Stalin became obsessive, and well before fascism went down to defeat, he was staking out his claim to be the first and foremost of the cold warriors. In Forrestal's eyes, Stalin was not merely the head of a huge nation-state, he was also the chief priest of a messianic religion that was spreading across the globe like wildfire. There might be a new world order in the postwar era, but that order, warned Forrestal, would not be inspired by American ideals.

During March 1947, Forrestal summarized his worst fears in a memo to President Truman: "Of the strategic battlegrounds of the present struggle, we have already lost Poland, Yugoslavia, Romania, Bulgaria, and a number of others; Greece is in imminent peril; after Greece, France and Italy may follow; and after France and Italy, Great Britain, South America, and ourselves."[32] The course of events, Forrestal warned, was leading to another terrible war, a war whose inevitability was being disregarded in Washington and all around the world. Feeling like a voice crying in the wilderness, Forrestal did all he could to awaken the United States to its peril and prepare its armed forces for an apocalyptic clash.

Despite his overwrought analysis of the world situation, Forrestal was appointed by President Truman to head the new Department of Defense, becoming secretary on September 17, 1947. He never considered the position a plum, and a month after assuming his new duties he predicted that "this office will probably be the greatest cemetery for dead cats in history."[33] He was soon describing the job of defense secretary as "too big for any one man."[34] Sadly, it proved too big for James Forrestal. When he closed his office door at the Pentagon for the last time on March 28, 1949, he was a physical and mental wreck. The president had eased him out of the job with great tact, but Forrestal had not been provided with the medical care that he obviously needed. No sooner had he left office than he experienced a complete mental breakdown.

Depressed and suicidal and severely psychotic, he told his friends that Stalinist agents had infiltrated the White House and the defense establishment— and were on the verge of invading and conquering the United States. Forrestal, who expected to be liquidated at an early stage in the Soviet occupation of the United States, was not alone in his hysteria. President Truman would later record of this period that "many good people actually believed that we were in imminent danger of being taken over by the communists."[35] Sent to be with friends in a Florida resort, Forrestal tried, without success, to forestall his imaginary enemies by killing himself. On April 2, he was brought back to the nation's capital and committed to a psychiatric ward at Bethesda Naval Hospital, but he distressed his new attendants by saying that he would never leave the grounds alive.

He made his own prophecy come true. Early in the morning of Sunday, May 22, James Forrestal committed suicide by jumping from the hospital's sixteenth floor. Three days later his body was carried with full military honors to Arlington National Cemetery. There, in the central amphitheater, waited a crowd of 6,500 that was rich in dignitaries, including President Truman and Vice President Alben Barkley.

The president had already told the nation how he conceived of Forrestal's death: "This able and devoted public servant was as truly a casualty of the war as if he had died on the firing line."[36] *The Washington Post* was less laudatory, finding that Forrestal had exaggerated the threat to America's national existence: "In this respect he succumbed partly to military badgering for all that the traffic would bear, partly to an obsession that the Cold War was the prelude to a shooting war. This obsession became an *idée fixe* as time went on."[37]

Joseph McCarthy, a man of enormous energy and amazing stamina, was another member of America's power elite to suffer from fixed ideas about Stalinism. Born and raised on a farm in Wisconsin, McCarthy contrived to become a circuit judge in his home state at the age of thirty. While serving as a marine intelligence officer in the Pacific during World War II, he fabricated a legend that led the folks back home to think of him as a fearless combat veteran called Tail-Gunner Joe. Always ambitious and hungry for publicity, McCarthy stood for little but his own ego, and was willing to use whatever popular issue came along to advance his fortunes. He was only thirty-seven years old when elected to the U.S. Senate.

Stalin's postwar belligerency was a political godsend for McCarthy. A man who considered James Forrestal one of the great authorities on the Communist menace, McCarthy soon began to turn up the heat under his own right-wing campaign. "I am firmly convinced," he wrote in a letter to one of his constituents, "that Stalin is no more bluffing in his promise to take over the entire world than was Hitler when he proclaimed his plans of world domination in *Mein Kampf*."[38] These words, penned in the same month that Forrestal was relieved as secretary of defense, were precursors to McCarthy's wilder claims—claims that would set the country on its ear.

McCarthyism's true advent came when he delivered a Lincoln Day speech to a Republican women's club in Wheeling, West Virginia, on February 9, 1950. Near its beginning, he made an obligatory reference to the cruelty of the Russian dictator:

> The great difference between our western Christian world and the atheistic communist world . . . lies in the religion of immoralism—invented by Marx, preached feverishly by Lenin, and carried to unimaginable extremes by Stalin. This religion of immoralism, if the Red half of the world wins—and well it may—this religion of immoralism will more deeply wound and damage mankind than any conceivable economic or political system.[39]

Such remarks were the standard fare of the day, and by themselves would have attracted little attention. What made the speech notorious, and set off a prolonged crisis in the American political system, was McCarthy's claim that the U.S. State Department was "thoroughly infested with communists." McCarthy bolstered his credibility by putting a number to the alleged conspiracy: "I have in my hand 57 cases of individuals who would appear to be either card-carrying members or certainly loyal to the communist party, but who nevertheless are still helping to shape our foreign policy."[40] McCarthy's claims, which were never substantiated, made a much bigger splash than he had anticipated. Almost overnight, he found himself widely accepted as a paragon of patriotism who deserved to be at the head of freedom's crusade.

In the congressional elections of 1946, the Republicans had made an enormous amount of political capital from claims that the long reign of Franklin Roosevelt had left the federal government riddled with Communist influence. Attempting to put the issue to rest in March 1947, Truman had ordered the publication of a list of subversive organizations and established a loyalty program to tighten security within the federal bureaucracy. Such measures failed to satisfy the fervent anti-Communists who credited McCarthy's view that the United States was losing its struggle with Stalin "at a tremendous pace."[41]

When the Korean War broke out in June 1950, McCarthy was more than ever the man of the hour, a seer who had predicted that Stalin would eventually move from mere subversion to a more violent offensive against the Free World. As the fighting went on, McCarthy tended to overshadow the president, who despite his toughness was perceived by many Americans to be soft on communism. Truman's failure to bring the war to a satisfactory conclusion was crucial in keeping McCarthy's stock high across the nation. As the senator continued to blast the president's policies and accuse his administration of consciously abetting treason, Truman learned to hate McCarthy, now an obvious contender for the White House, like no one else in Washington.

In his memoirs, Truman would clumsily define McCarthyism as "unwarranted persecution by demagogues on false charges and gossip about people they dislike."[42] At the time, he was much more evocative and colorful: When McCarthy became a household name, Truman denounced him publicly as "the greatest asset the Kremlin has."[43] But McCarthy seemed immune to the president's criticism—or anyone else's. Again and again he brazened his way out of tight corners and bulled on ahead, ruining reputations left and right. Anyone who was even faintly liberal had reason to fear the political vision of Joseph McCarthy, who saw Communists everywhere. His success was a dreadful measure of how much stress the cold war had produced in the American body politic. For McCarthy was a man who could only thrive by exploiting the deep-rooted sense of insecurity caused by endless rumors of war. It is no accident that he rose to prominence a few months after the Russians acquired the atomic bomb.

McCarthy had one great failing: He never knew when to quit. Even after General Eisenhower, his own party's candidate, captured the White House in the election of 1952, McCarthy refused to tone down his rhetoric. In the forefront of those Republicans who were calling for a rollback of Soviet power in eastern Europe, McCarthy continued to play for headlines. Eisenhower, though he had endorsed a rollback during the presidential campaign, chaffed under the dangerous pressure that McCarthy's demands placed on his administration.

Finally, McCarthy took on the U.S. Army and came out second best, failing to find disloyal officers in its ranks. As they watched McCarthy perform during televised hearings before a Senate subcommittee, millions of Americans could see for themselves what the man had become: an abrasive buffoon. Acknowledging that his antics had gone to ridiculous extremes, on December 2, 1954, the Senate voted 67–22 to find McCarthy guilty of actions that were "contrary to senatorial ethics and tended to bring the Senate into dishonor and disrepute, to obstruct the constitutional processes of the Senate, and to impair its dignity; and such conduct is hereby condemned."[44]

The curse proved effective. Whenever the censured senator, who refused to resign, rose to address his colleagues, they would head for the exits. "The difference between McCarthy before censure and McCarthy after censure," observed Senator Mike Monroney, "is the difference between getting headlines on page one and being buried back with the classified ads."[45] In May 1957, Joseph McCarthy, still a senator by law if not in fact, was literally buried, destroyed at the age of forty-eight by a lethal combination of hepatitis and alcoholism.

Fortunately, U.S. foreign policy was not greatly hindered by extremists like Forrestal and McCarthy. Effectively advised by men like Dean Acheson and George Kennan, Truman had been able to avoid the extremes of appeasement on the one hand and overreaction on the other. By and large, the foreign policy consensus that he forged would serve American interests well into the 1960s. But Truman was his own best eulogist. In January 1953, during his last address to the nation from the White House, he noted that "we have averted World

War III up to now, and we may have already succeeded in establishing conditions which can keep that war from happening as far ahead as man can see."[46]

Less than two months later Stalin died, but Stalinism would live on. As late as the 1980s, Ronald Reagan spent the better part of two terms fighting the dictator's fearful ghost. And it was not until December 1990 that the last statue of Stalin in an Eastern Europe capital—it stood in Tirana, Albania—was brought crashing to the ground.

11

Chairman Mao and the Paper Tiger

For sheer numbers of people involved, Mao Zedong's revolution in China was far and away the greatest event in political history. It was also one of the least expected. Though Mao's forces had been steadily advancing on Beijing for over a year, most Americans experienced his capture of the city in 1949 as a bolt out of the blue—a bolt that meant disaster for the future of U.S. influence in the Far East. Secretary of State Dean Acheson summed up the underlying horror by describing Mao's China as a "tool of Russian imperialism."[1]

When Mao visited Moscow from December 1949 to February 1950, he was chairman of both the Chinese Communist party and the central government. With the help of his premier, Zhou Enlai, he negotiated a treaty "of friendship and alliance" with Stalin, and the Chinese socialist bureaucracy soon learned to copy most of the features of the Soviet apparatus.

A terrible strategic nightmare came true when Mao hailed Stalin as "the teacher of the world revolution, best friend of the Chinese people."[2] U.S. planners found themselves looking at a huge Eurasian landmass—the world's geopolitical heartland by most calculations—that had succumbed to totalitarianism. Since international communism appeared robust, expansionist, and monolithic, it almost seemed as if World War II had been lost, not won. Pessimists in Washington perceived Mao's victory as an irreversible setback in America's quest for world order.

But concealed behind the facade of Communist unity lay China's own nightmare: Mao's real relationship with Stalin, who treated him more like an Oriental satrap than a chief of state. Stalin had always considered Chinese Marxism to be suspect, and he had consistently supported the Nationalist cause of Chiang Kai-shek over Mao's. Early and late, Mao would ponder Stalin's arrogant initiatives, which included stripping Manchuria of its Japanese-built industries in 1945 and 1946, thereby severely impeding China's postwar recovery. Mao would eventually admit that extracting foreign aid from the Soviets possessed all the charms of "taking meat from the mouth of a tiger."[3]

Although the Chinese revolution closely mimicked its Soviet predecessor until Stalin's death, the Russians tended to see Mao as an "agrarian reformer" whose programs had little to do with Marxism-Leninism. After all, the great Lenin himself had decreed that "only the industrial proletariat can liberate the toiling masses in the countryside,"[4] a process that had manifestly *not* occurred in China, where peasant armies had made all the difference. In general, western Marxists have looked upon peasants as small-scale capitalists who happen to be operating in a rural base. When Mao made them central to the Chinese revolution, he inadvertently fathered a major Marxist heresy.

Mao answered Moscow's doubts about his orthodoxy by denying that the peasant origins of the Chinese revolution did anything to undermine its authority. What really mattered was that Mao had moved Marxism into "a higher and completely new stage."[5] When Moscow remained skeptical, Mao was not surprised. The Soviets had ignored the greatest task facing socialism: to create a new morality for the entire population—or so thought Chairman Mao.

Theoretically, the people could be made to forget their own selfish needs and serve the state with full hearts and fervent faith, making it possible to construct an earthly paradise. "I have witnessed," Mao said, "the tremendous energy of the masses. On this foundation it is possible to accomplish any task whatsoever."[6] Mao's was the most obviously "spiritual" interpretation of Marxism that had ever been floated. What were its origins—and what would be its fate in the real world?

Born in December 1893, Mao Zedong was a native of Hunan, a fertile province in central China. His mother, a gentle woman, devoutly worshiped the Buddha. His father, a strict and stingy man, worked hard to acquire three acres of rice fields—a modest domain but one that made him seem rich compared to the other farmers in the neighborhood. As Mao grew up, his father added to the family holdings until he could fairly be described as a rich peasant. He was not above hoarding grain to drive up prices. "The first capitalist I struggled against," Mao liked to say, "was my father."[7]

Books obsessed Mao throughout his life. His reading as a teenager convinced him that China cried out for reform and renewal. In 1911, at the age of seventeen, he left home against his father's wishes and went off to continue his studies at better schools beyond the rural backwater of his youth. That same year, a revolutionary movement inspired by Sun Yat-sen overthrew the Manchus, China's last imperial dynasty. Mao responded by enlisting in the new republican army; but soon, supposing that the great events had quickly run their course, he was back in civilian clothes.

At twenty he enrolled in a teacher's college, where he was described as a "tall, clumsy, dirtily dressed young man whose shoes badly needed repairing."[8] After graduation he passed beyond the borders of Hunan for the first time, journeying to Beijing, where he got a temporary position as an assistant at the university library. During a second stay in the capital, he read the *Communist Manifesto* and began to study Marxism with real enthusiasm. On the side, he wrote poetry in the classical mode.

Returning to his home province at the age of twenty-seven, he immersed himself in radical politics, making a reputation for himself as a political writer and Communist organizer, one of the earliest in all China. He supported his comrades' decision, urged upon them by Soviet advisers, to join in a united front with the Chinese Nationalists and their rising young general Chiang. But he also embarked on a program of his own by convincing thirty-two Hunan peasants to form a rural branch of the Communist party. This part of Mao's career took place against a backdrop of general disorder throughout China, a semifeudal country whose peace was disturbed by the marches and counter-marches of one predatory warlord after another. It was a state of affairs that would eventually tempt the Japanese to establish a large military presence in Manchuria and to begin their long attempt to conquer all of China.

In 1927, Chiang Kai-shek turned on the Marxists in his midst and massacred as many as he could lay hands on, including Mao's first wife, his brother, and adoptive sister, and many of his closest friends. Mao and a battered remnant of his comrades—the core of the future Red Army—sought refuge in the hills of Hunan and Jiangxi provinces. There they set up a Chinese Soviet Republic with Mao as the chairman of its provisional central government. Within a few years, the number of his fighters had grown tremendously—to around 100,000. They repeatedly blunted the attacks of the Nationalists' much larger army, but Chiang Kai-shek, who had sworn to exterminate the Communists, would never admit defeat.

Chiang closed in from all sides during the climactic campaign of 1934, forcing the Red Army to break out toward the west. This was the beginning of the epic year-long journey known as the Long March. A retreat of more than six thousand miles across eleven provinces, twenty-four rivers, and eighteen mountain ranges, the ordeal threatened to become the death march of Chinese communism. Chiang's army kept on the Red Army's heels, and his air force harried it along with bombs and machine-gun bullets. The soldiers of ten war-lords also had to be overcome. There were still other enemies that gave the Red Army little rest—like cold, hunger, and disease. Of those who set out, only one in twenty finished.

Mao's position in the Chinese Communist party had been threatened several times during the 1920s and 1930s; at one point he was even deprived of his seat on the Central Committee. But his inspiring performance during the Long

March, which he had initially opposed, enabled him to consolidate his leadership. Time and again he reminded his comrades that their suffering was about more than mere survival. It was about freeing China from the foreign invader, and the route of the march was partially determined by Mao's "very deliberate desire to put ourselves in a position where we could fight the Japanese."[9] Mao and the Red Army ended up as cave dwellers in the region of the Great Wall at Yan'an in Shaanxi Province. From there they did indeed launch an offensive against the Japanese, though for years Mao would show more interest in expanding his power base than in risking his poorly armed troops in battle.

To protect his southern flank, Mao sent Zhou Enlai to negotiate a united front with Chiang Kai-shek against Japan. Under duress, Chiang agreed to cooperate with the Communists. Yet in spite of this new agreement, 450,000 Nationalist soldiers spent most of World War II avoiding the Japanese invaders and bottling up the Red Army. It was a situation that vexed Franklin Roosevelt, who had done so much to help the Nationalists.

Roosevelt tried repeatedly to get Chiang and Mao to work together against Tojo. Toward this end, in the middle of 1944, a transport plane landed a mission of U.S. diplomats and military men at Mao's headquarters in Yan'an. Mao welcomed them and made arrangements to host a formal U.S. Army Observer Group. Hoping to receive vast shipments of U.S. arms, Mao agreed to join the Nationalists in an anti-Japanese coalition that would include, at the very least, one U.S. paratroop division. He even approved of an American plan that would put Chiang's chief of staff, the U.S. Army general Joseph Stilwell, in command of the coalition forces.

Always wary of Mao's intentions, Chiang bridled at the very thought of cooperating with his old enemy. The Nationalist armies had become a tragic laughingstock as the Japanese drove deeper and deeper into China, but Chiang was still able to block the American initiative, thereby insuring that Communist influence in his wartime government would be kept to an absolute minimum.

As U.S. forces in the Pacific island-hopped toward their victory over Japan, Mao and Chiang maneuvered toward a decisive postwar conflict. The tilt decreed by Washington was distinctly toward the Nationalists, as shown by General MacArthur's order that only Chiang's government would be authorized to accept the surrender of Japanese troops in China proper. U.S. ships and transport planes entered the country and were used to ferry Nationalist soldiers into strategic areas of northern and eastern China, where they could frustrate Mao's plans to enlarge the Red Army's sphere of influence.

Wherever he did manage to exert his power, Mao was winning the sympathies of the peasants by dispossessing their landlords and giving the fields to the people who actually tilled the soil. Chiang, who hated Western-style democracy just as much as communism, seemed to stand for little beyond his own authority. During a moment of unusual candor, Chiang had admitted in 1930 that "it is impossible to find a single Kuomintang [Nationalist] headquarters which really administers to the welfare of the people: all are stigmatized for corruption, bribery, scrambling for power."[10] During the war years, Chiang's administration, by all accounts, had only gotten worse. Mao had taken his opponent's measure and was sure that communism would triumph. Chiang "is merely a corpse," Mao observed with scorn at the end of World War II, "and no one believes him anymore."[11]

In a bid for a more evenhanded U.S. policy, Mao and Zhou Enlai had proposed in January 1945 that they travel to Washington and meet with President Roosevelt. No response to their request was ever received, but American aid to Chiang Kai-shek, who professed to being a sincere Christian of the Methodist strain, kept pouring in.

After inheriting the White House, President Truman hoped to resolve the China crisis by assigning Gen. George C. Marshall to act as a mediator. Marshall spent all of 1946 in the country trying to effect a compromise that would satisfy both parties, but all his efforts were in vain. As Mao lost faith in Marshall's mission, his anti-American tendencies, which were always reinforced by Marxist ideology, came to the fore. In 1947 he bitterly suggested that "the American toiling masses have had enough of capitalist oppression. . . . When the next depression comes, they'll march on Washington and overthrow the Wall Street government."[12]

With the civil war heating up, Mao evacuated Yan'an, the sacred city of Chinese communism, in March 1947—a strategic retreat that bred overconfidence in Chiang. Yet Mao's own confidence was unshaken, and by the end of the year he had ordered the Red Army to take the offensive. The $3 billion in U.S. military and economic aid that Chiang had received after the defeat of Japan could not save the Nationalists, whom even Truman described as a gang of "grafters and crooks."[13] While Chiang's bureaucrats were busy robbing the till, the Red Army, now styled the People's Liberation Army (PLA), was crushing Nationalist power and marching on Beijing. When Mao's troops entered the capital they were well supplied with tanks and trucks, artillery and ambulances—the great bulk of which had been made in the U.S.A. and captured from Chiang's faltering legions.

Before the arrival of his fifty-sixth birthday, Mao had installed himself and his ambitious third wife, Jiang Qing, in a Ming dynasty villa within the old Imperial City at Beijing. On October 1, 1949, standing on the Gate of Heavenly Peace, overlooking a delirious crowd, he consummated thirty years of struggle by proclaiming the foundation of the People's Republic of China. The man whom Chiang Kai-shek had so often dismissed as a mere bandit was now the ruler of 4 million square miles and 550 million souls—a quarter of the world's population.

The Soviet Union recognized the People's Republic at once. It would be fully thirty years before the United States followed suit.

Three million Chinese had perished in the struggle between Mao and Chiang, but there was plenty more misery to come. At six in the morning on June 25,

1950, all hell broke loose on the Korean peninsula. Divided since the end of World War II into a northern zone protected by Stalin and a southern zone where U.S. influence prevailed, Korea consisted of two mutually antagonistic halves that had been threatening to explode from month to month. When the North Koreans under their Marxist premier, Kim Il Sung, attacked across the 38th parallel, they did so with an overwhelming force that included 90,000 men and 150 Soviet-made tanks. Within three days they had captured Seoul and sent the lightly equipped South Koreans, who had literally been caught sleeping, into a headlong retreat toward the southern coast.

The cold war was in full play by the summer of 1950. Since tensions were at a high level across the globe, it was natural for Truman to suspect that Stalin had ordered his North Korean proxy to attack the south as a diversion for a major Soviet offensive in Europe or the Middle East. The possibility existed that the South Koreans would have to be sacrificed while the United States defended more important resources. But when Stalin made no overt moves elsewhere, Truman became determined to win back the ground lost on the Korean peninsula.

South Korea was not a democracy by any stretch of the imagination. Truman was determined to save the country in order to demonstrate that he was ready to meet any Communist challenge anywhere on earth. As he put it in his memoirs, "[W]e considered the Korean situation vital as a symbol of the strength and determination of the West."[14] Domestically, the president was loathe to face Republican charges that another piece of the globe had been snatched away by the Marxists, especially in an election year. China had gone in 1949; South Korea would *not* be the next domino to fall. And the salvation of Seoul would tend to protect Japan from aggression.

To insure victory, Truman called scores of National Guard and reserve units to active duty. Local draft boards were also kept busy as the armed forces nearly tripled in size during the first year of the war. A cornucopia of new federal spending buoyed the prospects of defense contractors.

Since the Korean peninsula was a terra incognita for the vast majority of Americans, they expressed some confusion over Truman's call to arms. Even the U.S. forces serving with General MacArthur's Army of Occupation in Japan were bewildered by the unexpected developments. Lacy Barnett, a corporal in a medical company, remembered that "when word reached us in Japan on that rainy Sunday, the first reaction by many members of my unit was, 'Where is Korea?'"[15]

Of course, Gen. Douglas MacArthur had a thorough knowledge of the area's geography, but he had trouble imagining how the Truman administration would respond to the Communist attack. "What is United States policy in Asia?"[16] was the first question that came to his mind when he heard the bad news from Korea. Still, as supreme commander for the Allied powers in the Far East, MacArthur was the man whom Truman ordered to save the day. In tones redolent of melodrama and flirting with self-pity, the general later wrote that "once again I was being thrust into the breach against almost insuperable odds."[17]

It is certainly true that MacArthur was starting from behind. Initially, all the ground forces that he possessed to counter North Korea's seven divisions were four undermanned and unready divisions of the U.S. Army. Softened by occupation duty in postwar Japan, the American troops were transported across the Korea Strait and hustled into the front lines—to be badly bloodied by the North Koreans. As the summer of 1950 came to an end, it seemed that MacArthur might be forced to abandon the peninsula altogether. "The Cassandras of the world," as the general would later record, "gloomily speculated on a vast Asiatic Dunkirk."[18]

Instead of a disastrous withdrawal there was a masterful counteroffensive. MacArthur's amphibious landing on September 15 at Inchon, well behind Communist lines, led to the rapid disintegration of the North Korean army. The 1st Marine Division, which took Inchon, went on to liberate Seoul just over three months later, and the entire area below the 38th parallel was cleared of enemy troops shortly thereafter. At that point the Truman administration might well have been content to return to the status quo; instead, it decided to adopt the Communist goal of unifying Korea by force. On October 7, 1950, U.S. troops crossed the 38th parallel; by October 19, they had occupied the North Korean capital of Pyongyang. Two weeks before, the People's Republic of China had warned that it would intervene in Korea if the United States pursued such a course.

Chairman Mao now had to try reading MacArthur's mind. Was the U.S. Army's northward thrust a prelude to a more ambitious project? Mao could by no means discount the possibility that the Americans would continue north, crossing the Yalu River into China proper in an attempt to overthrow his new regime in Beijing. He approved contingency plans that envisioned a huge U.S. thrust, preparing his armies, as Zhou Enlai put it, "to retreat from the coastal provinces to the interior and to make the northwest and southwest the bases for planning a long war."[19] Even more important, he developed tactics for hitting MacArthur before he could advance into China.

While Mao marshaled his forces for a protracted conflict, MacArthur's troops were congratulating themselves on winning big in short order. By late October, "everyone," according to Corp. Lacy Barnett, "including our commanders, thought the war was over."[20] Everyone—and that especially included Douglas MacArthur—was wrong. The war started up all over again as Mao's "volunteers" crossed the Yalu and descended in force on the Americans.

Its bugles blaring, the PLA engaged U.S. troops for the first time at the beginning of November. By the middle of the month almost a third of a million Chinese troops were inside North Korea. Mao's commanders had managed to move a huge mass of men into Korea from Manchuria without being detected by U.S. reconnaissance aircraft. MacArthur, using the grandiose rhetoric that the world had come to expect from him, condemned the Chinese success as one of history's "most offensive acts of international lawlessness."[21] In Washington, both houses of Congress passed a resolution in January 1951 that condemned the Chinese as aggressors; on February 1, the U.N. General Assembly agreed.

These exercises in diplomacy made little difference to the soldiers in the field. Priv. Victor Fox of the 5th Cavalry Regiment would describe the situation at the front as the PLA began to spring its trap: "We felt the presence of the Chinese all around. We heard stories about hordes of them appearing suddenly on all sides, decimating units, then breaking contact and mysteriously fading away into the wilderness."[22] But it was not for classical guerrilla fighting that the PLA made its name during the Korean War. What history remembers are the "human-wave" tactics. Terribly profligate with the lives of their men, Mao's commanders would sacrifice hundreds of Chinese soldiers to take minor objectives. As a frigid Korean winter set in, the Chinese losses mounted but their advance continued. The Americans and their Allies had air cover and tanks and artillery; the Chinese had the numbers, and they used them to win mile after mile of Korean terrain.

On November 30, 1950, a rattled Truman told the press that his administration was giving serious consideration to the use of the atomic bomb. Heedless of their peril, the Chinese pushed the Allies back across the 38th parallel and then evicted them from Seoul and Inchon in early January. The disarray on the battlefield created disarray in the U.S. high command. In a rage that events had escaped his control, MacArthur made endless demands on the administration. He wanted "ground reinforcements of the greatest magnitude";[23] he wanted the Chinese staging areas in Manchuria to be devastated by U.S. air power; he wanted the bridges over the Yalu bombed; he wanted the entire Chinese coast to be blockaded.

MacArthur not only developed plans that risked igniting World War III, he also revealed their broad outlines—and his complaints about the administration—to the press. Finally, Truman tired of MacArthur's insubordination and, on April 11, 1951, fired him. Americans were incredulous at the news, and an amazing hubbub reverberated from coast to coast. U.S. flags were flown at halfmast or upside down.

Public opinion execrated Truman and celebrated MacArthur, who would soon be home to address Congress and ride through avalanches of ticker tape. Some of the general's admirers demanded Truman's impeachment, while Joseph McCarthy called MacArthur's dismissal "perhaps the greatest victory the Communists have ever won."[24] As usual, the president assailed his critics in plain English and followed his own game plan. Yet the critics had soured Truman on the presidency, and as the war became increasingly unpopular with the American people, he would decide against seeking another term in 1952.

At least the United States was not alone in Korea, for under the auspices of the United Nations, fifteen other nations sent combat troops to fight in the war. Compared to the 5,720,000 Americans who served in the Korean theater, the other U.N. forces were tiny, totaling only 40,000. Still, they participated in key battles and helped assure the American public that world opinion was on the right side.

Before the fighting ended, the Allies retook Seoul and Mao lost his eldest son, Anying, dead at the age of twenty-nine in a U.S. bombing raid on a Chinese army headquarters in the hills of Korea. Anying's death was symbolic of the high price Mao paid for joining in the war. Myriads of Chinese soldiers were killed in Korea, including the 100,000 who were lost in a reckless five-day offensive during May 1951. America's ability to decimate the PLA reinforced Mao's sense of technological inferiority and left him with a legacy of bitterness against the United States. It also put severe strains on the Chinese economy. Mao himself admitted that "what we spent on the war to resist U.S. aggression and aid Korea [in 1951] more or less equaled our expenditures for national construction."[25] The war helped inspire Mao to launch a fierce campaign of domestic "thought reform" and social regimentation, and to strike out against "counterrevolutionaries," which resulted in the deaths by execution of a million or more Chinese, many of them former supporters of Chiang Kai-shek.

Thirty-three thousand Americans were killed in combat or died in Communist captivity before negotiations brought the Korean War to an end in July 1953—six months after Dwight Eisenhower had taken the oath of office. The new president responded soberly to this achievement, noting that "we had won an armistice on a single battleground, not peace in the world."[26] Eisenhower's words were borne out at the Geneva Conference on Korea and Vietnam in 1954. There, his secretary of state, John Foster Dulles, refused to countenance a direct meeting with Mao's representative, Zhou Enlai; he would speak to Zhou "only if our cars collide in the street."[27] When the two diplomats suddenly came face-to-face before a formal session, Zhou extended his hand to Dulles, who muttered "I cannot" and strided rapidly away—or so runs a story that has gone down in history. By the end of the year, Zhou was calling the United States "the most arrogant aggressor ever known"[28]—a measure of just how threatened the People's Republic felt by the Eisenhower administration.

During the Korean War, essentially every inhabitant on the Chinese mainland had been subjected to a virulent propaganda campaign that presented the United States as an insanely cruel country. Meetings were held in every village and neighborhood to denounce Truman and MacArthur and everything they stood for. The substance of these meetings was echoed in an official Chinese publication that characterized the United States as a

> paradise of gangsters, swindlers, rascals, special agents, fascist germs, speculators, debauchers and all the dregs of mankind. . . . Everyone who does not want the people of [China] contaminated by these criminal phenomena is charged with the responsibility of arising to condemn [America], curse her, hate her and despise her.[29]

Chairman Mao's own pronouncements on the United States were delivered in more measured tones, but they did nothing to relieve international tensions. In 1957 he taught that the Chinese emperor, the Russian czar, Adolf Hitler, and the Japanese imperialists "were all paper tigers. As we know, they were all overthrown." Mao's words proceeded to a predictable conclusion: "U.S. imperialism . . . also will be overthrown. It, too, is a paper tiger."[30]

After Chiang Kai-shek lost the mainland in 1949, his consolation prize had been the presidency of the Republic of China on Formosa (Taiwan), where he ruthlessly imposed his rule on the large island's indigenous people. Truman had not been impressed. In January 1950, before relations between Beijing and Washington had hardened into real hostility, the president told the world that "the United States government will not provide military aid or advice to Chinese forces in Formosa."[31]

Coming out of the White House, such words could easily be read as an invitation for Mao to take Taiwan. By that summer, after war had broken out in the Korean peninsula, the president saw matters in a different light. At that point he announced that "the occupation of Formosa by Communist forces would be a direct threat to the security of the Pacific area";[32] so Chiang was back on the list of American arms recipients. The Nationalist regime had won its reprieve, yet it would keep Taiwan under martial law for nearly forty years.

MacArthur had proposed two roles for Chiang's soldiers during the war in Korea: On the one hand he wanted them to join with U.N. troops in fighting the Chinese on Korean soil, on the other he urged that Chiang be allowed to send an expeditionary force to begin the liberation of the mainland. During the 1952 presidential campaign, General Eisenhower seconded MacArthur's suggestion for a Nationalist invasion of China proper. It was more rhetoric than a real possibility, but immediately after becoming president Eisenhower did allow Chiang to launch hit-and-run raids across the Taiwan Strait. The president contributed to Mao's paranoia whenever possible, believing through a tortuous logic that Chinese fears would cause them to ask for excessive amounts of Soviet aid, thereby straining relations between the Communist giants.

A prolonged dispute over a handful of islands off the Chinese mainland caused severe tension between the People's Republic and the United States throughout the 1950s. In January 1955, after months of preliminary skirmishing, an actual shooting war broke out when the Maoists invaded Yijiang Island, where they defeated a thousand Nationalist troops and their eight American advisers. Chiang Kai-shek retaliated, with the advice and consent of Eisenhower, by bombing some of Mao's cities.

It now seemed possible that the PLA would launch an amphibious assault with the aim of subduing Taiwan itself—a goal that Mao had originally hoped to achieve in 1950, but which the Korean War had delayed. Remembering how MacArthur had been taken off guard by the Chinese attack in Korea, Eisenhower was determined to brook no repetition. Positioned in the Taiwan Strait, the U.S. Seventh Fleet entered a state of high alert, but the president doubted that it had the power to deter Maoist aggression. He ordered the Joint Chiefs of Staff to prepare detailed plans for a nuclear attack on the Chinese mainland by B-36 bombers of the U.S. Air Force, which would launch their missions from the American base on the island of Guam. During a press conference on March 16, 1955, Eisenhower, who, like Truman, had threatened to use A-bombs to end the Korean War, alarmed the nation and the world when he stated that nuclear weapons should "be used just exactly as you would use a bullet or anything else."[33]

The Eisenhower administration had been preaching the doctrine of "massive retaliation" for months. Now the president was steeling himself to put that doctrine into practice. It seemed an extreme reaction, and it was. Behind it lay the curious conviction that the loss of any more little coastal islands would lead to the triumph of communism throughout Asia. In the event, Mao and his colleagues failed to force Eisenhower's hand. Since China had no weapons of mass destruction, and since the Soviet Union refused to counter Washington's nuclear threats by offering to use its own atomic arsenal against the United States in China's behalf, Mao had no alternative but to climb down.

Another crisis over the offshore islands occurred in 1958, but this time Eisenhower refrained from making direct nuclear threats. Instead, he sent a huge armada of six aircraft carriers and forty destroyers to Chinese waters. Much to the relief of a worried international community, the situation simmered down. Nevertheless, Mao continued to take a hard line, voicing support for a world revolution that would destroy U.S. power at a time when Nikita Khrushchev and his Russian colleagues had decided that the existence of nuclear weapons meant that capitalism and communism would have to coexist peacefully or perish in the same hellish holocaust.

The Sino-Soviet split was well developed by the time that Eisenhower left office. In January 1962, President John F. Kennedy possessed hard evidence that, as a State Department research paper put it, "monolithic unity and control no longer exist in the communist camp. . . . There is no single line of command, no prime source of authority, no common program of action, no ideological uniformity."[34] Not long before, the large corps of Russian technicians who had been vital to Chinese industrial development was ordered home. By January 1963, the CIA was reporting that "the USSR and China are now two separate powers whose interests conflict on almost every major issue."[35]

John Kennedy's relief over the breakup of the Sino-Soviet bloc was tempered by his concern over China's nuclear weapons program. Desperate to keep the People's Republic a nonnuclear power, he was tempted to seek Khrushchev's approval for a joint U.S.-USSR bombing mission against Mao's nuclear facilities in northwestern China—facilities for which Soviet know-how had laid the foundations during the 1950s. But the proposal never went forward to Moscow, which is just as well, since it would have been dismissed out of hand by Khrushchev.

Mao did cultivate a cavalier attitude toward the possibility of nuclear war. If atomic fire killed half of humanity, "the other half would remain," as Mao blithely supposed, "while imperialism would be razed to the ground. . . . [T]he victorious people would very swiftly create on the ruins of imperialism a civilization thousands of times higher than the capitalist system."[36] Mao's frightening assertions about China's willingness to sacrifice millions of lives in a nuclear exchange resounded throughout the 1960s, making the Soviet leaders just as uncomfortable as America's power elite. Still, Mao was far from insane. His threats, and the Chinese nuclear program in general, were meant, as he quietly admitted, to "boost our courage and scare others."[37] They were also meant to "oppose the U.S. imperialist policy of nuclear blackmail."[38]

Chinese scientists exploded Mao's first nuclear device in October 1964. Watchers on the Potomac, who were able to study detailed photographs of China's nuclear facilities from the cameras of U-2 spy planes, took little consolation from Beijing's solemn pledge that it would "never at any time or under any circumstances be the first to use nuclear weapons."[39] Two years later, they had to fret over the implications of the test flight in Xinjiang Province of a Chinese East Wind 2 missile, which successfully carried a Hiroshima-size nuclear warhead five hundred miles downrange, where it detonated squarely on target.

In June 1967 the Chinese dropped their first H-bomb from a Hong 6 bomber, a feat that was greeted throughout China with fireworks and gongs and drums and frenzied cries of "Long Live Chairman Mao!" The source of this glee is easy to understand. The Chinese had been colonized, intimidated, and put upon by the West for decades. Now, at long last, they had the technology to hold their own in the world. To enhance their country's growing capabilities, Chinese scientists worked to perfect a series of nuclear-tipped missiles that would reach, progressively, American military bases in Japan, the Philippines, Guam, Hawaii, and the continental United States. In 1969, targets in Soviet Russia were added to Mao's nuclear hit list. In April 1970, China launched its first satellite, which played the Maoist anthem ("The east is red . . . Chairman Mao loves the people") as it circled the planet.

If Mao added to anxieties abroad, he also created chaos at home, for his belief in perpetual revolution meant that his harried people would never be left in peace. They were treated to a succession of centrally controlled campaigns that sought to obliterate all vestiges of Chinese feudalism and capitalism. The price that was paid for this pursuit of ideological purity was the crippling of the national economy and the coming of famine.

The Great Leap Forward was a disastrous failure that caused perhaps 25 million Chinese to starve to death in the late 1950s and early 1960s. "Revolution," Mao had warned, "is not a dinner party. . . ."[40] Indeed it was not—especially after his government herded China's peasants into huge, inefficient communes that were soon beset by record floods in some parts of the country and record droughts in others. In the cities, the regime's hasty industrialization programs failed almost as dismally as their rural counterparts.

When Mao died in 1976 at the age of eighty-two, the *New York Times* reported that China had "achieved enormous economic progress"[41] during his rule. The record suggests that most of the progress was made in spite of the Chinese Communist party. Mao himself admitted that "I don't understand industrial planning. So don't write about my wise leadership, since I had not even taken charge of these matters."[42] It was nevertheless apparent that Mao had been the direct inspiration for the Great Leap Forward and had traced out its broad outlines.

For his errors and ill fortune he was forced to pay a price. Capitalist practices that he had hoped to bury forever were revived, and in 1959, Mao lost his job as chairman of the People's Republic to the moderate Liu Shaoqi. However, he remained in his post as chairman of the Chinese Communist party. Though that would remain his only official post for the rest of his life, he was still very much the ruler of China in 1964, when Lyndon Johnson escalated the war in Vietnam.

President Johnson's course of action in Southeast Asia was guided, first and last, by his dread of Chinese expansionism. For his part, Mao feared that the United States would use its bases in Vietnam as launching pads for an offensive against China. As more and more American troops poured into the region, the Chinese grew less and less comfortable. And the U.S. military presence in Asia was hardly limited to Vietnam. American installations traced out an arc that ran through Pakistan, Thailand, the Philippines, Taiwan, Korea, and Japan—and China's coastal waters could be tightly blockaded by the peerless U.S. Navy in the event of a crisis. If the United States were ever to make common cause with the Soviets, Mao's neck would be caught in a very uncomfortable noose.

Johnson remained largely impervious to China's strategic dilemma. He had trouble seeing Vietnamese communism as much more than a stalking-horse for the hordes of the mad chairman in Beijing. For their part, the members of the president's cabinet were given to speculating on when the PLA would move south and, as in Korea, begin to grapple directly with U.S. forces in Vietnam.

It is a matter of record that Mao sent forty thousand Chinese to help advance Ho Chi Minh's war against the United States, but they were technicians and workers, not combat troops. Johnson would soon possess reliable intelligence about this fact, and in the spring of 1966, his anxieties were further alleviated when he received word from Mao that the Chinese would not directly intervene in the Vietnam War if U.S. ground forces stayed out of North Vietnam. The president apparently signaled his agreement. At any rate, he stopped telling the world that the real inspiration for the Vietnamese revolution lay in Beijing.

Later in 1966, Mao launched the Great Proletarian Cultural Revolution with huge, electrifying rallies like those staged at Nuremberg by the Nazis before World War II. The Cultural Revolution soon got out of hand and threatened to reduce China to civil war. Mao was seeking to purge his own party's gargantuan bureaucracy and purify Chinese Marxism, but the overwhelming result of his great push was to turn the People's Republic into an ideological madhouse.

Identified as the grand high muckamuck of the reactionaries, Mao's old rival Liu Shaoqi was ejected from power and harried into an early grave. Major monuments of China's cultural heritage were vandalized. "Bourgeois" and foreign influences were anathema; one pianist had his fingers broken for daring to perform Chopin. Mao's cult of personality came into play with a vengeance. Printing presses churned out 740 million copies of *Quotations from Chairman Mao Tse-tung*, a.k.a. the "little red book." His portrait was enshrined throughout the vast nation, and individual Chinese began and ended their day by bowing to his image and reciting his thoughts. Mao, who was both the Lenin and the Stalin of the Chinese Revolution, became a living god; the most sacred vows to serve the people were made in his name.

When Mao presented a gift of mangoes to Quinghua University in 1968, all China became maniacal about the tropical fruit. Plastic mangoes were carried aloft through the streets of Chinese cities, where enraptured masses hailed them as objects worthy of religious veneration. With mangoes or without, Mao was presented as a universal figure: "the great truth, the light of dawn, the savior of mankind and the hope of the world . . . the reddest, reddest sun in the hearts of the people."[43] But it was often difficult to prove to the rampaging Red Guards that Mao's light shone in one's own heart. For the average Chinese, political survival came down to knowing when to shout which slogan—and woe to the comrade who was cursing the Soviet Union when he should have been condemning the United States.

After months of confusion, it gradually emerged that the chief external target of the Cultural Revolution was in fact the USSR, which in Mao's view had betrayed communism and become imperialist in its own right. Since he had grown even more disaffected with the Soviets than with the leaders of the West, toward the end of his long life Mao conducted a policy of reconciliation with the United States. It was not a matter of his mellowing with age; though growing feeble in body, Mao was anything but mellow in spirit. When he heard that antiwar protests had reached new levels of intensity on the home front after the U.S. invasion of Cambodia in the spring of 1970, he crowed that "Nixon's fascist atrocities have kindled the revolutionary mass movement in the United States."[44] Mao continued to be a proponent of world revolution, but he also perceived that the U.S. debacle in Indochina would probably prevent a return of American military forces to the mainland of Asia during the twentieth century. Accordingly, his worries about the United States had largely evaporated.

The Soviets were a very different story. As the inheritors of czarist imperialism, they were sitting on millions of square miles of territory that Mao, reviving territorial claims from the Manchu dynasty, believed to be China's own. In the lexicon of Maoist propaganda, the Marxist rulers of Russia had become the "new czars." During the late 1960s, as Soviet and Chinese troops engaged in large-scale clashes along their six-thousand-mile-long common border, it looked as though a very bloody and excruciating war between the two Communist giants might be sparked off at any time. Both parties hoped to win the sympathy of the Americans.

In the United States, the Vietnam stalemate created pressures that favored an opening to the Chinese, for the Soviet Union, which had gained in might and status during this period of American eclipse, was threatening to undo the international balance of power. Therefore, President Richard Nixon and his national security adviser, Henry Kissinger, politely knocked on China's door. As for Mao, he would be content to host the lords of capitalism. The year was 1972. It was time for Nixon to visit Beijing.

12

Bearding Fidel in His Den

It is difficult to convey the horror that Fidel Castro's revolution inspired in the American establishment during the 1960s. Castro was seen as a terrible harbinger. If a Communist leader could stand up and defy the United States in an underdeveloped nation only ninety miles from Florida, the entire resource-rich Third World might find the appeal of Marxism decisive. And in truth, Cuba was well positioned to threaten U.S. interests. Possessed of a potentially contagious ideology, it also occupied one of the most strategic pieces of real estate in the Western Hemisphere. A tropical island that reaches over seven hundred miles from tip to tip, it might have been hand-placed to control the sea approaches to the southern United States.

Presidents as early as Thomas Jefferson had expected the federal government to absorb Cuba sooner or later, and the United States made several futile attempts to purchase it from Spain in the middle of the nineteenth century. Had the Confederacy defeated the Union, Jefferson Davis would have moved to add Cuba, "the pearl of the Antilles," to his southern domain. U.S. capital flowed into Cuba after the Civil War, and by the mid-1880s the dollar investment there totaled over 50 million. This economic clout was reinforced by military action in 1898, when major battles between the forces of Spain and the United States were fought on Cuban soil and in the waters around the island.

The U.S. victory in the Spanish-American War was theoretically meant to make President William McKinley the guarantor of Cuban independence, but Cuba had to struggle to gain more than semicolonial status. Its new role would be formalized in the Platt Amendment (1903), by which the United States reserved the right to intervene in Cuba's internal affairs whenever it determined that disorder was threatening. Showing the spirit of a large and overpowering brother, Washington also proposed to supervise Havana's foreign policy. Cuban resentment over these provisions mounted with the years; even after Franklin Roosevelt renounced the Platt Amendment in 1934, many Cubans still felt put upon by Yankee imperialism.

Others learned to profit from the colossus of the north. Fidel Castro's father was pleased to do business with the United Fruit Company, the Boston-based corporation that began operating in Cuba before the turn of the century. The senior Castro was a native of Spain who (as one tradition claims) had first come to Cuba as a soldier in the Spanish-American War. Turning himself into a wealthy landowner, he developed a certain immunity to public criticism. The climax of his life seems to have arrived when he forsook his legal wife in favor of a young housemaid named Lina Ruz.

Born out of wedlock on August 13, 1926 (the year 1927 is also given), Fidel Alejandro Castro Ruz would struggle hard to achieve a sense of legitimacy during his headstrong, tempestuous youth. Though radicalized as a law student in the mid-1940s at the University of Havana, the young Castro seems to have been more interested in power for its own sake than in any cause. He became accustomed to violence by fighting in the gangland-style wars that raged on the Havana campus. During an interlude from his more dangerous activities, he married an Americanized young woman, Mirta Díaz-Balart, whose family had made good by working for the ubiquitous capitalists of United Fruit. The Díaz-Balarts also enjoyed profitable links to the once and future Cuban dictator, Fulgencio Batista.

Fidel and Mirta agreed that their honeymoon should include a trip to New York. While there he thought about staying on and enrolling as a student at Columbia University. Instead, he returned with Mirta to Havana, where he prepared to take his place on the national political scene by finishing his doctor of laws degree in 1950. The year before, Fidel and Mirta became the parents of a son they called Fidelito, but the marriage floundered, ultimately ending in divorce. Castro's lust for life made it impossible for him to settle for anything resembling a conventional existence.

He would soon abandon his legal and political career in favor of direct action. On July 26, 1953, Castro led over a hundred of his followers in a dawn raid on the Cuban army's second-largest installation, the Moncada barracks at Santiago de Cuba. "We did not expect to defeat the Batista tyranny . . .," Castro said later. "But we did think that this handful of men could seize the first arms to begin arming the people."[1] Although Castro's attack was carefully planned, it was clumsily executed. His vanguard was cut down by the garrison's firepower, and some of those taken prisoner were tortured to death. Castro himself was captured and indicted by the Batista government. Acting as his own lawyer during the trial that followed, he created a propaganda sensation that roughly matched Hitler's performance thirty years earlier as a defendant in Munich. While the Cuban newspapers drew excellent copy from the proceedings, the court listened to Castro with a cynical ear—and imposed a sentence of fifteen years.

Castro's imprisonment would last only one year and seven months—until May 1955—but it was a bitter experience. Much of his time behind bars was spent in solitary confinement. "I only have company," he complained, "when some dead prisoner, who may have been mysteriously hanged or strangely assassinated . . . is laid out in the small mortuary facing my cell."[2] Amnestied as a result of the public pressure that his sympathizers applied to Batista, Castro took himself off to Mexico City, where he organized a group of revolutionaries that would soon include an Argentine doctor named Ernesto ("Che") Guevara.

By early December 1956, Castro and his comrades were back in Cuba. Eighty-one men strong, they landed in Oriente Province from a thirty-eight-foot yacht called, undramatically, the *Granma*. After struggling to terra firma through muddy shoalwater and a mangrove swamp, they were nearly wiped out on their fourth day by Batista's Rural Guard. Castro and a handful of survivors escaped with their lives and little else to the green heights of the Sierra Maestra. There they revived their endangered cause by winning the sympathies of the local peasants, who were among the poorest in Cuba. These people provided Castro with the initial support that he so desperately needed—and their kind eventually became the chief beneficiaries of his revolution.

Even at this early stage he aspired to be an international figure, and his Robin Hood image was something that he knew how to manipulate for a much wider audience. Having enticed Herbert Matthews of *The New York Times* into the Sierra, Castro used him to send a misleading message abroad: "We have no animosity toward the United States and the American people. Above all, we are fighting for a democratic Cuba and an end to the dictatorship."[3] To prove that he was a regular guy, Castro liked to impress American visitors to his mountain fastness with his knowledge of major league baseball.

Some journalists would join Matthews in characterizing the Cuban upstart as a romantic idealist with laudable aims, but in general the American press remained skeptical of what Castro could do for his own people—and fearful of what he might mean for U.S. interests in the Caribbean. Philip Bonsal, the new ambassador that President Eisenhower would send to Cuba in 1959, was not alone in worrying about "disquieting elements in Castro's past."[4]

If Castro actually felt a residue, however slight, of warmth toward the United States when he arrived in the Sierra, it was soon lost in his armed struggle against Cuba's old order. His feelings are easy to understand, for his men were attacked by military aircraft that the Eisenhower administration not only supplied to Batista but even loaded with ammunition and bombs and rockets at Guantánamo, the U.S. naval base at the foot of the Sierra Maestra. Castro vowed to avenge himself on the United States for such deadly opposition. "When this war is over," he wrote in a letter to his mistress and helpmate, Celia Sánchez, "a much wider and bigger war will commence for me: the war that I am going to wage against [the Americans]. . . . [T]his is my true destiny."[5]

In response to Castro's successes, Batista intensified his use of torture, imprisonment, and executions, but the added brutality only quickened the erosion of his authority. Soon his regime would crumble altogether. In one of the most unlikely campaigns in military history, three hundred of Castro's *barbudos* (bearded men) descended from the Sierra Maestra in the autumn of 1958 and began their final offensive against Batista's army of forty thousand. By the end of the year, the forces of the government were retreating everywhere, and on January 1, 1959, Batista fled to the Dominican Republic. He left with a grudge against the United States that would almost rival Castro's, for Eisenhower had refused to provide Batista with an American refuge. As the president put it, the United States would not serve "as a haven for displaced dictators who have robbed their countries."[6] Unfortunately, it was a bit late in the day to wax indignant over the governing practices of Fulgencio Batista.

Rather than making a beeline for the seat of power in Havana, Castro indulged himself in a leisurely triumphal progress along the roads from his headquarters in Oriente Province to the capital. Everywhere he was fêted as Cuba's savior, and by the time he got to Havana, the crowds were delirious with hero worship. The revolution was consummated when Castro addressed a huge gathering at Camp Columbia in northwestern Havana. At the end of his speech, a white dove swooped down and landed on Castro's shoulder. The ecstatic onlookers felt they had witnessed a visitation. This tall young man who had come down out of the mountains, was he not a political sorcerer, a magical soldier of hope and destiny? Was he not godlike? Would he not lead Cuba toward a glorious future?

Early on, Castro increased his domestic popularity, and alienated American public opinion, by summarily executing a number of Batista's henchmen. He interpreted U.S. protests over the work of his firing squads as evidence that the Eisenhower administration was worried about his plans for American investments. Certainly there was reason for Washington to be concerned. Under Batista, U.S. companies owned 90 percent of Cuba's mines, 80 percent of its power grid, and 40 percent of its canefields. The Pentagon could have preserved these assets by crushing Castro's revolution in a fortnight, but only at the expense of the U.S.'s international reputation.

One other calculation was at least as basic: the high cost in American dead and wounded that war in Cuba would create. Behind Castro stood thousands of Cubans who were not only chanting *"Patria o muerte!"* ("Fatherland or death!") but, if push came to shove, would be willing to lay down their lives for the new regime. Cuba's leader appreciated this fact better than anyone else. He had not been in power for a month when he rashly predicted that "200,000 gringos will die if the United States sends marines to Cuba."[7] By provoking U.S. hostility and then using that hostility to tighten his hold on the Cuban people, he instituted his own brand of dictatorship and frustrated American desires at every turn.

Seeing the Yankee hand at work throughout Latin America, Castro vowed to inaugurate a new era of Hispanic pride. "The shame of every Latin head of state," he pronounced, "is that he goes to Washington, begs and sells out."[8] Apparently there was no shame in going to Moscow—and great virtue in having Moscow come to him. On February 4, 1960, the first of many Soviet luminaries visited the Caribbean. Anastas Mikoyan, the USSR's vice premier, found in

Castro a man who was ready to swap his sugar for Soviet oil, and the first deals were done in short order. This Russian economic penetration of the New World came as a profound shock to the United States. For the most part, Cuba's richer citizens perceived which way the wind was blowing and abandoned their native island in droves.

Month after month, Castro solidified his Soviet connection and played the role of David to the North American Goliath with increasing panache. In Eisenhower's reading of events, "Castro begins to look like a madman."[9] U.S. officials did have grounds for complaint. In November 1959, Che Guevara assumed the presidency of Cuba's national bank at Castro's behest and began to nationalize what would eventually amount to $3 billion worth of American property. During the second annual May Day celebrations in 1960, Castro encouraged a huge crowd of his people to chant themselves into a frenzy with the words, "Cuba sí, Yanqui no!" Well aware that he was tempting the fates, Castro petitioned the Soviet Union to help him defend his regime against the inevitable reaction from the north.

As first secretary of the Soviet Communist party and chairman of the Council of Ministers of the USSR, Nikita Khrushchev observed that the United States "feared, as much as we [Russians] hoped, that a socialist Cuba might become a magnet that would attract other Latin American countries to socialism."[10] Still, the Soviets had to proceed with tremendous caution. Not only would supporting Cuba be expensive, it would also be hazardous. So far from Russia and so close to the United States, the island was not the sort of place that the Soviet general staff would have chosen to defend. But letting a leader like Fidel Castro be overwhelmed by a U.S.-inspired counterrevolution would dampen the spirits of Communists everywhere—and put Moscow on the receiving end of a withering barrage of criticism from Mao in Beijing.

In September 1960, Castro journeyed to New York to address the United Nations. History remembers what he did better than what he said: He led his rugged entourage into Harlem and showed his solidarity with American blacks by checking in at the Hotel Theresa on 125th Street and Seventh Avenue. In short order another foreign visitor, one who was also in town to speak before the General Assembly, would come to Harlem to meet his new comrade-in-arms. It was the rotund Russian himself, blissfully exchanging bear hugs with his Cuban admirer while a volley of flash bulbs popped. Later that same day, Khrushchev and Castro staged a repeat performance on the floor of the General Assembly, and within hours their shining visages would stare at startled Americans from the front pages of newspapers across the nation.

Eisenhower was not amused. Already in July he had made it unlawful for American companies to import Cuban sugar. That autumn he upped the ante by clamping strict controls on almost all U.S. trade with Cuba. Two weeks before leaving office in January 1961, he severed diplomatic relations with Havana.

As Castro understood perfectly well, the unfulfilled aim of the outgoing administration had been his speedy overthrow. On Eisenhower's orders, the

CIA had launched a secret war against the *Fidelistas*. Miami became the agency's base for its operations against Cuba, with so many personnel flowing in that they helped fuel a boom in the local economy—a boom also fed by the huge dollar amounts that had come out of Cuba with the new anti-Castro exiles.

In homage to the origins of its wealth, Miami became the great American bastion of anticommunism. In the city's Little Havana district, the initials CIA were said to stand for Cuban Invasion Authority. Beyond Miami's city limits was an arc of noisy training schools where young Spanish-speaking exiles passed their days practicing marksmanship and learning demolition techniques; alumni went on to Central American destinations for their advanced studies. On another secret front, the CIA's Technical Services Division prepared to poison Castro with thallium salts, which would cause his beard to fall out and, presumably, his charisma to evaporate.

Vice president under Eisenhower and the Republican nominee in the presidential election of 1960, Richard Nixon had to watch while John Kennedy made political hay out of the developing nightmare on the island that was only "eight jet minutes from the coast of Florida."[11] During a campaign appearance in Cincinnati on October 6, Kennedy solemnly accentuated the negative: "For the present, Cuba is gone. Our policies of neglect and indifference have let it slip behind the Iron Curtain—and for the present no magic formula will bring it back."[12] But Cuba was hardly Candidate Nixon's only vulnerability. The closing year of Eisenhower's second term had been a disaster on several fronts. It had seen the downing of the U-2 spy plane over Russia and the subsequent collapse of the Paris summit between the Western leaders and Khrushchev. The Soviets were still ahead in the space race. Plus, the U.S. economy would be in a recession on election day.

Nixon desperately needed a grand finale for the Eisenhower administration, so he pressed for going ahead with a U.S.-assisted invasion of Cuba to overthrow Castro and, possibly, insure his victory over Kennedy in November. But as the election approached, no October surprise was in the offing. Exasperated, Nixon asked an assistant why the CIA was so tardy in bringing Castro to bay: "Are they falling dead over there? What in the world are they doing that takes months?"[13] Part of what they were doing was worrying about Eisenhower's reaction to their plans, since the president had issued a warning that the United States "could lose all of South America" if it failed to "conduct itself in precisely the right way vis-à-vis Cuba."[14]

The presidential race was a squeaker, and Nixon might well have won if Castro had been ousted before Americans went to the polls. Always paranoid in defeat, Nixon was loathe to criticize Eisenhower, preferring to blame the "liberals" in the CIA who had supposedly dragged their feet on Cuba to help put Jack Kennedy in the White House. Now, at any rate, the storm over Cuba would darken the wide horizon of Kennedy's New Frontier. To begin with, there was the old dilemma: Any overt use of U.S. force to topple Castro would earn Kennedy a resounding chorus of condemnation from world leaders. Even more to the point, Kennedy feared that Khrushchev would retaliate for an obvious U.S. move in the Caribbean by trying to strangle the beleaguered city of West Berlin—an eventuality that might have led to World War III.

But Kennedy's chief problem was invisible to himself and his advisers: It was their misperception that, with a little prompting from CIA agents and collaborators who were already in place, anti-Communist uprisings would break out all over the island whenever Castro was challenged by an invasion of well-armed Cuban exiles. Kennedy also believed that, if defeated in their first engagements, the exiles could melt into the mountains and begin a guerrilla war against Castro. In fact, there were no mountains in the immediate vicinity of the chosen invasion site at the Bay of Pigs, and the CIA had not trained its anti-Castro campaigners in irregular warfare. But on the strength of his false expectations, Kennedy gave the go-ahead for fifteen hundred exiles to land in Cuba.

Without American help of a size that would be impossible to disguise, the exiles faced an overwhelming task. If they ever had the ghost of a chance for success, their fate was sealed when, on April 15, 1961, a bombing force piloted by exile pilots in CIA aircraft failed to destroy Castro's tiny air force. The reason for this setback lay in the astute planning of the Maximum Leader himself; foreseeing the rough outline of the events that would now unfold, Castro had ordered his planes to be dispersed to airfields throughout Cuba. As a result, eight of his thirteen aircraft survived the CIA bombing missions.

Since Kennedy would not risk revealing the U.S. role by providing effective air cover for the little invasion armada, Castro's eight aircraft were enough to sink the supply ships of the exiles, leaving them stranded on the shore, easy prey for the new Cuban army. The beachhead at the Bay of Pigs collapsed completely after only three days. According to Philip Bonsal, the defeat of the exiles "consolidated Castro's regime and was a determining factor in giving it the long life it has enjoyed."[15] In short, American opposition was a godsend for Fidel Castro. And ever since the spring of 1961, the mosquito-rich Bay of Pigs has been a minor tourist attraction for the Cuban people, with their government billing it as the place that saw "the first defeat of imperialism in America."[16]

Kennedy was appalled at the extent to which he had underestimated Castro's hold on power, and he took the exiles' failure hard. According to his brother Robert, he was extremely disheartened in its aftermath: "He felt very strongly that the Cuba operation had materially affected . . . his standing as president and the standing of the United States in public opinion throughout the world."[17] Kennedy's friend Charles Spalding recalled how the incident changed the entire tenor of the new administration: "Before the Bay of Pigs, everything was a glorious adventure, onward and upward. Afterward, it was a series of ups and downs, with terrible pitfalls. . . ."[18]

But the Bay of Pigs was only the start of Kennedy's obsession with the Cuban leader. As Robert Kennedy told Richard Helms, the CIA's deputy director for plans, in January 1962, the destruction of "that son-of-a-bitch with the beard" would be "the top priority in the U.S. government. . . . No time, money, effort, or manpower is to be spared."[19] With Bobby monitoring its every move, the CIA launched a thousand little initiatives against Castroism. On occasion, agency pilots in unmarked B-26 bombers flew missions against the island from airfields in southern Florida. Almost nightly, CIA boats shuttled secret agents and saboteurs in and out of Cuba.

These acts were part of the largest covert operation in American history, code-named Mongoose. U.S. operatives damaged Castro's factories and mines, contaminated shipments of his sugar, counterfeited his currency, and attacked his coastal shipping. The goal was to incite "an open revolt and overthrow of the communist regime"[20] by the autumn of 1962. With U.S. opposition and his inner circle's mismanagement placing Cuba's economy in double jeopardy, Castro had to face reality and order food rationing to begin on July 1 of that year. A long generation later, Cubans would still be standing in line for their daily bread.

Castro's assassination was slated to be the centerpiece of Operation Mongoose. This goal had not originated with the New Frontier. Already in 1960, the Eisenhower administration had developed plans to physically eliminate Castro from the scene, and a Mafia chieftain named Johnny Roselli, who had once managed the Sans Souci casino in Batista's Havana, was recruited by the CIA. Apparently paid $150,000 to arrange Castro's murder, Roselli pooled his resources with other underworld figures like Sam Giancana. But in this case the U.S. government's blood money produced no blood: All of the Mafia's repeated attempts to kill the Cuban leader failed.

A masterful propagandist, Nikita Khrushchev had used the triumphs of the Soviet space program to convince the world that the USSR possessed a nuclear arsenal that was second to none, and he prided himself in thinking that even America was fooled by his claims. But in October 1961 the Kennedy administration called his bluff by announcing that "the destructive power which the United States could bring to bear even after a Soviet surprise attack upon our forces would be as great as, perhaps greater than, the total undamaged force which the enemy can threaten to launch against the United States in a first strike."[21] In short, America possessed a clear and unquestionable nuclear superiority—a fact of which Fidel Castro, by his own later account, would be unaware during the coming crisis.

The Soviets were enraged that Kennedy had dared to expose their pretensions. Two days later, in the far reaches of Siberia, they set a fearful record by exploding a nuclear test device equivalent to 30 million tons of TNT. Dramatic as it was, their riposte could not restore the general perception of nuclear balance. Lacking the long-range missiles to make good on his promise to burn the United States to cinders in the event of World War III, Khrushchev turned to his shorter-range missiles, of which he had enough to annihilate the NATO allies in Western Europe. Now he would be tempted to move some of those weapons far forward—all the way to Cuba—so that they would be capable of devastating the United States. If such a move were made, Khrushchev would have at least partially rectified the imbalance of forces, which favored the United States even more than President Kennedy realized.

Conditions seemed ripe for the introduction of nuclear missiles into Cuba.

Buoyed by his victory over Kennedy at the Bay of Pigs, Castro had announced in December 1961 that "I am a Marxist-Leninist, and shall remain a Marxist-Leninist until the day I die."[22] Accepting an aggressive interpretation of what Marxism required him to do, he aimed to spread his revolution far and wide, making Havana the new capital of a "liberated" Third World. Huber Matos, a former Cuban commander, believes that Castro forsook democracy because communism "offered him the opportunity of becoming the undisputed ruler of the country for the rest of his life."[23] Whatever his deepest motives, he had to insure that his Cuban base was safe before he could step up the pace of the international revolution. And so he pricked up his ears when the Soviets mentioned the possibility of stationing nuclear missiles in Cuba.

Sending in the missiles would be risky, but Khrushchev saw that their presence might serve as a formidable shield for Castro at the same time that it would create a new nuclear balance. Convinced that John Kennedy could be tricked and outmaneuvered, he persuaded the Politburo to approve the transfer of the missiles and their technicians to Cuba. The United States had already installed similar weapons in Britain, Italy, and Turkey, and to Khrushchev's mind, one bad turn deserved another. "It was high time," he believed, that "America learned what it feels like to have her own land and her own people threatened."[24] As for Castro, he saw a psychological upside for himself and his comrades: "We preferred the risks . . . of great tension, a great crisis, to the risks of . . . having to wait, impotently, for a United States invasion of Cuba."[25] And Castro agreed to the Soviets sending some forty thousand troops to his island as well—to serve as protection for their technical cadre and to help defend the Cuban revolution.

While Kennedy believed that Russian personnel on Cuba numbered fewer than ten thousand, the key fact about the alien presence—that it included weapons capable of destroying entire American cities—was revealed to him by the U-2s of the U.S. Air Force's 4080th Strategic Reconnaissance Wing. His national security adviser, McGeorge Bundy, entered the family quarters in the White House at 8:30 in the morning on October 16, 1962, to tell Kennedy the bad news. The president looked up from his breakfast with eyes full of distress and outrage, but he was not wholly unprepared for this turn of events. Rumors about Soviet missiles in Cuba had been rumbling along the Potomac during the late summer of 1962, and Kennedy's new head of the CIA, John McCone, had quietly warned the president that Khrushchev was on the verge of taking a disastrous new initiative in the Caribbean.

Kennedy had hardly dreamed that Khrushchev would actually plant such provocative weaponry among the tall palms of Castro's isle. But he wanted to show his critics in the Republican party that his administration was not relaxing its vigilance, so in September the president had publicly warned the Soviets against shipping advanced warheads and delivery systems to Cuba. Now, in October, the crisis arrived. Waiting in the wings was a nuclear war that would destroy Soviet power for decades at the cost of perhaps 10 million American lives—and, probably, a much higher toll of dead in Western Europe.

For the duration, Kennedy formed his most trusted advisers into an Executive Committee of the National Security Council (Ex Comm) and urged them to develop options for dealing with the crisis. A consensus of opinion proved hard to come by. As Secretary of Defense Robert McNamara recalled, "[T]here was tremendous tension between those who wanted to use the opportunity to get rid of Castro and those who thought it too dangerous, and between those who thought that the Soviet deployment meant a massive shift in the strategic balance and those who didn't."[26]

John McCone and the Joint Chiefs of Staff felt that the missiles on Cuba *did* upset the balance of terror, but neither the president nor McNamara believed that they posed a significant new threat to U.S. security. For Kennedy and his secretary of defense, the main complications were political, not military. Kennedy had already promised the American people that any nuclear warheads moved into Cuba would be neutralized, and he was determined to be as good as his word. He perceived that failure in a matter of such moment might lead to his impeachment.

During his televised address on October 22, the president revealed Khrushchev's "sudden, clandestine decision to station strategic weapons for the first time outside of Soviet soil."[27] Kennedy spoke mainly to his fellow citizens, but he was also keenly aware of the need to influence world opinion. He even directed part of his speech "to the captive people of Cuba," telling them that men like Castro were "no longer Cuban leaders inspired by Cuban ideals. They are puppets and agents of an international conspiracy which has turned Cuba . . . into the first Latin American country to become a target for nuclear war. . . ."[28]

The climax of his speech came when the president announced that it "shall be the policy of this nation to regard any nuclear missile launched from Cuba against any nation in the Western Hemisphere as an attack by the Soviet Union on the United States, requiring a full retaliatory response upon the Soviet Union."[29] These final words were the most dramatic threat ever to come out of the White House. Khrushchev denounced them and the rest of Kennedy's crisis diplomacy as "the folly of degenerate imperialism" and reminded the president that "with the advent of modern types of armament, the U.S.A. has fully lost its invulnerability."[30] Despite his public truculence, Khrushchev seemed convinced that the missiles in Cuba were purely defensive. To describe them as offensive and demand their removal was, to his mind, a travesty.

Kennedy's secretary of state, Dean Rusk, called the missile crisis the most perilous passage in world history. During its course, the president, who was under intense pressure from the right to invade Cuba, brought the armed forces of the United States to the maximum level of combat readiness. For the first time since the Korean War, U.S. military commands around the globe were placed on high alert. The army's 1st Armored Division was moved from Fort Hood, Texas, to Fort Stewart, Georgia, as a first step toward invading Cuba. Those long-range bombers of the Strategic Air Command that were not aloft on airborne alert were dispersed to civilian airfields, lest they be destroyed in a Soviet preemptive attack. The U.S. Navy's fleet of Polaris missile submarines were ordered to launching positions close to Soviet shores. NATO forces were also placed on a war footing.

On the diplomatic front, the language had rarely been more intense. The U.S. ambassador to the United Nations, Adlai Stevenson, told the Security Council that Castro's Cuba "has aided and abetted an invasion of this hemisphere," and so identified itself as "an accomplice in the communist enterprise of world domination."[31] A limited naval blockade (Kennedy called it a "quarantine") was thrown around Cuba, arousing the Soviets to issue charges of piracy on the high seas. Their howls grew louder when six Russian submarines were harried to the surface by U.S. destroyers.

The crisis assumed even more frightening dimensions on Saturday, October 27. "To add to the feeling of foreboding and gloom," as Robert Kennedy remembered, "Secretary McNamara reported increased evidence that the Russians in Cuba were now working day and night, intensifying their efforts on all the missile sites. . . ."[32] Later that day, a U-2 was shot down by Russian technicians, killing the pilot, Maj. Rudolf Anderson. When word of this first blood got around, the urban population of Cuba ran wild with joy in the streets. Monitoring such activity in Moscow, Khrushchev detected "a smell of burning in the air."[33]

Stress took its toll. When John Kennedy signed the formal order for the naval quarantine on the evening of the twenty-second, he had to ask his staff to remind him of the day's date not once but three times. As his brother later put it, the president was painfully conscious that he "had initiated the course of events, but . . . no longer had control over them."[34] Through the long days of uncertainty, the American scene remained preternaturally quiet. People went about their business. There were essentially no demonstrations of public distress; if the president's competence to deal with the crisis was being questioned, little was audible above private murmurs.

In a message broadcast over Radio Moscow on October 27, Khrushchev insisted that his missiles in Cuba would not be removed unless similar U.S. weapons were taken out of Turkey. Later that day Robert Kennedy informed Soviet ambassador Anatoly Zobrynin of the president's final, non-negotiable position: Khrushchev had only twenty-four hours to promise that the Soviet missiles would be speedily disassembled and returned to Russia. Otherwise, U.S. warplanes would destroy them. As for the U.S. missiles in Turkey, Robert told Zobrynin that their continued presence was a kind of fluke: The president "had ordered their removal some time ago, and it was our judgment that, within a short time after this crisis was over, those missiles would be gone."[35]

On October 28, Khrushchev climbed down. That Sunday at nine in the morning Washington time, Moscow Radio announced that "the Soviet government . . . has given a new order to dismantle the arms which you described as offensive, and to crate and return them to the Soviet Union."[36] The president was intensely relieved. "I feel like a new man," he confided to his assistant David Powers. "Do you realize that we had an air strike all arranged for Tuesday? Thank God it's all over."[37]

Khrushchev and Kennedy had made a deal that traded the removal of the offensive weapons (about forty missiles and thirty-six nuclear warheads) from Cuba for an American guarantee to refrain from attacking the island. It was not a deal of which Castro would approve. In fact, he was shocked when he learned of the U.S.-USSR agreement, for "it had really never crossed my mind that the option of withdrawing the missiles was conceivable."[38] Because Castro refused to allow United Nations inspectors to oversee the dismantling of the missiles, Kennedy was never to issue a formal noninvasion pledge. But knowledgeable observers understood that the missile crisis had all but guaranteed Castro's survival as dictator of Cuba.

Whatever dangers his presence on the international scene has created, Castro remains a commanding figure. He is a man who reads English with near-perfect comprehension but speaks it with a heavy accent. Hating the struggle with bureaucracy and paperwork, he has spent perhaps a quarter of his working life in interviews and conversations of doubtful worth. His speeches still stretch out toward the end of time. If capitalism could be talked to death, Castro would have finished it off years ago.

A self-professed Christian who has had his differences with the Catholic church, he claims to get along famously with God—in spite of his underlying Marxism. He is known for donning peasants' garb, picking up a machete, and joining in the sugar cane harvest. As the commander of a garrison state, he prefers to wear olive-green fatigues rather than a more formal uniform with a blouse and a tie. Late in 1985, Castro shocked the Cuban tobacco industry by giving up cigars. He has always been tireless and remains so, irrepressible in his seventh decade of life. His most useful *campañero* is his brother Raúl, the Cuban defense minister.

His intensely personal style of government may mean that his achievement will perish with him. In the meantime, undeniable advances have been made under Castro; for instance, the percentage of literate Cubans has increased dramatically, and the medical care given free to his people is said to be of good quality. But these advances have taken place within the worrisome context of a full-blown Marxist apparatus.

Castro had an enviable laboratory for his experiment in socialism: an island that was relatively easy to defend; a powerful enemy lurking nearby to unite the people; a mentor state that was willing to bankroll his ever-failing economy; his own indefatigable and charismatic personality; an adoring population eager to help him build a new Cuba; and a messianic icon, soon to be conveniently dead, in the person of Che Guevara. As head of the Cuban government, first secretary of the Cuban Communist party, and commander in chief of the Cuban armed forces, Castro could give orders to anyone about anything. Under his auspices, all Cuba was organized as though it were his private army—with the Soviets winning temporary control of certain key regiments.

Yet he could not construct a new society, much less the informal world empire to which he seemed to aspire. Cuban socialism saddled Castro with the problem that all Marxist leaders share: a woefully inefficient command economy. Though his people do not wear rags or live in shanties, Castro's Cuba shambles along—when it moves at all—with a pronounced limp. The country's transportation system creaks with age and neglect. On the political front, human rights are routinely violated. Personal freedom is even more strictly rationed than foodstuffs, but Castro's jails are rich in dissenters.

In 1990, Castro's situation worsened when, due to the process of German unification, it lost the aid of East Germany. With the end of the Soviet empire, the $5 billion in annual support he has received from his comrades in Moscow has virtually disappeared, and the average Cuban is keenly aware that the island's economic circumstances have been straitened by a severe energy crisis. Despite these setbacks, Castro appears to be just as resistant to reform as Mao's heirs in China. Which means that his popularity at home is on the wane.

The extent of Cuba's growing unrest was dramatized as early as 1980, when he announced that any Cuban who wanted to leave for the United States was free to go. Over 125,000 people came forward to request transportation to America. Enraged that so many Cubans would desert his island paradise for the capitalist wasteland to the north, Castro vowed "to turn this shit against the United States."[39] His tactic was to contaminate the hopeful mass of voluntary exiles, who exited Cuba from the port of Mariel, with the criminals and mental patients that he called *escoria* (scum). And many such individuals were allowed to enter American society before the danger was recognized.

If, as suggested by the Mariel boat lift, the Cuban revolution is an internal failure, its external machinations have often produced results. Panamanian leaders like Manuel Noriega helped Castro circumvent the U.S. trade embargo and were given Cuban aid in return. Guerrilla warriors trained in Cuba have been active from Grenada to Angola, from Yemen to El Salvador, from Columbia to Ethiopia. The Sandinistas in Nicaragua might never have achieved power without Castro's aid and comfort. Often the USSR has helped to direct his foreign adventures, but the Soviet machine has never been able to integrate Cuba's military capabilities into a worldwide Communist offensive.

A case in point was the Soviet-Cuban failure to consolidate their advantage on the Caribbean island of Grenada. The Marxists who seized power there in 1979 got help from Cuban advisers with Soviet arms, but their rule proved fleeting. When the United States invaded in October 1983, the battle was quickly—if clumsily—won. Twenty-four years of unremitting hostility between the United States and Cuba had passed without the armed forces of the two countries ever coming into direct conflict. When the inevitable finally happened on Grenada, the cost to Castro was twenty-four dead and fifty-nine wounded. The Grenada invasion renewed Castro's old fears that Cuba would soon be treated likewise. He sent his high defense budget to even higher levels, placing added strains on the Cuban economy.

There has never been a foreign leader whose career was so completely centered on his fear of and disdain for the United States. In Castro's view, his northern neighbor is either directly or indirectly responsible for the lion's share of the world's poverty, militarism, and racism. Given this perception, it strikes him as only fair that the United States be hit with every weapon that he is able to command. From the early years of his regime, Castro has used the drug trade to harm U.S. society—and to help finance the export of revolution from Cuba to other Third World countries. But it was only in the mid-1970s that drug-running became a pillar of the Cuban economy, a source of much-needed American dollars.

In particular, Castro cut a deal with the drug lords of Colombia that called for him to share the enormous profits of the cocaine trade in exchange for the use of Cuba as a depot, point of transit, and shelter for drug-running missions into U.S. territory. Some of Castro's leading bureaucrats lived up to their part of the agreement. Their activities received public recognition on November 15, 1982, when a federal grand jury in Miami returned an indictment that accused four high-ranking officials of the Cuban Communist party, among others, of expediting the delivery of illegal drugs from Colombia to the United States.

Not that Castro's use of the drug trade is indiscriminate. As the head of the U.S. Drug Enforcement Agency told a congressional task force in February 1984, "the Cubans apparently deal only with those drug smugglers they trust or those who can provide some benefit or service to Cuba such as smuggling weapons."[40] These requirements were met by Noriega as well as the leaders of the Medellín cartel. On the flip side of these Castroite scandals are American crimes and misdemeanors, for U.S. operatives have also worked with members of the Colombian cartel. Their purpose: to raise funds for arming such anti-Communist guerrillas as the Nicaraguan contras.

A confidential U.S. government document reported in 1986 that "Castro's officials not only provided equipment and chemicals to refine . . . cocaine, but . . . set up [the operation] on an armed military base, offering maximum security."[41] In July 1989, to divert attention from his own apparent responsibility for such activities, Castro had four of his comrades, including Gen. Arnaldo Ochoa Sánchez, put to death on charges of corruption and involvement in the drug trade. Ochoa had begun to shape up as a political rival to Castro, so his execution removed a potential opponent at the same time that it perpetuated the myth of Cuba's severe treatment of drug offenders. In fact, with his financial woes, there is more pressure on Castro in the 1990s to sustain his revolution with drug money than at any time in the recent past.

Understandably, Castro expects the United States to repay him in full for all the nightmares he has caused the American establishment. A recurring theme of his rule has been the imminence of a Yankee invasion. In this sense Ronald Reagan was a blessing to the Cuban Communists. Given Reagan's reputation, it was that much easier for Castro to keep the people frightened and mobilized—and in no mood to question the authority of their Maximum Leader. The real threat to his regime will come when and if Cubans quit believing that the United States has military designs on their island. Castro, the old master of *machismo-leninismo*, could get along without Third World allies. He can probably endure even though his old friends in Moscow are gone. But he could not survive without the United States as an external enemy.

13

On the Trail of Ho Chi Minh

To the mind of its 36th president, Lyndon Baines Johnson, the American order was threatened by a host of enemies. His attitude, so strikingly suggestive of paranoia, was revealed in November 1966 when he said that

> there are 3 billion people in the world and we have only 200 million of them. We are outnumbered 15 to one. If might did make right they would sweep over the United States and take what we have. . . . We are showing right now it can't be done in Vietnam. Four hundred thousand of our young men, the flower of our manhood, the very tops, are out there.[1]

Marxists had a different point of view about the war in Vietnam. Che Guevara, for one, saw in Ho Chi Minh's resistance to U.S. pressure a harbinger of international revolution. His slogan—"Two, three, *many* Vietnams!"—became a rallying cry for guerrillas around the world. While Guevara's excitement about the bloody mess in Southeast Asia was hardly out of character, it seems strange that Vietnam could have achieved such strategic importance in American eyes. Yet Lyndon Johnson's inner circle resolved to make the struggle there a pivotal event in the cold war. McGeorge Bundy, the assistant for National Security that Johnson had inherited from John Kennedy, went to Vietnam in 1964 and returned to report that the "international prestige of the United States, and a substantial part of our influence, are directly at risk in Vietnam."[2]

Johnson himself thought the triumph of Ho Chi Minh would "shatter my presidency, kill my administration and damage our democracy."[3] And he embraced the domino theory in one of its most extreme forms:

> You see, I was as sure as any man could be that once we showed how weak we were [by withdrawing from Vietnam], Moscow and Peking would move in a flash to exploit our weakness . . . whether through nuclear blackmail, through subversion, with regular armed forces or in some other manner. . . . And so would begin World War III.[4]

Before the Communist successes of the Tet offensive, which began on January 31, 1968, Americans tended to credit Johnson's repeated assertions that the war was well on its way to being won. After Tet, with its assaults on thirty-six provincial capitals, sixty-four district towns, and a dozen large U.S. installations, Americans didn't know what to believe, but they wished that they had never heard of places like Quang Tri and Pleiku and Bien Hoa. The light at the end of the tunnel had become an ever-receding will-o'-the-wisp.

At the same time that the Vietcong and the North Vietnamese army were advancing their fortunes in the field, American reporters were drawing a bead on the government of South Vietnam, exposing it as corrupt and inefficient. Although Ho's regime in Hanoi was rich in its own brand of brutes, it still seemed unsullied in comparison to that gang of mediocrities in Saigon, and Ho himself was lionized by a large minority of the American people—most of them young.

But his popularity represented a vote of no-confidence in the war rather than an informed opinion, for it was hard to determine whether such a distant, controversial man was an admirable character or not. As one U.S. ambassador to South Vietnam, Gen. Maxwell Taylor, would put it, "Who was Ho Chi Minh? Nobody really knew."[5] Few Americans realized that Chi Minh, the last of Ho's many noms de guerre, means "he who enlightens,"[6] or that Ho had visited Harlem as a young man, or that he had been an assistant pastry cook in a ritzy London hotel on the eve of World War I, or that he had tried to present the case for Vietnamese self-determination to Woodrow Wilson at the Versailles Peace Conference in 1919.

Ho was born Nguyen Sinh Cung in central Vietnam in 1890, the son of a nonconformist intellectual father, Nguyen Sinh Sac, who once served as a court official at Vietnam's old imperial capital, Hué. Ho's mother died when he was ten years old. At the age of twenty-one, he sailed from Saigon as a galley boy on a French freighter—and did not return to Vietnam for thirty years. He first gained notoriety as a Communist opponent of the French empire builders who had occupied his country since the second half of the nineteenth century. Notoriously soft-spoken but capable of wit and irony, he once wrote that "Madame Justice . . . has had such a rough passage on her voyage [from France] to Indochina that she's lost everything except her sword."[7]

Converting himself into a Marxist thinker at the end of World War I, Ho became a founding member of the French Communist party. Later, his name would also appear on the rolls of the Soviet, Chinese, Indochinese, and Vietnamese parties. Over the years Ho became fluent in English as well as French,

Russian, and several dialects of Chinese. In 1923 he moved to the Soviet Union and, a few months later, was given space in a black-bordered edition of *Pravda* to eulogize Lenin: "In his lifetime he was our father, teacher, comrade and advisor. Now he is our guiding star. . . . Lenin lives on in our actions. He is immortal."[8]

It is said that Ho became friends with Stalin, who took a special interest in colonized peoples at the same time that he was cruelly suppressing the national minorities of the emerging Soviet Union. Ho's activism and sincerity impressed a wide range of his comrades. A German Marxist named Ruth Fischer, who knew Ho in Moscow in 1924, said that he "played a very big part in things, bigger than some of the better-known Asian leaders of the time—Mao did not come to the fore till later."[9] Pleased to exploit Ho's talents, the Soviets sent him to China in 1925 as an agent of the Communist international.

The coming years would see him working the left-wing circuit through much of Southeast Asia. Widely recognized as a professional revolutionary, he served time under British jailers in Hong Kong and Chinese jailers in Guangxi Province. His trials and tribulations, as he wrote in a prison poem, "turned my mind into steel."[10] Finally returning to his homeland in 1941, he founded the nationalist organization that he called the Vietminh. His goal was to resist Vietnam's most recent occupiers, the Japanese, and their Vichy French collaborators.

After making contact in 1945 with the U.S. Office of Strategic Services (the OSS, which would later become the CIA), Ho collected useful intelligence about Japanese military installations and troop movements in Indochina and sent it to American agents stationed in Kunming, China. As a reward, the Vietminh received modest supplies of U.S. weapons. Ho's relationship with the United States was only a marriage of convenience, but it worked reasonably well. After the defeat of Japan, he wrote that "I feel only sorry that all our American friends have to leave us so soon."[11] Of course, their return to Southeast Asia would distress him far more than their departure. In the 1960s, stroking his thin goatee, he asked if the Statue of Liberty was still standing, and then added, "Sometimes it seems to me it must be standing on its head."[12]

Throughout his maturity, Ho's health was troubled by tuberculosis and malaria, yet he proved tireless in his pursuit of Vietnamese independence. One of his comrades described Ho as "taut and vibrant. . . . He had only one thought in his head—and it has, I think, obsessed him all his life long. His country. Vietnam."[13] As Ho himself said, "[I]t was patriotism and not communism that originally inspired me."[14] He never married and had no children, but he became "Uncle Ho" to his entire nation. He was almost monklike in the simplicity of his daily existence, preferring to live in a small cottage rather than occupy his official residence, a large French-built palace in Hanoi.

When Ho pronounced Vietnam free from foreign rule in September 1945, he bracketed his Marxism long enough to quote from the American Declaration of Independence, for he hoped that U.S. backing would guarantee his country's permanent separation from France. He even went so far as to ask that Vietnam be made an American protectorate as a step toward complete autonomy. If Franklin Roosevelt had lived for another year, he and Ho might have struck a deal. The Truman administration, however, was predictably repelled by Ho's ideological orientation and felt forced to support France, a nation that could help keep the Soviets out of Western Europe. After Mao prevailed in China, the United States supplied the French armed forces with the money and weaponry to resubjugate the Vietnamese. This tilt toward an outdated brand of European colonialism came as a deep disappointment to Ho.

Beijing and Moscow recognized Ho's Democratic Republic of Vietnam in early 1950. Dean Acheson, the U.S. secretary of state, responded by calling Ho "the mortal enemy of native independence in Indochina."[15] For many years, U.S. policymakers continued to believe—or professed to believe—that Ho was essentially a puppet of the Soviets or the Maoists or both. This became one of the most disastrous misperceptions ever to plague U.S. foreign policy, for it lent Ho's revolution a symbolic importance that did not correspond to its real role in international politics.

Events conspired to keep American illusions intact. When war came to Korea in the summer of 1950, President Truman feared a general Communist offensive around the periphery of China and increased his backing of France's effort to suppress Ho's nationalist movement. By 1954, U.S. military assistance to French colonialism totaled over $2.5 billion.

After France met its Indochinese Waterloo at Dienbienphu in May 1954, the Geneva Conference decreed that elections be held in both parts of Vietnam two years later as a precursor to national unification. Since Ngo Dinh Diem, the Roman Catholic president of South Vietnam, was no match for Ho in popularity, Diem refused to play the unification game. He ignored the Geneva accords and went about the business of making his regime an Asian beacon of anticommunism.

Encouraged by an open and vigorous American commitment to his survival, Diem declared the Republic of Vietnam, with Saigon as its capital, on October 26, 1955. The situation might have been stabilized along the lines that he desired, for in January 1957 the Soviet Union suggested that the separation of the two Vietnams be made permanent and recognized by the entry of each into the United Nations. The Eisenhower administration missed an extraordinary opportunity by letting the Soviet proposal drop.

President Eisenhower had hoped that U.S. preponderance in nuclear weapons would secure the American world order by dampening Marxist ardor everywhere. Under threat of "massive retaliation," even for small insurrections, Communists were supposed to curb their evil ways and keep them curbed. As the 1950s ran on, it became more and more obvious that such a stance was scarcely credible. When John Kennedy's turn to deal with Ho came, he was ready with a new anti-Communist strategy. A system of "graduated response" to Marxist offensives would be developed; the punishment would then fit the crime, and the U.S. struggle for a stable international order would seem just and reasonable. The United States would continue to need its doomsday arsenal to deter a Soviet nuclear attack, but the outcome of the global contest was more likely to depend on the Pentagon's use of counterinsurgency to defeat the irregular warfare practiced by Mao, Castro, and Ho in the Third World.

Calculations of this kind caused many Americans to see the war in Vietnam as a matter of life and death. If John Kennedy could frustrate Ho's ambitions, the United States might go on to secure the blessings of freedom for the entire planet; if Ho prevailed, the counsel for capitalism would be one of despair. While no one can imagine how Kennedy's Vietnam policy might have evolved during a second term, he was not the sort of man to back away from a challenge. At the time of his assassination, more than sixty thousand American military "advisers" were operating in Vietnam. As he succeeded Kennedy, Lyndon Johnson had begun to suspect that it would take a far greater force to win this war.

On August 2, 1964, an American destroyer on a reconnaissance mission off North Vietnam, the USS *Maddox,* was engaged by several of Ho's torpedo boats, which were overcome by the destroyer's guns and by aircraft from a nearby U.S. carrier, the *Ticonderoga.* This so-called Gulf of Tonkin incident provided Johnson with a pretext to expand the U.S. role in Vietnam. After a second incident occurred on August 4, Johnson extracted from Congress what was essentially a blank check to carry the war to Ho. In the Senate, the tally in favor of the Gulf of Tonkin Resolution was 88–2, while the House vote was unanimous. Congress thereby agreed that the president should "take all necessary measures to repel any armed attack against the forces of the United States and to prevent further aggression. . . ."[16] On August 7, navy warplanes attacked the bases used by the offending patrol boats. These were the first of tens of thousands of American bombing sorties that would be flown against North Vietnam, and opinion polls indicated that 85 percent of the U.S. population approved of Johnson's tactics.

The United States was escalating the war in the midst of a deteriorating situation. After President Diem was murdered in a military coup during the autumn of 1963, the Saigon government became a revolving door crowded with incompetent generals. By November 1964, U.S. ambassador Maxwell Taylor was reporting that Communist gains in the northern part of South Vietnam "have been so serious that once more we are threatened with a partition of the country by a Vietcong salient driven to the sea."[17] The army of the Republic of Vietnam had, in short, failed to defend its own territory. The Johnson administration foresaw an early end to the country's independence if its rulers were left to their own devices.

The broad outlines of the plan to Americanize the war were formulated in February 1965 by McGeorge Bundy, who successfully pressed President Johnson to initiate "a policy of sustained reprisal against North Vietnam—a policy in which air and naval action against the North is justified by and related to the whole Vietcong campaign of violence and terror in the South."[18] This offensive against Hanoi was coupled with the beginnings of a huge U.S. military presence in support of Saigon. The first regular American combat troops, 3,500 marines organized in two battalions, waded ashore at Da Nang on March 8, 1965, their assignment to protect the U.S. air base there from Vietcong attack. They were greeted by, among others, the local women, who hung garlands of flowers around their necks. Thereafter Vietnam would soak up American manpower like a bloody sponge.

Lyndon Johnson ran his war from the White House in detail; he was hardly exaggerating when he said that U.S. forces "can't even bomb an outhouse without my approval."[19] He controlled the pace and tempo of the war as he controlled its intensity and scope. By 1965, he had determined not to go all-out, exactly, but to make a very large effort. In April he told an audience at Johns Hopkins University that abandoning South Vietnam "to its enemies, and to the terror that must follow, would be an unforgivable wrong."[20]

Predictably, the president referred to America's larger ambitions:

> We are also there to strengthen world order. Around the globe, from Berlin to Thailand, are people whose well-being rests in part on the belief that they can count on us. . . . To leave Vietnam to its fate would shake the confidence of all these people in the value of an American commitment and in the value of America's word.[21]

Besides, shying away from the fight in Southeast Asia would only lead to greater perplexities later on: "The battle would be renewed in one country and then in another. The central lesson of our time is that the appetite of aggression is never satisfied."[22]

Ho Chi Minh saw the war in equally cosmic terms. He, too, was out to save the world from tyranny; he, too, had come to see the war in terms of a much larger plot. The Americans, he wrote in November 1965, "are using South Vietnam as a testing ground for a new type war of aggression as well as for new kinds of modern weapons . . . which will be eventually employed in other countries with a view to . . . establishing U.S. rule over the world."[23] According to Ho, his people were in the forefront of the battle against an insatiable imperialism, and he prosecuted the war as if the fate of the international revolution depended on its outcome.

Given their mutually inflated views of what was at stake in Vietnam, Johnson and Ho were bound to fail as peacemakers. But Johnson was under far more domestic pressure to stop the fighting, so he became the wooer, and Ho the wooed. Time and again Johnson would invite the North Vietnamese to join him in ending the war. His inducements to negotiation included funds for the development of Southeast Asia's peacetime economy. "We're going," he promised in 1966, "to turn the Mekong into a Tennessee Valley."[24] Publicly he berated Hanoi for its refusal to make peace, but privately the president expressed his admiration: "If I were Ho Chi Minh, I would never negotiate."[25] For his part, Ho denounced the administration's overtures as "deceitful talk" from men who were obsessed with causing "ever greater devastation, in order to compel the Vietnamese people to lay down their arms and give up their legitimate aspirations."[26]

Rallying around their wartime leader, the North Vietnamese liked to think of Ho as an honest, kindly man who was rigid only in matters of national self-defense. But their president was also a hard-line Marxist who had given the North's peasants fits with his program of "land reform." He would send his divisions down the Ho Chi Minh Trail through Laos to fight in the south, yet he would instruct his prime minister to denounce American reports of their presence as "a myth fabricated by the U.S. imperialists to justify their war of aggression."[27] Another major fact of the fighting that Ho preferred to obscure was the interdependence of the Vietcong and the North Vietnamese.

The United States had never been clearly defeated by a foreign foe. It seemed ridiculous that American pride would finally bow before a little leftist with a wispy beard who ruled over an underdeveloped domain a quarter the size of Texas. Lyndon Johnson believed that the war was being lost on the propaganda front more than anywhere else. In September 1967 he said in an interview that "I can prove that Ho is a son-of-a bitch . . . but they want *me* to be the son-of-a-bitch."[28]

Since political considerations made it impossible to launch an all-out offensive against Hanoi, Gen. William Westmoreland, the head of U.S. combat forces in Vietnam from 1964 to 1968, was forced to run what was essentially a war of attrition. Yet as Defense Secretary McNamara pointed out, Ho Chi Minh had become a master of "attriting *our* national will,"[29] and what wore down first was not the Communists' ability to take punishment but the patience of the American people. As the opinion polls showed, support for the war began to cool as early as the summer of 1965. But antiwar sentiment was slow to prevail, and the troop buildup went on. So did the fighting. During 1968, Johnson's last full year in office, 14,589 Americans were killed in action in Vietnam—the highest one-year toll of the war. Postwar studies suggested that it was this mounting list of casualties rather than negative reporting by U.S. war correspondents that destroyed domestic tolerance for Johnson's policies.

The president's dismay deepened in the wake of the 1968 Tet offensive, which was launched because, as one North Vietnamese officer put it, "Uncle Ho was very old and we had to liberate the south before his death."[30] Though Tet involved seventy thousand Communist warriors, it fell short of its most optimistic goal: to set up a new coalition regime in Saigon that would evict the U.S. expeditionary force from Vietnam and prepare the way for the country's unification under the auspices of Ho Chi Minh. The cold numbers show Tet in a very poor light: Communist ranks were depleted by perhaps forty thousand, while the United States lost two thousand and the South Vietnamese four thousand men.

There was a palpable sense of disappointment in Hanoi that Tet had fallen so far short of decisive victory. But in terms of its impact on the American psyche, the offensive was a huge success for Ho Chi Minh. Even the U.S. embassy in the heart of Saigon had been attacked, and it took over six hours for the embassy compound to be resecured. Now, for the first time since Harry Truman dismissed Douglas MacArthur, there was a massive, simultaneous loss of confidence by the American people in their president's ability to govern. Lyndon Johnson's popularity had been slipping for some time, but in the wake of Tet it collapsed.

Trying to deflect some of the disappointment, Johnson told his colleagues that Ho Chi Minh "is like Hitler in many ways. . . . [W]e, the president and the cabinet, are called murderers and they never say anything about Mr. Ho."[31] Johnson's repeated assertions that Tet had been a disaster for the Communists did little to hearten the American public, who began to recognize the immensity of Ho's willpower. They were seeing his cruel strength—as the French had seen it long before, when Ho told them that "You will kill ten of our men, and we will kill one of yours. Yet, in the end, it is you who will tire."[32]

For the American soldiers who fought this war and sustained the casualties, the standard one-year tour of duty seemed to be never-ending: "Eighty days have September, April, June, and November," ran one rendition of how time passed in Vietnam. "All the rest have 93, except the last month which has 140."[33] Saigon was literally halfway around the world from Washington. The enemy was nowhere and everywhere; the front could be a bar in downtown Saigon as surely as it could be a Vietcong village just this side of Cambodia. Progress on the battlefield was measured in terms of grim body counts. Psychological disorientation was suffered by almost every American in the country. For Vietnam veterans, the struggle to deal with post-traumatic stress disorder (known in earlier wars as shell shock and combat fatigue) would become a nightmare from which it would sometimes seem impossible to awake.

On the home front, it was a war that combined with general affluence to create a youthful counterculture, launching a thousand books on disarmament, yoga, organic gardening, anarchism, UFOs, drug use, astrology, and teepee lore. Draft cards were not the only things that burned in the 1960s; severe rioting punctuated the dismal life of the nation's black ghettos. Because the war had largely been financed through deficit spending, inflation became a problem. People stopped believing Lyndon Johnson's claims that his social programs would cure all the nation's ills. Both of his wars—the war on poverty and the war in Vietnam—were looking like losers.

A "credibility gap" had opened between president and people. In a televised speech on March 31, 1968, Johnson buckled under an overload of stress and recognized defeat. He restricted the bombing campaign against North Vietnam, offered to send a delegation to meet Ho's representatives at the peace table, and declined to run again for the presidency. In mid-May, direct talks between American and North Vietnamese diplomats began in Paris.

Nursing his wounds in retirement, the former president had plenty of time to ponder his relationship with the "raggedy-ass little fourth-rate country"[34] that had caused him to conduct a futile war and tear his own country apart. Few mourned the passing of the Johnson administration, even though it was Richard Nixon who came to power in January 1969. When Ho died of a heart attack seven months later at the age of seventy-nine, America's international reputation had reached an all-time low.

The Nixon that America elected president over Democrat Hubert Humphrey in November 1968 did not seem to be the same man who came out swinging after his inauguration. Candidate Nixon had clearly run on the promise to end the war as quickly as possible; he even claimed that he had a "secret plan" ready to implement as soon as he entered the White House. Perhaps Ho's death helped convince him that the worst passages of the Vietnam debacle were over; at any rate, he soon expanded the war.

Despite Ho's passing, there were worthy opponents to fight Nixon's plans, including Gen. Vo Nguyen Giap, the man who had long directed North Vietnam's military operations. Giap and the other Communist leaders who succeeded Ho pledged themselves to carry on in his honor until the Americans were completely driven out. Nixon was undaunted by their determination.

As Nixon realized, Lyndon Johnson had failed to fight the war in Vietnam to the hilt, for Johnson felt that both the risks and the costs of escalation *à outrance* would have been too high. The incredible devastation wrought by a total war would have aroused worldwide condemnation, and domestic opposition would have risen to a fever pitch. There was the possibility that the Korean tragedy would be repeated, with up to half a million Maoist soldiers charging down from China to reinforce the Vietnamese—and taking a tremendous toll in American lives. The protests of the Soviet Union might have created a general crisis in international relations. The huge dollar amounts of a victory budget for the Pentagon would have gutted the Great Society programs on which Johnson's historical reputation largely rested, and that prospect surely appalled him. (Even so, Johnson saw his domestic reforms suffer significant cuts as the fighting escalated.)

For Nixon, these considerations soon became passé. He would weather all antiwar protest so successfully that his victory in the 1972 election would be an overwhelming landslide. With little stake in the kind of social engineering that was dear to Johnson's heart, Nixon was unconcerned about sacrificing domestic reform to the goal of prevailing in Vietnam, and he slashed away at Johnson's Great Society programs with gusto. Abroad, Nixon found Mao and Zhou Enlai so unperturbed by his continued prosecution of the war that they welcomed him to Beijing in the midst of it. While continuing to supply the North Vietnamese war machine, the Soviets were eager to placate Nixon in order to reach an agreement on limiting the nuclear arms race, and they also pursued improved relations with Washington because they needed U.S. grain to feed their people.

There was another weighty reason why Hanoi received only qualified support from the leaders of world communism. Moscow and Beijing, especially in the period around 1969, were threatening to engage each other in a disastrous war along the length of their common border, and each needed to curry American favor in the event that worse came to worst. When Lyndon Johnson bombed the North in 1964, he had to fear the Soviet and Chinese reaction. By 1972, Nixon knew that the Communist giants would combat his moves against the North with little more than rhetoric. In short, Nixon was free to prosecute the war in ways Johnson had not been.

On April 30, 1969, three months into Nixon's first term, U.S. forces reached their peak strength: just over 543,000. Although he was pledged to bring U.S. troops home as soon as possible, Nixon wanted to persevere until the continued existence of South Vietnam was guaranteed. The emphasis of Henry Kissinger, Nixon's national security adviser, was more on the side of securing the best possible truce—and then damning Communist perfidy when it all came apart with the fall of Saigon. At any rate, both Nixon and Kissinger wanted to achieve the "Vietnamization" of the war. They hoped to persuade North Vietnam to withdraw its troops from the South at the same time that the United States was reducing its commitment to Saigon. But Hanoi was having none of it. Instead, it insisted that the United States abandon Nguyen Van Thieu, who had been clinging to power as South Vietnam's president since 1967.

To help insure Thieu's survival, Nixon took new and radical departures. From the spring of 1969 to the spring of 1970, he approved of 3,630 bombing missions against the Ho Chi Minh Trail and other targets in Cambodia. His orders were unconstitutional, for they were drawn up and executed without congressional authorization—and when questioned on the matter, the president publicly denied that any such bombing was taking place. As April 1970 drew to a close, Nixon rushed in where Lyndon Johnson had feared to tread. He openly joined a ground war to his secret air war, ordering thousands of U.S. and South Vietnamese soldiers across the border into Cambodia. These forces would try to do what the bombing had failed to accomplish: destroy the sanctuaries that the Communists had been using to support their troops in South Vietnam.

This unexpected widening of the American role caused unprecedented expressions of outrage on the home front. And then real tragedy struck. Never before in American history had university students been killed while protesting their nation's foreign policy. Now it happened twice in the course of a fortnight: four students were shot dead on May 4, 1970, by members of the National Guard at Kent State University in Ohio, and two students died on May 15 when police opened fire on demonstrators at Jackson State College in Mississippi. It was a wonder that more students were not killed, for the typical campus had become a dangerous battleground where unarmed protesters faced well-armed cops. Not since the Civil War had the United States found itself in such domestic disarray.

National divisiveness started at the top. Like his predecessor's, Nixon's sense of enemies, both foreign and domestic, was highly developed. His list of American foes was headed by Daniel Ellsberg, a renegade defense intellectual who released the Pentagon Papers to *The New York Times*. When both the *Times* and *The Washington Post* published large excerpts, the public was able to read a detailed account of the Johnson administration's internal struggles to hit on the right response to the challenge posed by Ho Chi Minh. Richard Nixon was outraged that confidential memoranda of the federal government could be exposed to the eyes of the world by a handful of dissenting individuals. His mood was not improved by the fact that he kept discovering allusions to the secret maneuvers of his diplomatic corps in the national press.

After losing a battle in the Supreme Court to keep the Pentagon Papers from being published, Nixon ordered a secret investigative unit to be set up and quartered in the basement of the Executive Office Building—just across West Executive Avenue from the West Wing of the White House, the site of the Oval Office. The task: to gather intelligence on Ellsberg and the administration's other domestic bugbears. Nixon's "plumbers" would expand their illegal activities to include, in June 1972, a break-in at the Democratic party's national committee headquarters in the Watergate complex on the Potomac. As luck would have it, five of the six plumbers involved in the crime were apprehended on the premises.

On June 23, six days after the break-in, Nixon violated the law of the land by instructing his chief of staff, H. R. Haldeman, to use the influence of the CIA to call off the FBI's investigation of the incident. Brought before judge and jury, the plumbers, some of whom were Cuban exiles, claimed that they were on a secret mission to quash the machinations of Fidel Castro. The final outcome of this bungled burglary and all the revelations that flowed out of it is well known: the destruction by Richard Nixon of his own presidency.

Haldeman would eventually trace it all back to Southeast Asia: "Without the Vietnam war there would have been no Watergate."[35] And the fact that Nixon was preoccupied in 1973 (when farcical cease-fire agreements were signed by U.S. and North Vietnamese representatives in Paris) and 1974 by the worst political scandal in American history allowed Hanoi to advance toward victory at an accelerated pace. By 1975, the year that North Vietnam consummated its "Ho Chi Minh Campaign" by capturing Saigon, most Americans felt little more than a shamed relief that the long ordeal was finally over. On May 3, Saigon was officially renamed Ho Chi Minh City. Soon it would host Vietnam's official American War Crimes Museum.

There is one great military debate about Vietnam that continues to this day, and it concerns the use and misuse of air power during the war. The record is unambiguous about one thing: Attacks by U.S. tactical aircraft constantly supported the struggle of U.S. ground forces in South Vietnam. It is impossible to argue that a wider use of "close air support" would have been justified; even as it was, more South Vietnamese civilians than Vietcong warriors were killed by close air support and American artillery. The argument that the war might have been won by a wider use of air power can only refer to the bombing campaigns against North Vietnam.

Certainly the U.S. Air Force and the air arms of the navy and Marine Corps operated under major restrictions when dealing with North Vietnam. Consider, for instance, that the North was subjected to no large-scale bombing campaigns from the autumn of 1968 to the spring of 1972. Consider that the North's largest port facilities, located at Haiphong, were not extensively bombed or mined until nearly eight years after the Gulf of Tonkin incident, for fear that the East bloc ships that supplied the port almost continuously would be damaged—as they finally were, without causing more than an expression of formal outrage from Moscow.

Richard Nixon would live to regret his role in the bombing strategy. In April 1988, he told a national television audience that the greatest mistake of his presidency had nothing to do with Watergate, but consisted of his failure to blast the North during his first year in office. Already in 1969, Gen. William W. Momyer had spoken for most of his colleagues in the air force when he wrote that "We had the force, skill, and intelligence [to win the war through air power], but our civilian betters wouldn't turn us loose."[36]

On the other side were those like Secretary McNamara who believed that the basically rural nature of North Vietnamese society ruled out "an economic collapse as a result of the bombing."[37] McNamara was to testify before the Senate Armed Services Committee in August 1967 that "Enemy operations in the south cannot . . . be stopped by air bombardment—short, that is, of the virtual annihilation of North Vietnam and its people."[38]

Even with the relative restraint exercised by Johnson and Nixon, the tonnage of bombs dropped by U.S. aircraft in the course of the war amounted to several times the total tonnage expended around the globe during World War II. All this ordnance came nowhere close to crushing the Communists' spirit. Col. David Hackworth, one of the U.S. Army's premier fighting men in Vietnam, has recorded that, all too often, the enemy's "fortified positions were manned by hard-core mothers who didn't give up even after their eardrums had burst from the concussion of our bombs and blood was pouring out of their noses and ears. . . ." The bombing made such soldiers "hate us even more, and become that much more determined."[39]

As for the U.S. airmen, they could speak with one voice about the rigors of hitting the enemy. Thanks to the antiaircraft batteries, surface-to-air missiles, and radar systems provided by the Soviets, the North Vietnamese put up fierce resistance to American bombing campaigns. After the war, one U.S. pilot attested that "99 percent of the time as I dropped bombs, somebody was shooting at me."[40] By 1973, Hanoi would be holding nearly six hundred downed airmen as prisoners of war, while hundreds of others had been killed in action. Clearly, carrying the air offensive to the North had taken its toll. In the South, on the other hand, the areas controlled by the Vietcong possessed no effective antiaircraft defenses. So it was in the South that the really dreadful damage to the people of Vietnam was done. But no amount of high-tech destruction could overcome guerrilla warriors who were so willing to lay down their lives for their cause.

A week before his death, Ho Chi Minh had expressed sympathy for "the growing number of young Americans who are dying senselessly in Vietnam."[41] The overall toll of this, America's longest war, *was* stunningly high. In terms of deaths in the theater of operations, it was the fourth most fatal conflict in U.S. history, surpassed only by the very high numbers of the Civil War and the two world wars. The U.S. armed forces sustained a total of nearly sixty thousand dead, while Vietnamese fatalities, military and civilian, probably numbered over a million. All the death and destruction cost American taxpayers something over $250 billion.

As Ho saw it, he was leading his people through a rain of fire toward a future of great good fortune; his last will and testament promised that, once the United States was driven out, "we will build a country ten times more beautiful."[42] But what of the new, united Vietnam that Ho never lived to see? Did it win the peace as well as the war? The answer was given years after the American withdrawal by the man who had been Ho's closest associate, the Vietnamese prime minister, Pham Van Dong: "Yes, we defeated the United States. But now we are plagued by problems. We do not have enough to eat. We are a poor, underdeveloped nation. . . . [W]aging a war is simple, but running a country is very difficult."[43]

In general, reconstruction has suffered from the common Communist mistake of stressing ideological purity over simple economic efficiency. To make conditions still worse, Ho Chi Minh's old comrades from the north have treated the south like a conquered country, fitting it out with a gulag of "reeducation" camps. A strict economic embargo by the United States has added to the strain. Soviet aid was of limited value. China, far from being a useful ally, became Vietnam's archenemy and ravaged its northern provinces in 1979. While capitalist neighbors like Taiwan, Singapore, and Thailand boomed, Vietnam got poorer. Since the end of the war, hundreds of thousands of refugees have risked their lives to flee from the decrees of its Marxist cadres. "Open the doors," as even one Communist official in Ho Chi Minh City has admitted, "and everyone would leave overnight."[44]

As it entered the 1990s, Vietnam did seem eager to introduce a limited market economy and attract foreign investment. Above all, it needed to normalize relations with the United States, since institutions like the International Monetary Fund are shy—or incapable—of loaning the Vietnamese low-interest money for development without U.S. approval.

Despite their disillusionment, most Vietnamese still cherish the memory of Uncle Ho. He is seen as the only real hero in the ashen wasteland of recent Vietnamese history. Built six years after his death, his large, Lenin-like tomb is a holy site in the middle of Hanoi—although he requested a simple burial in his last will. Neither his mausoleum nor his society reflect the kind of outcome that Ho had cherished in his lifelong dream of a socialist and independent fatherland. Were he alive today, he might agree with those who describe the prolonged agony in Vietnam as the war that nobody won.

14

Saddam Makes His Move

Had U.S. policymakers in 1961 foreseen that Vietnam was a lost cause, they might have despaired of America's future. But when defeat in Southeast Asia finally came, it was taken in stride. For the triumph of the Vietnamese revolution was no longer seen as part and parcel of a worldwide Marxist offensive. Undoubtedly, it was a major setback for the U.S. vision of world order, but as seen from Washington in 1975, communism no longer represented an unbearable threat. With détente between East and West a fact of life, with the Sino-Soviet split apparently irreparable, and with Marxist initiatives stalling out through most of the world, Ho's revolution appeared not as a harbinger of capitalist collapse but as a special case—and a very isolated success.

Although the era of obsessive fear was over, Washington was still vexed by the rise of "nonaligned" leaders who, while distancing themselves from doctrinaire communism, nevertheless embraced one form or other of socialism. It was a world in which Karl Marx enjoyed much more vogue than Adam Smith; and after Vietnam, the United States found itself facing broad challenges in a largely hostile international environment. This was the situation that carried the improbable figure of Ronald Reagan into the White House in January 1981—and led to the massive budget deficits that were partly due to overbuilding in the defense sector of the U.S. economy.

American leaders had always hoped that socialism would disintegrate under the weight of its own contradictions, but few observers at the beginning of Reagan's first term expected Marxist power to wane before the end of the twentieth century. And then, during the second half of the 1980s, communism went into a precipitous decline. It was not just that it had failed to link up its disparate movements in a worldwide alliance that would carry all before it. What

184

happened was exactly the opposite of what Marxist propaganda had been preaching for decades.

Instead of capitalism rotting from within, it was communism that fell apart almost spontaneously, like a huge fearful beast infected with a deadly virus. With this sudden, unanticipated retreat of Marxism, it was widely believed in the United States that a new era of international tranquility and cooperation could begin. But it was not to be. Though Communist imperialism no longer posed an ongoing threat, expansionist nationalism was still stalking the planet. Nowhere was this more evident than in Iraq.

Before the beginning of the Gulf War, a grim joke placed the population of the country at 36 million: 18 million Iraqis plus 18 million portraits of Saddam Hussein. Certainly Saddam's image was everywhere in Iraq, and the list of his epithets stretched out toward the horizon. The Iraqi media called him "the Knight of the Arab Nation" and "the Hero of National Liberation,"[1] and even "the Leader with a Strategic Mind and Precise Calculations."[2]

In 1981 the Iraqi dictator would dramatize his authority by claiming that "A law is a piece of paper on which we write one or two lines and sign underneath it Saddam Hussein, President of the Republic."[3] Formally, he was both premier and president of Iraq, as well as the commander in chief of its armed forces, which were the world's fourth largest in the autumn of 1990. He chaired, and dictated to, Iraq's most powerful governing body, the Revolutionary Command Council of the Baath Party.

A decade of his personal rule submerged his people in a twilight realm of propaganda and repression. Kanan Makiya, the astute Iraqi exile who writes under the name of Samir al-Khalil, observed in 1989 that "The public's ability to judge what is right or wrong about its affairs, what is real as opposed to mere illusion, has broken down completely."[4] Small wonder. Every urban neighborhood in Iraq had long contained a government surveillance center where terrible things happened. Taking many of its cues from the methods of Joseph Stalin, Saddam's police state developed the control of the masses into a brutal science. Many of his critics were silenced by being tortured to death.

Blandly, Saddam would justify his methods to one Western visitor by stating that "Weakness doesn't assure achieving the objectives required by a leader."[5] With the help of a political elite that abounded in his relatives by blood and marriage, he turned his country into a totalitarian nightmare. For Saddam, terrorism began at home; in Saddam's Iraq, every year was 1984.

Early in his rule the dictator had his media announce that he was directly descended from the Prophet Mohammed. However that may be, Saddam was born into a very poor peasant family in April 1937 at a village on the upper Tigris River called al-Auja, close to the town of Takrit. Eight hundred years before his birth, Takrit had seen the advent of the fabled sultan Saladin—a coincidence that Saddam used to enhance his cult of personality. In 1958, Takrit witnessed his first prominent political act, and it was indicative of what would follow: He assassinated a supporter of Abdul Karim Kassem, the brigadier general who had just overthrown the Iraqi monarchy.

At the age of twenty-two Saddam moved to Baghdad and took part in a conspiracy to gun down Kassem himself. The plot miscarried and Saddam, who sustained a leg wound, was forced to leave Iraq and live in Syria and Egypt for three years. His premature return to his homeland toward the middle of the 1960s resulted in his prompt arrest. After two years behind bars he escaped and went into hiding, and the triumph of his Baath party soon placed the prisons of Iraq at the ex-prisoner's disposal.

His army uniforms with their field marshal's insignia were Saddam's favorite attire. It was only a matter of time before this thoroughgoing militarist found his first major war, which began when he ordered his troops to invade Iran in September 1980. Despite his early victories, Saddam was forced to recognize that Iraq would not prevail unless it received far more help from abroad. Loosening his ties with international terrorists, he began a worldwide effort to gain new support; and the United States, with its potent sense of grievance against the Ayatollah Khomeini and its fear that Islamic fundamentalism might engulf the Middle East, was among those who tilted toward Saddam. There was, after all, no doubt that the Ayatollah's regime had attempted to subvert Baathist rule in Iraq. More to the point, Iran was obviously striving to spread its revolutionary fervor to the large population of Saudi Arabian Shiites who lived harrowingly close to the largest oil fields in the Middle East.

Normal diplomatic relations between the United States and Iraq, broken since Israel's victory over the Arabs in 1967, were restored in the autumn of 1984. After toning down his anti-American rhetoric, Saddam stepped up his acquisition of high-tech items from U.S. companies through both legal and illegal means. Mostly the means were legal, for during the 1980s the Department of Commerce approved Iraqi requests to purchase millions of dollars worth of American products—many of which had military applications, even for use in chemical, biological, and nuclear warfare.

The flow of trade moved in both directions. By the end of the 1980s, the United States had imported over $5 billion worth of Iraqi oil. During the second Reagan administration, some of this oil had been taken out of the Persian Gulf in Kuwaiti tankers that were flying the American flag and escorted by warships of the U.S. Navy, lest they be attacked by the Iranians. Iraq was an enemy that the United States tried hard *not* to make.

But dealings with the United States were only a small part of Saddam's international network. The Soviet Union, France, and China did far more war-related business in Iraq than the United States; military supplies from the Poles, West Germans, and Czechs also helped Saddam keep the Iranians at bay.

Perhaps the most scandalous story to come out of Iraq was investigated by German reporter E. R. Koch. British journalist Simon Henderson would relay the information in his 1991 book on Saddam, *Instant Empire*:

[West] German companies . . . were more involved than other foreign firms in helping the Iraqis set up chemical weapons factories. . . . [I]n one Iraqi research facility, German engineers installed a chamber large enough for humans. The purpose of the chamber . . . was to test gas masks and protection equipment. It was reported that Iranian prisoners of war were used in these tests, and many of them died during the experiments.[6]

Predictably, Iraq's cruel use of advanced weaponry, especially its chemical weapons, proved to be of more military value than Iran's fundamentalist fervor. Also of exceptional importance were the new long-range Scud missiles that Saddam began to rain on Tehran and other Iranian cities in the winter of 1988. The ceasefire that both sides agreed to in August of that year was widely interpreted as a victory for Saddam.

The Bush administration apparently felt that Iraq as well as Iran had been exhausted by their eight-year struggle. Saddam was recognized as a mean customer, but Iraq had suffered as many as half a million casualties and had seen a treasury brimming with $30 billion turn into a debt of $80 billion.

Among his creditors was the United States Department of Agriculture, which, in December 1982 alone, had guaranteed $300 million in loans to Iraq so that Saddam could buy American grain. It seemed unreasonable to expect such a "victor" to cause a regional, much less an international, crisis for the foreseeable future. An official of the Bush administration described U.S. Iraq policy in 1989 as a continuation of the approach adopted by the Reaganites: "Try to use carrots, rather than sticks, in moderating [Iraqi] behavior."[7]

To rebuild its shattered economy and make itself the leading power in the Gulf, Iraq needed its oil revenues to rise. When they did not, Saddam pinned the blame on Kuwait's ruling al-Sabah clan. The Iraqi line was soon familiar throughout the Middle East: By overproducing and keeping world oil prices down, the emir of Kuwait was making it impossible for Iraq, which possesses the world's second-largest oil reserves, to recover from its Iranian debacle. Kuwait also aroused Saddam's ire by refusing to write off the $10 billion that it had loaned Iraq to fight the war. Saddam and his cohorts seemed genuinely puzzled: Wasn't it clear that Iraq's costly conflict with Khomeini had saved pleasure-loving little Kuwait from becoming a part of Iran? In the vision of Iraqi propaganda, the emir was "stabbing Iraq in the back with a poisoned dagger."[8]

During the eighteen months following the end of the war with Iran, Saddam survived four assassination attempts and watched his economy teeter toward collapse. He needed to project Iraq's inevitable postwar unrest outward, and the road to Kuwait was open. The alternative to taking the emirate, according to Saddam, was economic disaster for Iraq and the end of his regime.

When it came, the invasion was far more than a military exercise. Beginning on August 2, 1990, Saddam's troops brutalized Kuwait's people and stripped the emirate of anything of value that would move; even traffic lights were taken down and shipped back to Baghdad. Iraq, whose major port of Basra can only be approached up a narrow, insecure waterway shared with the Iranians, now controlled the capacious natural harbor of Kuwait City, the best on the Persian Gulf. On August 8, Saddam declared that his conquest would henceforth be incorporated into Iraq as "province number 19."

Initially, Kuwait's military governor would be his cousin Ali Hasan al-Majid, who commanded the forces that had used nerve gas on the Kurdish villagers of eastern Iraq in 1988.

The first major crisis of the post–cold war era was on. What really intensified international concern was the number of troops that Saddam had put into Kuwait: 100,000. Half that many would have won the emirate for Saddam. One hundred thousand would be capable of driving right on through Kuwait and defeating the Saudi military of seventy thousand as it seized the Saudi oil fields. The CIA believed that, if Saddam took the plunge, his forces could grab both the oil and Riyadh, the Saudi capital, inside of three days.

At the end of September, Christopher Flavin of the Worldwatch Institute presented a summary of the perils offered by the Gulf crisis. Flavin wrote that severe damage to the Saudi oil fields ("right in the middle of the area of conflict") might devastate the international banking system and lead to outright collapse among the Third World's struggling economies. "Not even at the start of World War II," Flavin concluded, "was the world economy on the line the way it is now."[9]

Approaching the situation with a different emphasis, Alfonse D'Amato, Republican senator from New York, had stressed the apocalyptic dangers of refusing to take action against Iraq. "Imagine the Middle East," challenged D'Amato, "with Saddam Hussein in command of a multimillion-man army, equipped with chemical, biological and nuclear weapons, and intercontinental missiles to deliver them. Unless Mr. Hussein is destroyed now, that is what we will face in the future."[10] Actually, Saddam lacked the population base to organize a "multimillion-man" armed force, but concern about his unconventional weapons was very much to the point.

Such anxieties were particularly acute in Jerusalem, for Saddam had threatened in the spring of 1990 to use his chemical weapons to "eat up half of Israel if it tries anything against Iraq."[11] The Israelis were even more worried about the potential nuclear threat presented by Iraq. Their apprehensions were not misplaced. Obsessed with Israel's nuclear capability, Saddam pushed Iraq's own nuclear and ballistic missile programs, which were presided over by his son-in-law, Gen. Hussein Kamil Hasan al-Majid, the minister for military industrialization. Iraq is said to have spent $1 billion in developing missiles alone, and some of the results were announced before the war. In December of 1989, Saddam told the world that his scientists had successfully tested a forty-eight-ton booster capable of carrying satellites into orbit. With the help of a legion of nations, progress was also being made on the warheads that Saddam hoped to mate to his missiles. Even money from U.S. grain loans ended up in Saddam's nuclear program.

Iraq and Israel have been in a formal state of war with each other since the founding of the Jewish state in 1948, when Iraqi troops helped stop an Israeli drive into the West Bank. The Israelis, who bombed the Osirak nuclear reactor near Baghdad on June 7, 1981, saw nuclear weapons in the hands of Saddam Hussein as an intolerable threat. Their point was well taken. According to British expert Frank Barnaby, three nuclear warheads "would be enough to decimate Israel's main population centers and industry, and to destroy its most important military command centers."[12]

The Jewish state possesses enough nuclear weapons to destroy Iraq's cities and vitrify much of the rubble, but that fact fails to console the Israelis. The Scud attacks on Israel during the winter of 1991 drastically heightened the country's sense of vulnerability. Saddam intended these attacks to draw Israel into the Gulf War, thereby igniting the Arab world, destroying the Allied coalition, and turning his conquest of Kuwait into a jihad against the Jewish and Christian infidels. As Saddam reportedly told Yasser Arafat, "Israel involvement in the conflict will change everyone's attitude in the Arab world. . . ."[13]

Determined to frustrate Saddam's strategy, George Bush took extraordinary measures to keep the Israelis out of the fighting. Three days after the beginning of the war, he sent them U.S. Patriot antimissile batteries, but Jerusalem saw the move as an inadequate fix. And, in truth, the Patriot record was very mixed; in Israel, more Scuds got through to hit their targets (thirteen) than were intercepted by the Patriots (eleven). Direct hits on the body of an incoming missile did not guarantee the neutralization of its warhead. Although only 4 Israelis died as a direct result of the Scuds, 289 more were wounded and 11,727 apartments were destroyed or damaged. From a historical point of view, the introduction of the Patriots was mainly significant because it was the first instance of U.S. troops directly participating in the defense of Israel.

Of course the conventional warheads on the Scuds were mere bee stings compared to nuclear warheads. Though there was little evidence to confirm Saddam's claim to CNN reporter Peter Arnett on January 28, 1991, that he already possessed operational nuclear weapons, steps were taken to hit his reactors and research facilities early in the war. His factories for producing chemical and biological weapons were also bombed by the coalition air forces. But the Allied offensive failed to destroy many of the unconventional weapons in the Iraqi armory and high-tech facilities in the country.

Factors other than fear of Saddam's growing technological sophistication helped to justify offensive action against Iraq. The overriding concern was a secret to no one. On September 11, 1990, George Bush noted before a joint session of Congress that "Iraq itself controls 10 percent of the world's proven oil reserves. Iraq plus Kuwait controls twice that. . . . We cannot permit a resource so vital to be dominated by one so ruthless."[14] Having orchestrated a United Nations economic embargo against Saddam, Bush underscored his hope that a "new world order"[15] would grow out of the confrontation. To initiate this new order, Bush approved plans for what Gen. Colin Powell, chairman of the Joint Chiefs of Staff, would describe as "the largest, most complex, rapid deployment of U.S. forces since World War II."[16] These forces included thousands of reservists who were called to active duty for the duration. The total number of American lives—military and civilian—directly impacted by the Gulf War would soon run into the millions.

On November 8, two days after the national elections, and even as the U.S.

economy was skidding deeper into recession, Bush announced his decision to send enough additional personnel to the Persian Gulf "to insure that the coalition has an adequate offensive military option should that be necessary to achieve our common goals."[17] The new game plan meant that the number of U.S. personnel in the Gulf region would rise from 238,000 to about 540,000—uncannily close to the number of Americans in Vietnam at the height of the war in 1969. Desert Shield was fated to become Desert Storm, and not even the release of all the Western hostages in Iraq could change that fact.

For the Pentagon, the stakes had rarely seemed higher. Secretary of Defense Dick Cheney apparently remarked that "The military is finished in this society, if we screw this up."[18] Some observers were convinced that Bush had written the United States a prescription for disaster. In a syndicated column published in the middle of September, Patrick Buchanan had discussed the downside possibilities. A ground invasion of Kuwait, he projected, would cost "tens of thousands of U.S. dead." An air war would cost "planes, pilots, hostages." To invade Iraqi and Kuwaiti territory at the same time "could require a million troops—as the Arab world exploded."[19] Saddam did what he could to make such an explosion more likely, telling the world that the Moslem holy city of Mecca had become "the captive of the spears of the Americans and the Zionists. . . ."[20] He repeatedly dashed hopes for peace by taking the line that Iraq would pull out of Kuwait only if Israel withdrew from the West Bank and Gaza Strip.

There is a sense in which the planning for this war began as far back as 1979, at the time of the Iranian revolution, when President Jimmy Carter concluded that the Soviets might take advantage of the chaos caused by the overthrow of the shah to seize some of the Persian Gulf's major oil fields. Responding to this perceived threat, Carter ordered the Pentagon to set up the Rapid Deployment Joint Task Force to project U.S. power into the region. In 1983 this organization became the U.S. Central Command; late in 1990 it established its headquarters in Riyadh.

As U.S. forces became powerful enough to develop an offensive against Saddam, the liberation of Kuwait called for by U.N. Resolution 678 seemed too modest an aim. Now Bush, who time and again denounced Saddam as another Hitler, said that the war could not be considered truly won until the dictator had been overthrown. For his part, Saddam promised the Americans such a bloody fight that his own triumph would be assured: "When the deaths and dead mount on them, the infidels will leave and the flag of [Allah] will fly over the mother of all battles."[21]

In spite of his bluster, Saddam never expected to win a clear victory on the battlefield. What he wanted was to inflict such heavy casualties on U.S. forces that Bush would decide to abandon the attempt to free Kuwait. Iraqi officials warned the Allied coalition that it might be able to outkill Saddam's soldiers, but it would never be able to outdie them. Kuwait would, in short, turn out to be a desert version of Vietnam, and on its barren ground American resolve would perish. Central Command had very different expectations. Weeks before the war began, Gen. H. Norman Schwarzkopf promised that U.S. forces "would be using capabilities that are far more lethal, far more accurate and far more effective than anything we have ever used."[22]

In its only war vote since passing the Gulf of Tonkin resolution in 1964, the U.S. Congress on January 12, 1991, authorized George Bush to use force to liberate Kuwait, though the margin favoring passage in the Senate was only five votes. The United States would not have to stand alone. Due largely to the personal efforts of Bush and Secretary of State James Baker, twenty-eight nations—many of them Arab—were persuaded to join the anti-Iraq coalition. With the United States leading the way, they forged a victory that may change the way wars are fought in the future, for during Desert Storm the use of air power had a decisive impact in a large theater of operations for the first time.

A Vietnam-like strategy of slow escalation of aerial warfare was rejected. From day one in the middle of January, the air attack on Iraq was all-out; technologically speaking, it was the most complex, most intensive, and best executed aerial offensive in military history. Purely civilian targets were generally spared, but few Iraqi government buildings escaped damage. Ho Chi Minh's official residence in Hanoi had remained sacrosanct throughout the Vietnam War; Saddam's own palace in the middle of Baghdad was reduced to ruins during the first night of the Gulf War.

While he lacked long-range SAMs capable of knocking down aircraft at over ten thousand feet, Saddam did have plenty of short-range SAMS and antiaircraft artillery. Allied missions were carefully planned to maximize damage on Iraq while minimizing the number of planes shot down. Sophisticated coalition aircraft provided an invaluable SEAD (suppression of enemy air defense) capability. Livid over the poor performance of his air defense system (which may have been invaded by a CIA computer virus), Saddam apparently had his air defense commander executed.

The effectiveness of air power meant that the ground war, launched on February 23, 1991, could be wrapped up in a hundred hours. Advocates of aerial warfare had been predicting such a success for decades but, as Secretary Cheney pointed out, "air campaigns have frequently not achieved the results predicted for them."[23] Even the Pentagon's senior command must have been surprised at just how irresistible the Allied air attack proved to be. Because of its success, only 148 U.S. servicemen and women died in combat during the Gulf War, which lasted a total of forty-three days.

As for Saddam, he refused to buy into the concept of defeat. While Baghdad was being bombed and his army was being "attrited," he incessantly declared that the Iraqi people were achieving a great triumph. But he soon discovered that a very different interpretation had been placed on events by his chief internal enemies, the Shiites of southern Iraq and the Kurds in the north. When their rebellions threatened to fragment the country into several vulnerable new nations, a whole new tragedy began. The danger now was that Iran and Syria would bite off chunks of Iraqi territory; Iranian influence might even succeed in installing a radical Islamic regime in Baghdad, in which case the United States would have won the battle of Kuwait but lost the war for Iraq.

Saddam with the fourth-largest armed forces in the world and a budding nuclear capability had been one thing; Saddam clinging to power and bribing his Republican Guards to stay loyal to his person was another. As one unnamed high-ranking official in Washington told *The New York Times* in March 1991, "[I]t's far easier to deal with a tame Saddam than with an unknown quantity."[24]

So George Bush stayed the hand of Central Command, leaving Saddam with enough destructive power to defeat Kurd and Shiite alike. The "battle of annihilation" that General Schwarzkopf had planned for Iraq was stopped in its tracks. Ideally, the president wanted to see Saddam replaced by one of his more pliable generals; what Bush feared was the elimination of the Baath party and the chaos that might follow. As Theodore Draper would point out, it was as though Bush "had wanted the German Army and the Nazi party to overthrow the Führer and take charge of the country. . . ."[25]

When Mr. Bush was reminded of his earlier demand that Saddam be ousted, and the fact that the United States had initially used radio broadcasts and CIA operatives in the Middle East to help spark the revolt, the president countered with the statement that the war had really been about Kuwait, and that Iraq's designs on the little emirate had been decisively defeated.

Yet Saddam, as Milton Viorst reported from Baghdad in June 1991, displayed "no sign of remorse for bringing about the war, or of being chastened by its results."[26] The grotesque ecological damage wrought by the war apparently troubled him not at all. Still thinking of his country as merely one region of "the Arab homeland," Saddam soon started to rebuild his military machine— and to dream of the day when he has the resources to renew his pan-Arabic crusade. For his part, George Bush would be on the lookout for a cost-effective way to terminate Saddam's regime forever.

On the home front, the sense of a great victory quickly evaporated. As the economy continued its downward course, the concerns of the American people turned away from the world's first live-television war and back to the rigors of daily life. We were jarred by the news that more U.S. citizens had been murdered on America's streets during the hundred-hour ground war than were killed at the battlefront. It suddenly seemed that what we really lacked was a genuine domestic order. The riots that followed the Rodney King verdict threw the general crisis of our cities into high relief.

What, then, of the new *world* order? It is, of course, the latest reemergence of the great American theme: that the United States has a mission to save and regenerate the planet. Whatever his failings as a leader, Bush himself gave that mission one of its classic formulations in his victory speech to a joint session of Congress on March 6, 1991, when he said that he could see a new international reality "coming into view. . . . A world where the United Nations—freed from Cold War stalemate—is poised to fulfill the historic vision of its founders. A world in which freedom and respect for human rights find a home among all nations." The president went on to proclaim that "The Gulf War put this new world to its first test. And my fellow Americans, we passed that test."[27]

Bush's speech played to mixed reviews. In capitals from Paris to Tokyo, from

Beijing to Buenos Aires, the phrase "new world order" seemed to suggest that, with the Soviets out of the great game, the United States would use its military might to intervene abroad at will. But would such interventions create real stability? Observers around the world suggested that the new order might bear an uncanny resemblance to the old chaos.

At home, critics had plenty of complaints about Bush's stewardship of the American nation. They could recite a long list of problems that received little or no presidential attention during the war—problems from the budget deficit to the trade gap to the sorry state of the U.S. banking industry, the degradation of our natural environment, the physical decay of our infrastructure, the huge gaps in our programs of nonmilitary research and development, the maldistribution of our personal wealth, and the crisis of our educational and health-care systems.

Further, American critics could dash hopes for world order by saying that the special circumstances that frustrated Saddam's aggression were unlikely to be replicated at any time in the near future. They could lambast the Gulf War on the basis that it was what the president gave us instead of a comprehensive energy policy. In short, there were plenty of factors to magnify the disgruntlement that always follows in the wake of war, no matter how successful the outcome. And the galling fact of Saddam's survival in state power, however diminished, did nothing to improve the public's mood. Only a minority appeared to realize that Iraq would remain an international problem, and the Middle East a powder keg, whether Saddam is overthrown or not.

Iraq is hardly the only place where U.S. aims have been thwarted. Even at the height of its dominion the United States could not police the entire globe; it could only exert leadership that might or might not produce results. Though the Soviet Union has disappeared as a superpower, the relative decline of the United States, plus the structural weaknesses that are found throughout the U.S. and world economy, make the American millennium seem far, far off. As the year 2000 approaches, U.S. power is interdependent on the power of other nations as never before.

What does the past tell us to expect of the future? Overall, it says that we are fated to live from day to day and year to year. Certain principles and traditions have helped to shape our policies since 1776, but our national success has largely been the result of quick-fix solutions to short-term emergencies. The future will find us improvising new solutions to new threats. Then the threats will change, and the improvisation will begin again.

We will court new allies and antagonize new enemies—or revive old ones—because of changes in our vital interests and shifts in our national psyche. In every foe that we encounter abroad, we will seek the final enemy—the enemy whose defeat will inaugurate the new world order. But there is no such enemy, and no war to end war. Golden ages are easy to dream about, impossible to achieve. History, it seems, is a martial machine.

Notes and References

1. Enemies of the American Order

1. Hunt, *Ideology and U.S. Foreign Policy*, p. 31.
2. Ibid., p. 40.
3. Cherry, *God's New Israel*, p. 295.
4. Toynbee, *A Study of History*, vol 4, p. 115.
5. LaFeber, *The American Age*, p. 3.
6. Graebner, *Manifest Destiny*, p. 234.
7. Tuchman, *Stilwell and the American Experience in China*, p. 17.
8. Barnet, *The Rockets' Red Glare*, p. 144.
9. Cherry, p. 293.
10. Ibid., pp. 297–98.
11. Chace and Carr, *America Invulnerable*, p. 253.
12. Havel, "'Uncertain Strength,'" p. 6.

References

BARNET, RICHARD J. *The Rockets' Red Glare: When America Goes to War.* New York: Simon and Schuster, 1990.

CHACE, JAMES, and CALEB CARR. *America Invulnerable: The Quest for Absolute Security from 1812 to Star Wars.* New York: Summit Books, 1988.

CHERRY, CONRAD. *God's New Israel: Religious Interpretations of American Destiny.* Englewood Cliffs, N.J.: Prentice-Hall, 1971.

GRAEBNER, NORMAN A., ed. *Manifest Destiny.* Indianapolis, Ind.: Bobbs-Merrill, 1968.

HAVEL, VÁCLAV. "'Uncertain Strength': An Interview." *New York Review of Books,* August 15, 1991, pp. 6–8.

HUNT, MICHAEL H. *Ideology and U.S. Foreign Policy.* New Haven, Conn.: Yale University Press, 1987.

LaFeber, Walter. *The American Age: United States Foreign Policy at Home and Abroad since 1750.* New York: W. W. Norton, 1989.

Toynbee, Arnold J. *A Study of History,* vol. 4. Oxford University Press, 1939.

Tuchman, Barbara W. *Stilwell and the American Experience in China, 1911–45.* New York: Macmillan, 1971.

2. The Royal Brute of Britain

1. Ryan, *Salute to Courage,* p. 33.
2. Commager and Morris, *Spirit of 'Seventy-Six,* vol. 1, p. 245.
3. Brooke, *King George III,* p. 131.
4. Ibid., p. 156.
5. Commager and Morris, vol. 1, p. 61.
6. Ibid., p. 97.
7. Fleming, *1776,* p. 326.
8. Commager and Morris, vol. 1, p. 467.
9. Mumby, *George III and the American Revolution,* p. 410.
10. Commager and Morris, vol. 1, p. 500.
11. Fleming, p. 430.
12. Emery, *Washington,* p. 187.
13. Fleming, p. 55.
14. Commager and Morris, vol. 1, p. 254.
15. Paine, *Common Sense and Other Political Writings,* p. 10.
16. Ibid., p. 14.
17. Ibid., p. 21.
18. Ibid., p. 27.
19. Ibid.
20. Ibid., p. 32.
21. Fleming, p. 266.
22. Ibid., p. 34.
23. Paine, p. 56.
24. Emery, p. 214.
25. Brooke, pp. 303–304.
26. Ibid., p. 304.
27. Ibid., p. 321.
28. Plumb, *The First Four Georges,* p. 126.
29. Tuchman, *The First Salute,* pp. 189–90.
30. Ibid., p. 213.
31. Brooke, p. 352.
32. Commager and Morris, vol. 2, pp. 1281–82.
33. Tuchman, *The March of Folly,* p. 228.
34. Smith, *John Adams,* vol. 2, p. 627.
35. Ibid., p. 629.
36. Macalpine and Hunter, *George III and the Mad-Business,* p. 3.
37. Ibid., p. 55.
38. Brooke, p. 7.
39. Ibid., p. 10.
40. Ibid.

References

BROOKE, JOHN. *King George III*. St. Albans, Hertfordshire: Granada Publishing Ltd., 1974.

COMMAGER, HENRY STEELE, and RICHARD B. MORRIS. *Spirit of 'Seventy-Six: The Story of the American Revolution as Told by Participants*, 2 vols. Indianapolis, Ind.: Bobbs-Merrill, 1958.

EMERY, NOEMIE. *Washington: A Biography*. New York: G. P. Putnam's Sons, 1976.

FLEMING, THOMAS. *1776: Year of Illusions*. New York: W. W. Norton, 1975.

LANGGUTH, A. J. *Patriots: The Men Who Started the American Revolution*. New York: Simon and Schuster, 1988.

MACALPINE, IDA, and RICHARD HUNTER. *George III and the Mad-Business*. New York: Pantheon Books, 1969.

MUMBY, FRANK ARTHUR. *George III and the American Revolution*. Boston: Houghton Mifflin, 1923.

PAINE, THOMAS. *Common Sense and Other Political Writings*, ed. by N. F. Adkins. Indianapolis, Ind.: Bobbs-Merrill Educational Publishing, 1976.

PLUMB, J. H. *The First Four Georges*. Glasgow, Scotland: William Collins Sons, 1983.

RYAN, DENNIS P., ed. *Salute to Courage: The American Revolution as Seen Through Wartime Writings of Officers of the Continental Army and Navy*. New York: Columbia University Press, 1979.

SMITH, PAGE. *John Adams*, 2 vols. Garden City, N.Y.: Doubleday, 1962.

TUCHMAN, BARBARA. *The First Salute*. New York: Knopf, 1988.

———. *The March of Folly: From Troy to Vietnam* (Chapter 4: "The British Lose America"). New York: Knopf, 1984.

3. A Pasha and His Pirates

1. Ray, "Horrors of Slavery," p. 328.
2. Tucker, *Dawn Like Thunder*, p. 253.
3. Ibid., p. 217.
4. Ray, p. 332.
5. Ibid., p. 333.
6. Ibid., p. 336.
7. Knox, *Naval Documents*, vol. 3, p. 347.
8. Ray, p. 415.
9. McKee, *Edward Preble*, p. 128.
10. Knox, vol. 1, pp. 35–36.
11. Symonds, *Navalists and Antinavalists*, p. 30.
12. Allen, *Our Navy and the Barbary Corsairs*, p. 58.
13. Albion and Pope, *Sea Lanes in Wartime*, p. 135.
14. Ray, p. 355.
15. Knox, vol. 3, p. 377.
16. Lewis, *The Romantic Decatur*, p. 42.
17. Fowler, *Jack Tars and Commodores*, p. 101.
18. McKee, p. 131.
19. Ray, p. 414.
20. Ibid., p. 370.
21. Ibid., p. 372.

22. Quoted in Ray, p. 387.
23. Allen, p. 212.
24. McKee, p. 312.
25. Tucker, p. 345.
26. Knox, vol. 5, p. 367.
27. Ibid., p. 433.
28. Ibid., p. 468.
29. Ibid., p. 469.
30. Ibid., p. 472.
31. Knox, vol. 6, p. 47.
32. Tucker, p. 426.
33. Knox, vol. 6, p. 162.
34. Irwin, *The Diplomatic Relations of the United States with the Barbary Powers*, p. 154.
35. Ray, p. 408.
36. Allen, p. 253.
37. Ibid., p. 254.
38. McKee, p. 336.

References

ALBION, ROBERT G., and JENNIE B. POPE. *Sea Lanes in Wartime: The American Experience, 1775–1942*. New York: W. W. Norton, 1942.

ALLEN, GARDNER W. *Our Navy and the Barbary Corsairs*. Boston: Houghton Mifflin, 1905.

FOWLER, WILLIAM M., JR. *Jack Tars and Commodores: The American Navy, 1783–1815*. Boston: Houghton Mifflin, 1984.

IRWIN, RAY W. *The Diplomatic Relations of the United States with the Barbary Powers, 1776–1816*. Chapel Hill: University of North Carolina Press, 1931.

KNOX, DUDLEY W., ed. *Naval Documents Related to the United States Wars with the Barbary Powers*, 6 vols. Washington, D.C.: U.S. Government Printing Office, 1939–44.

LEWIS, CHARLES LEE. *The Romantic Decatur*. Philadelphia: University of Pennsylvania Press, 1937.

MCKEE, CHRISTOPHER. *Edward Preble: A Naval Biography, 1761–1807*. Annapolis, Md.: Naval Institute Press, 1972.

RAY, WILLIAM. "Horrors of Slavery, or the American Tars in Tripoli." *The Magazine of History with Notes and Queries* 4, extra numbers 13–16 (1911): 247–526.

SYMONDS, CRAIG L. *Navalists and Antinavalists: The Naval Policy Debate in the United States, 1785–1827*. Newark: University of Delaware Press, 1980.

TUCKER, GLENN. *Dawn Like Thunder: The Barbary Wars and the Birth of the U.S. Navy*. Indianapolis, Ind.: Bobbs-Merrill, 1963.

4. Santa Anna: The Alamo and After

1. Fehrenbach, *Lone Star*, p. 208.
2. Lord, *A Time to Stand*, p. 62.
3. Long, *Duel of Eagles*, p. 111.
4. Ibid., p. 121.

5. De la Peña, *With Santa Anna in Texas*, p. 40.
6. Ibid., p. 42.
7. Long, p. 126.
8. Lord, p. 138.
9. Ibid., p. 144.
10. Santa Anna, *The Eagle*, p. 51.
11. Lord, p. 167.
12. Ibid., pp. 170–71.
13. De la Peña, p. 83.
14. Ibid., p. 178.
15. Callcott, *Santa Anna*, p. 145.
16. Santa Anna, p. 58.
17. Jones, *Santa Anna*, p. 80.
18. Ibid., p. 93.
19. Ibid., p. 94.
20. Eisenhower, *So Far from God*, p. 67.
21. Johannsen, *To the Halls of the Montezumas*, p. 145.
22. Jones, p. 110.
23. Weems, *To Conquer a Peace*, p. 297.
24. Nevins, *Polk: The Diary of a President*, p. 251.
25. Weems, p. 355.
26. Smith and Judah, *Chronicles of the Gringos*, p. 166.
27. Eisenhower, p. 311.
28. Ibid., p. 307.
29. Cf. Bauer, *The Mexican War*, p. 318.
30. Santa Anna, p. 108.
31. Smith and Judah, p. 264.
32. Eisenhower, p. 367.
33. Johannsen, p. 311.
34. Grant, *Personal Memoirs*, p. 38.

References

BAUER, K. JACK. *The Mexican War, 1846–1848*. New York: Macmillan, 1974.

CALLCOTT, WILFRID HARDY. *Santa Anna: The Story of an Enigma Who Once Was Mexico*. Norman: University of Oklahoma Press, 1936.

DE LA PEÑA, JOSÉ ENRIQUE. *With Santa Anna in Texas: A Personal Narrative of the Revolution*, trans. and ed. by Carmen Perry. College Station: Texas A&M University Press, 1975.

EISENHOWER, JOHN S. D. *So Far from God: The U.S. War with Mexico, 1846–1848*. New York: Random House, 1989.

FEHRENBACH, T. R. *Lone Star: A History of Texas and the Texans*. New York: Macmillan, 1968.

GRANT, ULYSSES S. *Personal Memoirs of U.S. Grant*. New York: AMS Press, 1972.

JOHANNSEN, ROBERT W. *To the Halls of the Montezumas: The Mexican War in the American Imagination*. New York: Oxford University Press, 1985.

JONES, OAKAH L., JR. *Santa Anna*. New York: Twayne, 1968.

LONG, JEFF. *Duel of Eagles: The Mexican and U.S. Fight for the Alamo*. New York: William Morrow, 1990.

LORD, WALTER. *A Time to Stand.* New York: Harper & Brothers, 1961.

NEVINS, ALLAN, ed. *Polk: The Diary of a President, 1845–1849.* London: Longmans, Green, 1929.

SANTA ANNA, ANTONIO LÓPEZ DE. *The Eagle: The Autobiography of Santa Anna,* ed. by Ann Fears Crawford. Austin, Tex.: The Pemberton Press, 1967.

SMITH, GEORGE WINSTON, and CHARLES JUDAH, eds. *Chronicles of the Gringos: The U.S. Army in the Mexican War, 1846–1848.* Albuquerque: University of New Mexico Press, 1968.

WEEMS, JOHN EDWARD. *To Conquer a Peace: The War Between the United States and Mexico.* Garden City, N.Y.: Doubleday, 1974.

5. The Ordeal of Emilio Aguinaldo

1. Dewey, *Autobiography,* p. 192.
2. Ibid., p. 214.
3. May, *Imperial Democracy,* p. 7.
4. O'Toole, *The Spanish War,* p. 185.
5. Dewey, p. 305.
6. Ibid., p. 289.
7. Ibid., p. v.
8. O'Toole, p. 189.
9. Dewey, p. 246.
10. Ibid., p. 247.
11. Aguinaldo, *My Memoirs,* p. 1.
12. Ibid.
13. *The Times* of London, July 23, 1920, p. 15 C.
14. Trask, *The War with Spain in 1898,* p. 404.
15. Ibid., p. 406.
16. Miller, *"Benevolent Assimilation,"* p. 37.
17. Ibid., p. 38.
18. Schirmer, *Republic or Empire,* p. 69.
19. Dewey, p. 269.
20. O'Toole, p. 371.
21. Karnow, *In Our Image,* p. 132.
22. Wolff, *Little Brown Brother,* p. 149.
23. Karnow, p. 138.
24. O'Toole, p. 386.
25. Ibid., p. 387.
26. Dewey, p. 175.
27. Aguinaldo, *A Second Look at America,* p. 100.
28. Bain, *Sitting in Darkness,* p. 12.
29. Wolff, p. 195.
30. Trask, p. 466.
31. Tompkins, *Anti-Imperialism in the United States,* p. 241.
32. Wolff, p. 210.
33. Schirmer, p. 129.
34. Ibid.
35. Aguinaldo, *A Second Look,* p. 100.
36. Wolff, p. 226.

37. Karnow, p. 142.
38. Alip, *In the Days of General Emilio Aguinaldo*, p. 95.
39. Karnow, p. 146.
40. Gates, *Schoolbooks and Krags*, p. 226.
41. Miller, p. 211.
42. Trask, p. 78.
43. Bain, p. 366.
44. Ibid., p. 370.
45. Aguinaldo, *A Second Look*, p. 16.
46. Miller, p. 171.
47. Aguinaldo, *A Second Look*, p. 128.
48. Ibid., p. 129.
49. Ibid., p. 186.

References

AGUINALDO, EMILIO, with VICENTE ALBANO PACIS. *A Second Look at America*. New York: Robert Speller & Sons, 1957.

————. *My Memoirs*, trans. by Luz Colendrino-Bucu. Manila, Philippines: 1967.

ALIP, EUFRONIO M. *In the Days of General Emilio Aguinaldo*. Manila, Philippines: Alip & Sons, 1969.

BAIN, DAVID HAWARD. *Sitting in Darkness: Americans in the Philippines*. Boston: Houghton Mifflin, 1984.

DEWEY, GEORGE. *Autobiography of George Dewey, Admiral of the Navy*. New York: Charles Scribner's Sons, 1913.

GATES, JOHN MORGAN. *Schoolbooks and Krags: The United States Army in the Philippines, 1898–1902*. Westport, Conn.: Greenwood Press, 1973.

KARNOW, STANLEY. *In Our Image: America's Empire in the Philippines*. New York: Random House, 1989.

MAY, ERNEST R. *Imperial Democracy: The Emergence of America as a Great Power*. New York: Harcourt, Brace & World, 1961.

MILLER, STUART CREIGHTON. *"Benevolent Assimilation": The American Conquest of the Philippines, 1899–1903*. New Haven, Conn.: Yale University Press, 1982.

O'TOOLE, G. J. A. *The Spanish War: An American Epic—1898*. New York: W. W. Norton, 1984.

QUIRINO, CARLOS. *The Young Aguinaldo*. Manila, Philippines: Aguinaldo Centennial Year, 1969.

SCHIRMER, DANIEL B. *Republic or Empire: American Resistance to the Philippine War*. Cambridge, Mass.: Schenkman Publishing, 1972.

TOMPKINS, E. BERKELEY. *Anti-Imperialism in the United States: The Great Debate, 1890–1920*. Philadelphia: University of Pennsylvania Press, 1970.

TRASK, DAVID F. *The War with Spain in 1898*. New York: Macmillan, 1981.

WOLFF, LEON. *Little Brown Brother: How the United States Purchased and Pacified the Philippine Islands at the Century's Turn*. Garden City, N.Y.: Doubleday, 1961.

6. Kaiser Billy and the War to End War

1. Cecil, *Wilhelm II*, p. 27.
2. Röhl and Sombart, *Kaiser Wilhelm II*, p. 47.

3. Balfour, *The Kaiser and His Times*, p. 119.
4. Cecil, p. 128.
5. Röhl and Sombart, p. 29.
6. Balfour, pp. 154–55.
7. Witcover, *Sabotage at Black Tom*, p. 37.
8. Wilhelm II, *My Memoirs*, pp. 243–44.
9. Ibid., p. 244.
10. Ibid., p. 293.
11. Kürenburg, *The Kaiser*, p. 308.
12. Palmer, *The Kaiser*, p. 175.
13. Balfour, p. 359.
14. Bailey and Ryan, *The Lusitania Disaster*, p. 150.
15. Ibid., p. 260.
16. Ibid., p. 265.
17. Link, *Wilson*, vol. 3, p. 50.
18. Ibid., p. 7.
19. Roosevelt, *The Works of Theodore Roosevelt*, vol. 21, p. 3.
20. Link, vol. 3, p. 51.
21. Ibid., p. 21.
22. Ibid., p. 33.
23. Ibid., p. 350.
24. Witcover, p. 24.
25. Ibid., p. 83.
26. Kennedy, *Over Here*, p. 5.
27. Link, *Wilson*, vol. 5, p. 247.
28. Ibid., p. 291.
29. Balfour, p. 370.
30. Link, vol. 5, p. 389.
31. Balfour, p. 359.
32. Cornebrise, *War as Advertised*, p. 38.
33. Ibid., p. 67.
34. Ibid., p. 42.
35. Ibid., p. 74.
36. Mock and Larson, *Words that Won the War*, facing p. 64.
37. Roosevelt, *The Works of Theodore Roosevelt*, vol. 20, p. xxiv.
38. Ibid., p. xxv.
39. Roosevelt, vol. 21, pp. 286–87.
40. Ibid., p. 361.
41. Bailey and Ryan, p. 261.
42. Roosevelt, vol. 21, p. xxi.
43. Ibid., p. xxii.
44. Pershing, *My Experiences in the World War*, vol. 1, p. 28.
45. Ibid., p. 30.
46. Ibid., p. 9.
47. Stallings, *The Doughboys*, p. 126.
48. Ibid., p. 134.
49. Pershing, *My Experiences in the World War*, vol. 2, p. 162.
50. Ibid., pp. 395–96.
51. Weintraub, *A Stillness Heard Round the World*, p. 307.

52. Kennedy, p. 367.
53. Balfour, p. 413.
54. Wilhelm II, p. 269.
55. Ibid., p. 283.
56. Ibid., p. 310.
57. Ibid., p. 314.
58. Cowles, *The Kaiser,* p. 408.
59. Röhl and Sombart, p. 32.
60. Cowles, p. 425.
61. Balfour, p. 419.

References

BAILEY, THOMAS A., and PAUL B. RYAN. *The Lusitania Disaster: An Episode in Modern Warfare and Diplomacy.* New York: Free Press, 1975.

BALFOUR, MICHAEL. *The Kaiser and His Times.* New York: W. W. Norton, 1972.

CECIL, LAMAR. *Wilhelm II: Prince and Emperor, 1859–1900.* Chapel Hill: University of North Carolina Press, 1989.

CORNEBISE, ALFRED E. *War as Advertised: The Four Minute Men and America's Crusade, 1917–1918.* Philadelphia: American Philosophical Society, 1984.

COWLES, VIRGINIA. *The Kaiser.* New York: Harper & Row, 1963.

KENNEDY, DAVID M. *Over Here: The First World War and American Society.* New York: Oxford University Press, 1980.

KÜRENBERG, JOACHIM VON. *The Kaiser: A Life of Wilhelm II, Last Emperor of Germany,* trans. by H. T. Russell and Herta Hagen. New York: Simon and Schuster, 1955.

LINK, ARTHUR S. *Wilson.* Vol. 3: *The Struggle for Neutrality, 1914–1915.* Princeton, N.J.: Princeton University Press, 1960.

————. *Wilson.* Vol. 5: *Campaigns for Progressivism and Peace, 1916–1917.* Princeton, N.J.: Princeton University Press, 1965.

MOCK, JAMES R., and CEDRIC LARSON. *Words that Won the War: The Story of the Committee on Public Information, 1917–1919.* Princeton, N.J.: Princeton University Press, 1939.

PALMER, ALAN. *The Kaiser: Warlord of the Second Reich.* London: Weidenfeld and Nicolson, 1978.

PERSHING, JOHN J. *My Experiences in the World War,* 2 vols. New York: Frederick A. Stokes, 1931.

RÖHL, JOHN C. G., and NICOLAUS SOMBART, eds. *Kaiser Wilhelm II: New Interpretations.* Cambridge, England: Cambridge University Press, 1982.

ROOSEVELT, THEODORE. *The Works of Theodore Roosevelt* (Memorial Edition), vols. 20–21. New York: Charles Scribner's Sons, 1925.

STALLINGS, LAURENCE. *The Doughboys: The Story of the A.E.F., 1917–1918.* New York: Harper & Row, 1963.

WEINTRAUB, STANLEY. *A Stillness Heard Round the World: The End of the Great War—November 1918.* New York: E. P. Dutton, 1985.

WILHELM II. *My Memoirs: 1878–1918.* London: Cassell, 1922.

WITCOVER, JULES. *Sabotage at Black Tom: Imperial Germany's Secret War in America, 1914–1917.* Chapel Hill, N.C.: Algonquin Books, 1989.

7. Comrade Lenin Sees It Through

1. Mason and Smith, *Lenin's Impact on the United States*, p. 69.
2. Murray, *Red Scare*, p. 65.
3. Ibid., p. 79.
4. Ibid., p. 17.
5. Ibid., p. 129.
6. Leiteizen, *Lenin on the United States*, p. 444.
7. Ackerman, *Trailing the Bolsheviki*, p. 7.
8. Murray, pp. 110–11.
9. Ibid., p. 83.
10. Ackerman, p. 252.
11. Levin, *Woodrow Wilson and World Politics*, pp. 233–34.
12. Maddox, *The Unknown War with Russia*, p. 123.
13. Krupskaya, *Reminiscences of Lenin*, p. 15.
14. Wilson, *To the Finland Station*, p. 426.
15. Leiteizen, p. 343.
16. Wilson, p. 522.
17. Payne, *The Life and Death of Lenin*, pp. 328–29.
18. Clark, *Lenin*, p. 271.
19. Cf. ibid., p. 268.
20. Pearlstien, *Revolution in Russia*, p. 236.
21. Kennan, *Soviet-American Relations*, vol. 1, p. 18.
22. Clark, p. 324.
23. Ibid.
24. Strakhovsky, *Origins of American Intervention*, p. 73.
25. Ibid., p. 74.
26. Kennan, vol. 1, p. 513.
27. Mason and Smith, p. 41.
28. Clark, p. 287.
29. Levin, pp. 127–28.
30. Leiteizen, p. 343.
31. Levin, p. 91.
32. Silverlight, *The Victors' Dilemma*, p. 44.
33. Kennan, *Soviet-American Relations*, vol. 2, p. 398.
34. Leiteizen, p. 336.
35. Ibid., p. 348.
36. Tumarkin, *Lenin Lives!*, p. 81.
37. Payne, p. 495.
38. Krupskaya, p. 482.
39. Clark, p. 374.
40. Mason and Smith, p. 68.
41. Payne, p. 497.
42. Pearlstien, pp. 253–54.
43. Silverlight, p. 196.
44. Ibid., p. 173.
45. Leiteizen, p. 381.
46. Strakhovsky, p. 75.
47. Silverlight, p. 165.

48. Maddox, p. 103.
49. Silverlight, p. 63.
50. Kennan, vol. 1, p. 156.

References

ACKERMAN, CARL W. *Trailing the Bolsheviki: Twelve Thousand Miles with the Allies in Siberia.* New York: Charles Scribner's Sons, 1919.

CLARK, RONALD. *Lenin: The Man Behind the Mask.* London: Faber and Faber, 1988.

KENNAN, GEORGE F. *Soviet-American Relations, 1917–1920.* Vol. 1: *Russia Leaves the War.* Princeton, N.J.: Princeton University Press, 1956.

———. *Soviet-American Relations, 1917–1920.* Vol. 2: *The Decision to Intervene.* Princeton, N.J.: Princeton University Press, 1958.

KRUPSKAYA, N. K. *Reminiscences of Lenin.* New York: International Publishers, 1970.

LEITEIZEN, C., ed. *Lenin on the United States: Selected Writings by V. I. Lenin.* New York: International Publishers, 1970.

LEVIN, N. GORDON, JR. *Woodrow Wilson and World Politics: America's Response to War and Revolution.* New York: Oxford University Press, 1968.

MADDOX, ROBERT J. *The Unknown War with Russia: Wilson's Siberian Intervention.* San Rafael, Calif.: Presidio Press, 1977.

MASON, DANIEL, and JESSICA SMITH, eds. *Lenin's Impact on the United States.* New York: NWR Publications, 1970.

MURRAY, ROBERT K. *Red Scare: A Study in National Hysteria, 1919–1920.* Minneapolis: University of Minnesota Press, 1955.

PAYNE, ROBERT. *The Life and Death of Lenin.* New York: Simon and Schuster, 1964.

PEARLSTIEN, EDWARD W., ed. *Revolution in Russia.* New York: Viking, 1967.

SILVERLIGHT, JOHN. *The Victors' Dilemma: Allied Intervention in the Russian Civil War.* New York: Weybright and Talley, 1970.

STRAKHOVSKY, LEONID I. *The Origins of American Intervention in North Russia (1918).* Princeton, N.J.: Princeton University Press, 1937.

TUMARKIN, NINA. *Lenin Lives! The Lenin Cult in Soviet Russia.* Cambridge, Mass.: Harvard University Press, 1983.

WILSON, EDMUND. *To the Finland Station: A Study in the Writing and Acting of History.* New York: Farrar, Straus and Giroux, 1985.

8. A Führer and His Reich

1. Herzstein, *Roosevelt and Hitler*, p. 233.
2. Ibid., p. 19.
3. Shirer, *The Rise and Fall of the Third Reich*, p. 636.
4. Ibid., p. 124.
5. Maser, *Hitler*, p. 83.
6. Ibid., pp. 87–88.
7. Fest, *Hitler*, p. 77.
8. Ibid., p. 78.
9. Ibid., p. 92.
10. Divine, *Roosevelt and World War II*, p. 35.
11. Toland, *Adolf Hitler*, p. 646.

12. Irving, *Hitler's War*, p. 254.
13. Ibid.
14. Divine, p. 44.
15. Shirer, p. 1154.
16. Larrabee, *Commander in Chief*, p. 56.
17. Ibid., p. 57.
18. Gannon, *Operation Drumbeat*, p. 85.
19. Toland, p. 693.
20. Irving, p. 291.
21. Ibid., p. 303.
22. Ibid., p. 352.
23. Shirer, p. 1171.
24. Ibid., p. 1173.
25. Bullock, *Hitler*, p. 663.
26. Toland, p. 695.
27. Gannon, pp. 378–79.
28. Irving, p. 353.
29. Larrabee, p. 176.
30. Gannon, p. 397.
31. Larrabee, p. 13.
32. Ibid., p. 4.
33. Halasz, *Roosevelt Through Foreign Eyes*, p. 243.
34. Divine, p. 39.
35. Davis, *Come as a Conqueror*, p. 37.
36. Murrow, *In Search of Light*, p. 81.
37. Irving, p. 774.
38. Ibid., pp. 675–76.
39. Halasz, p. 296.
40. Irving, p. 770.
41. Trevor-Roper, *The Last Days of Hitler*, pp. 110–11.
42. Murrow, p. 56.
43. Ibid., p. 57.
44. Trevor-Roper, p. 141.
45. Bullock, p. 781.
46. Irving, p. 793.
47. Davis, p. 197.
48. Fest, p. 718.
49. Irving, p. 822.
50. Bullock, p. 794.

References

BULLOCK, ALAN. *Hitler: A Study in Tyranny.* New York: Harper & Row, 1962 (completely revised edition).

DAVIS, FRANKLIN M., JR. *Come as a Conqueror: The United States Army's Occupation of Germany, 1945–1949.* New York: Macmillan, 1967.

DIVINE, ROBERT A. *Roosevelt and World War II.* Baltimore, Md.: The Johns Hopkins Press, 1969.

FEST, JOACHIM C. *Hitler*, trans. by Richard and Clara Winston. New York: Vintage Books, 1975.

GANNON, MICHAEL. *Operation Drumbeat*. New York: Harper & Row, 1990.

HALASZ, NICHOLAS. *Roosevelt Through Foreign Eyes*. Princeton, N.J.: D. Van Nostrand, 1961.

HERZSTEIN, ROBERT EDWIN. *Roosevelt and Hitler: Prelude to War*. New York: Paragon House, 1989.

IRVING, DAVID. *Hitler's War*. New York: Viking, 1977.

LARRABEE, ERIC. *Commander in Chief: Franklin Delano Roosevelt, His Lieutenants, and Their War*. New York: Harper & Row, 1987.

MASER, WERNER. *Hitler: Legend, Myth & Reality*, trans. by Peter and Betty Ross. New York: Harper & Row, 1973.

MURROW, EDWARD R. *In Search of Light: The Broadcasts of Edward R. Murrow, 1938–1961*, ed. by Edward Bliss, Jr. New York: Alfred A. Knopf, 1967.

SHIRER, WILLIAM L. *The Rise and Fall of the Third Reich*. New York: Fawcett Crest, 1960.

TOLAND, JOHN. *Adolf Hitler*. Garden City, N.Y.: Doubleday, 1976.

TREVOR-ROPER, H. R. *The Last Days of Hitler*. New York: Collier Books, 1972.

9. The Rising Sun of Hideki Tojo

1. Coox, *Tojo*, p. 11.
2. Browne, *Tojo: The Last Banzai*, p. 109.
3. Coox, p. 87.
4. Ibid., p. 115.
5. Browne, p. 108.
6. Slackman, *Target: Pearl Harbor*, p. 60.
7. Ibid., p. 58.
8. Ibid., p. 120.
9. Butow, *Tojo and the Coming of the War*, p. 407.
10. Slackman, p. 314.
11. Butow, p. 424.
12. Lingeman, *Don't You Know There's a War On?*, p. 28.
13. Ibid., p. 210.
14. *Time*, December 22, 1941, p. 33.
15. Stephan, *Hawaii Under the Rising Sun*, p. 125.
16. *Los Angeles Times*, February 25, 1942, p. 1.
17. Butow, p. 291.
18. Webber, *Silent Siege II*, p. 18.
19. Stephan, p. 114.
20. Webber, p. 148.
21. Ibid., p. 158.
22. Ibid., p. 159.
23. Ibid., p. 160.
24. Coox, p. 131.
25. Browne, p. 184.
26. Ibid., p. 197.
27. Ibid.

28. Lamont, *Day of Trinity*, p. 244.
29. Ibid., p. 261.
30. Thomas and Witts, *Enola Gay*, p. 307.
31. Ibid., p. 317.
32. Hachiya, *Hiroshima Diary*, p. 1.
33. Ibid., p. 5.
34. Ibid., p. 6.
35. Cave Brown and MacDonald, *The Secret History of the Atomic Bomb*, p. 550.
36. Hachiya, p. 48.
37. Cave Brown and MacDonald, p. 582.
38. Browne, p. 200.
39. Sheldon, *The Honorable Conquerors*, p. 96.
40. Ibid., p. 97.
41. Ibid.
42. Brackman, *The Other Nuremberg*, pp. 74–75.
43. Butow, p. 496.
44. Ibid.
45. Brackman, p. 350.
46. Coox, p. 153.
47. Mosley, *Hirohito, Emperor of Japan*, p. 341.
48. Hachiya, p. 88.
49. Ibid., p. 138.
50. Mosley, p. 347.
51. Sheldon, p. 140.

References

BRACKMAN, ARNOLD C. *The Other Nuremberg: The Untold Story of the Tokyo War Crimes Trials*. New York: William Morrow, 1987.

BROWNE, COURTNEY. *Tojo: The Last Banzai*. New York: Holt, Rinehart and Wilson, 1965.

BUTOW, ROBERT J. C. *Tojo and the Coming of the War*. Princeton, N.J.: Princeton University Press, 1961.

CAVE BROWN, ANTHONY, and CHARLES B. MACDONALD, eds. *Secret History of the Atomic Bomb*. New York: The Dial Press, 1977.

COOX, ALVIN D. *Tojo*. New York: Ballantine Books, 1975.

HACHIYA, MICHIHIKO. *Hiroshima Diary*, trans. and ed. by Warner Wells. Chapel Hill: The University of North Carolina Press, 1955.

LAMONT, LANSING. *Day of Trinity*. New York: Atheneum, 1965.

LINGEMAN, RICHARD R. *Don't You Know There's a War On? The American Home Front, 1941–1945*. New York: G. P. Putnam's Sons, 1970.

MOSLEY, LEONARD. *Hirohito, Emperor of Japan*. Englewood Cliffs, N.J.: Prentice-Hall, 1966.

SHELDON, WALT. *The Honorable Conquerors: The Occupation of Japan, 1945–1952*. New York: Macmillan, 1965.

SLACKMAN, MICHAEL. *Target: Pearl Harbor*. Honolulu: University of Hawaii Press, 1990.

STEPHAN, JOHN J. *Hawaii Under the Rising Sun: Japan's Plans for Conquest After Pearl Harbor*. Honolulu: University of Hawaii Press, 1984.

THOMAS, GORDON, AND MAX MORGAN WITTS. *Enola Gay.* New York: A Kangaroo Book, 1978.

WEBBER, BERT. *Silent Siege II: Japanese Attacks on North America in World War II.* Medford, Ore.: Webb Research Group, 1988.

10. Joseph Stalin's American Dream

1. Ulam, *Stalin,* p. 367.
2. Solzhenitsyn, *The First Circle,* p. 106.
3. Ulam, p. 560.
4. Nisbet, *Roosevelt and Stalin,* p. 6.
5. Ibid., p. 26.
6. Ibid., pp. 48–49.
7. Ibid., p. 51.
8. *Time,* February 5, 1945, p. 36.
9. Nisbet, p. 24.
10. McNeal, *Stalin,* p. 3.
11. Ibid., p. 4.
12. Smith, *The Young Stalin,* p. 128.
13. McNeal, p. 54.
14. Conquest, *The Great Terror,* p. 64.
15. Ibid., p. 56.
16. Ulam, p. 219.
17. Ibid., pp. 222–23.
18. Conquest, p. 56.
19. Solzhenitsyn, pp. 101–102.
20. Alliluyeva, *Twenty Letters to a Friend,* p. 222.
21. Ibid., p. 10.
22. Laqueur, *Stalin,* p. 15.
23. Truman, *Memoirs,* vol. 2, p. 2.
24. Maddox, *From War to Cold War,* p. 84.
25. Sherwin, *A World Destroyed,* p. 224.
26. Yergin, *Shattered Peace,* p. 188.
27. Maddox, p. 167.
28. Yergin, p. 279.
29. Sherwin, p. 155.
30. Rogow, *Victim of Duty,* p. 178.
31. Ibid., p. 174 n.
32. Ibid., p. 297.
33. Ibid., p. 210.
34. Ibid., p. 207.
35. Truman, vol. 2, p. 291.
36. Rogow, p. 19.
37. Ibid., p. 34.
38. Oshinsky, *A Conspiracy So Immense,* p. 82.
39. Thomas, *When Even Angels Wept,* p. 93.
40. Ibid., p. 96.
41. Oshinsky, p. 84.
42. Truman, vol. 2, p. 285.

43. Oshinsky, p. 143.
44. Ibid., p. 491.
45. Thomas, p. 628.
46. Truman, vol. 1, p. xi.

References

ALLILUYEVA, SVETLANA. *Twenty Letters to a Friend,* trans. by Priscilla J. McMillan. New York: Harper & Row, 1967.

CONQUEST, ROBERT. *The Great Terror: A Reassessment.* New York: Oxford University Press, 1990.

LAQUEUR, WALTER. *Stalin: The Glasnost Revelations.* New York: Charles Scribner's Sons, 1990.

MCNEAL, ROBERT H. *Stalin: Man and Ruler.* London: Macmillan, 1988.

MADDOX, ROBERT JAMES. *From War to Cold War: The Education of Harry S. Truman.* Boulder, Colo.: Westview Press, 1988.

NISBET, ROBERT. *Roosevelt and Stalin: The Failed Courtship.* Washington, D.C.: Regnery Gateway, 1988.

OSHINSKY, DAVID M. *A Conspiracy So Immense: The World of Joe McCarthy.* New York: The Free Press, 1983.

ROGOW, ARNOLD A. *Victim of Duty: A Study of James Forrestal.* London: Rupert Hart-Davis, 1966.

SHERWIN, MARTIN J. *A World Destroyed: The Atomic Bomb and the Grand Alliance.* New York: Vintage Books, 1977.

SMITH, EDWARD ELLIS. *The Young Stalin: The Early Years of an Elusive Revolutionary.* New York: Farrar, Straus and Giroux, 1967.

SOLZHENITSYN, ALEXANDER I. *The First Circle,* trans. by Thomas P. Whitney. New York: Harper & Row, 1968.

THOMAS, LATELY. *When Even Angels Wept: The Senator Joseph McCarthy Affair.* New York: William Morrow, 1973.

TRUMAN, HARRY S. *Memoirs,* 2 vols. Garden City, N.Y.: Doubleday, 1955 and 1956.

ULAM, ADAM B. *Stalin: The Man and His Era.* New York: Viking, 1973.

YERGIN, DANIEL. *Shattered Peace: The Origins of the Cold War and the National Security State.* Boston: Houghton Mifflin, 1977.

11. Chairman Mao and the Paper Tiger

1. Chang, *Friends and Enemies,* p. 37.
2. Ibid., p. 65.
3. Bloodworth, *The Messiah and the Mandarins,* p. 101.
4. Ibid., p. 52.
5. Lin Biao in *Quotations from Chairman Mao,* p. i.
6. Karnow, *Mao and China,* p. 96.
7. Terrill, *Mao,* p. 16.
8. Bloodworth, p. 22.
9. Terrill, p. 123.
10. Payne, *Chiang Kai-shek,* p. 156.
11. Terrill, p. 183.
12. Ibid., p. 176 n.

13. Chang, p. 13.
14. Whelan, *Drawing the Line*, p. 119.
15. Knox, *The Korean War: Pusan to Chosin*, p. 6.
16. MacArthur, *Reminiscences*, p. 328.
17. Ibid., p. 332.
18. Ibid., p. 345.
19. Wilson, *Chou*, p. 190.
20. Knox, p. 425.
21. Whelan, p. 253.
22. Knox, p. 459.
23. Whelan, p. 266.
24. Ibid., p. 304.
25. Terrill, p. 209.
26. Whelan, p. 370.
27. Wilson, p. 194.
28. Ibid., p. 200.
29. Stoessinger, *Nations in Darkness*, p. 48.
30. *Quotations from Chairman Mao*, p. 75.
31. Payne, p. 294.
32. MacArthur, p. 340.
33. Chang, p. 128.
34. Ibid., p. 222.
35. Ibid., p. 235.
36. Rice, *Mao's Way*, p. 153.
37. Lewis and Xue, *China Builds the Bomb*, p. 216.
38. Ibid., p. 1.
39. Ibid., p. 242.
40. *Quotations from Chairman Mao*, p. 11.
41. *New York Times*; September 10, 1976, p. A13.
42. Karnow, p. 121.
43. Rice, p. 497.
44. Ibid., p. 492.

References

BLOODWORTH, DENNIS. *The Messiah and the Mandarins: The Paradox of Mao's China.* London: Weidenfeld and Nicolson, 1982.

CHANG, GORDON H. *Friends and Enemies: The United States, China, and the Soviet Union, 1948–1972.* Stanford, Calif.: Stanford University Press, 1990.

KARNOW, STANLEY. *Mao and China: From Revolution to Revolution.* New York: Viking, 1972.

KNOX, DONALD. *The Korean War: Pusan to Chosin.* San Diego, Calif.: Harcourt Brace Jovanovich, 1985.

LEWIS, JOHN WILSON, AND XUE LITAI. *China Builds the Bomb.* Stanford, Calif.: Stanford University Press, 1988.

MACARTHUR, DOUGLAS. *Reminiscences.* New York: McGraw-Hill, 1964.

PAYNE, ROBERT. *Chiang Kai-shek.* New York: Weybright and Talley, 1969.

Quotations from Chairman Mao Tse-tung. Peking: Foreign Languages Press, 1967.

RICE, EDWARD E. *Mao's Way.* Berkeley: University of California Press, 1972.

STOESSINGER, JOHN G. *Nations in Darkness: China, Russia and America*. New York: Random House, 1975.

TERRILL, ROSS. *Mao: A Biography*. New York: Harper & Row, 1980.

WHELAN, RICHARD. *Drawing the Line: The Korean War, 1950–1953*. Boston: Little, Brown, 1990.

WILSON, DICK. *Chou: The Story of Zhou Enlai, 1898–1976*. London: Hutchinson, 1984.

12. Bearding Fidel in His Den

1. Szulc, *Fidel*, p. 242.
2. Ibid., p. 310.
3. Geyer, *Guerrilla Prince*, p. 169.
4. Bonsal, *Cuba, Castro, and the United States*, p. 29.
5. Bourne, *Fidel*, p. 155.
6. Ambrose, *Eisenhower*, p. 545.
7. Bourne, p. 167.
8. Geyer, p. 227.
9. Ambrose, p. 556.
10. Khrushchev, *Khrushchev Remembers*, p. 545.
11. Wyden, *Bay of Pigs*, p. 66.
12. Bonsal, p. 172.
13. Wyden, p. 29.
14. Ambrose, p. 583.
15. Bonsal, p. 186.
16. Wyden, p. 311.
17. Beschloss, *The Crisis Years*, p. 143.
18. Ibid., p. 144.
19. Ibid., p. 6.
20. Szulc, p. 573.
21. Beschloss, p. 330.
22. Bourne, p. 230.
23. Geyer, p. 192.
24. Khrushchev, p. 547.
25. Szulc, p. 582.
26. Blight and Welch, *On the Brink*, p. 51.
27. Kennedy, *Thirteen Days*, p. 166.
28. Ibid., p. 170.
29. Ibid., p. 168.
30. Beschloss, p. 501.
31. Blight and Welch, p. 380.
32. Kennedy, p. 94.
33. Beschloss, p. 571 n.
34. Kennedy, p. 71.
35. Ibid., p. 109.
36. Ibid., p. 205.
37. Beschloss, p. 542.
38. Szulc, p. 585.
39. Geyer, p. 368.

40. Ehrenfeld, *Narco-terrorism*, p. 34.
41. Ibid., p. 35.

References

AMBROSE, STEPHEN E. *Eisenhower: The President*. New York: Simon and Schuster, 1984.

BESCHLOSS, MICHAEL R. *The Crisis Years: Kennedy and Khrushchev, 1960–1963*. New York: HarperCollins, 1991.

BLIGHT, JAMES G., and DAVID A. WELCH. *On the Brink: Americans and Soviets Reexamine the Cuban Missile Crisis*. New York: Hill and Wang, 1989.

BONSAL, PHILIP W. *Cuba, Castro, and the United States*. Pittsburgh, Pa.: University of Pittsburgh Press, 1971.

BOURNE, PETER G. *Fidel: A Biography of Fidel Castro*. New York: Dodd, Mead, 1986.

EHRENFELD, RACHEL. *Narco-terrorism*. New York: Basic Books, 1990.

GEYER, GEORGIE ANNE. *Guerrilla Prince: The Untold Story of Fidel Castro*. Boston: Little, Brown, 1991.

KENNEDY, ROBERT. *Thirteen Days: A Memoir of the Cuban Missile Crisis*. New York: W. W. Norton, 1969.

KHRUSHCHEV, NIKITA S. *Khrushchev Remembers*, trans. and ed. by Strobe Talbott. New York: Bantam Books, 1971.

SZULC, TAD. *Fidel: A Critical Portrait*. New York: William Morrow, 1986.

WYDEN, PETER. *Bay of Pigs: The Untold Story*. New York: Simon and Schuster, 1979.

13. On the Trail of Ho Chi Minh

1. *Public Papers of the Presidents*, pp. 1287–88.
2. VanDeMark, *Into the Quagmire*, p. 66.
3. Goodwin, *Lyndon Johnson and the American Dream*, p. 252.
4. Ibid., p. 253.
5. Karnow, *Vietnam*, p. 19.
6. N. Khac Huyen, *Vision Accomplished?*, p. xiv.
7. Fenn, *Ho Chi Minh*, p. 31.
8. Neumann-Hoditz, *Portrait of Ho Chi Minh*, p. 81.
9. Lacouture, *Ho Chi Minh*, p. 44.
10. Ho Chi Minh, *Prison Diary*, p. 28.
11. Fenn, p. 83.
12. Ho Chi Minh, *Prison Diary*, p. ix.
13. Lacouture, pp. 62–63.
14. Karnow, p. 122.
15. Tuchman, *March of Folly*, p. 250.
16. VanDeMark, p. 18.
17. Pratt, *Vietnam Voices*, p. 179.
18. Ibid., p. 187.
19. Karnow, p. 415.
20. Pratt, p. 201.
21. Ibid., pp. 201–202.
22. Ibid., p. 202.

23. Ho Chi Minh, *Selected Articles and Speeches*, p. 163.
24. Goodwin, p. 267.
25. VanDeMark, p. 123.
26. Ho Chi Minh, *Selected Articles and Speeches*, p. 163.
27. Karnow, p. 330.
28. Berman, *Lyndon Johnson's War*, p. 183.
29. Ibid., p. 13.
30. Karnow, p. 514.
31. Berman, p. 174.
32. N. Khac Huyen, p. 155.
33. Pratt, p. 212.
34. Tuchman, p. 321.
35. Karnow, p. 577.
36. Clodfelter, *The Limits of Air Power*, p. 145.
37. Ibid., p. 144.
38. Karnow, p. 509.
39. Hackworth and Sherman, *About Face*, p. 505.
40. Karnow, p. 457.
41. Neumann-Hoditz, p. 171.
42. N. Khac Huyen, p. 316.
43. Karnow, pp. 27–28.
44. Ibid., p. 36.

References

BERMAN, LARRY. *Lyndon Johnson's War: The Road to Stalemate in Vietnam.* New York: W. W. Norton, 1989.

CLODFELTER, MARK. *The Limits of Air Power: The American Bombing of North Vietnam.* New York: The Free Press, 1989.

FENN, CHARLES. *Ho Chi Minh.* New York: Charles Scribner's Sons, 1973.

GOODWIN, DORIS KEARNS. *Lyndon Johnson and the American Dream.* New York: St. Martin's Press, 1991.

HACKWORTH, DAVID H., and JULIE SHERMAN. *About Face.* New York: Simon and Schuster, 1989.

HALLIN, DANIEL C. *The "Uncensored War": The Media and Vietnam.* New York: Oxford University Press, 1986.

HO CHI MINH. *Ho Chi Minh: Selected Articles and Speeches, 1920–1967,* ed. by Jack Woddis. New York: International Publishers, 1970.

———. *The Prison Diary of Ho Chi Minh,* trans. by Aileen Palmer. New York: Bantam Books, 1971.

N. KHAC HUYEN. *Vision Accomplished? The Enigma of Ho Chi Minh.* New York: Macmillan, 1971.

KARNOW, STANLEY. *Vietnam: A History.* New York: Viking, 1983.

LACOUTURE, JEAN. *Ho Chi Minh: A Political Biography,* trans. by Peter Wiles. New York: Random House, 1968.

NEUMANN-HODITZ, REINHOLD. *Portrait of Ho Chi Minh,* trans. by John Hargreaves. New York: Herder and Herder/McGraw-Hill, 1972.

PRATT, JOHN CLARK, ed. *Vietnam Voices: Perspectives on the War Years, 1941–1982.* New York: Viking, 1984.

Public Papers of the Presidents of the United States: Lyndon Johnson, 1966, Book II.
Washington, D.C.: Government Printing Office, 1967.

TUCHMAN, BARBARA W. *The March of Folly: From Troy to Vietnam* (Chapter 5: "America Betrays Herself in Vietnam"). New York: Alfred A. Knopf, 1984.

VANDEMARK, BRIAN. *Into the Quagmire: Lyndon Johnson and the Escalation of the Vietnam War.* New York: Oxford University Press, 1991.

14. Saddam Makes His Move

1. Khalil, *Republic of Fear,* p. 110.
2. CARDRI, *Saddam's Iraq,* p. 51.
3. Ibid., p. 250.
4. Khalil, p. 119.
5. Yergin, *The Prize,* p. 771.
6. Henderson, *Instant Empire,* p. 167.
7. Miller and Mylroie, *Saddam Hussein and the Crisis in the Gulf,* pp. 148–49.
8. Karsh and Rautsi, *Saddam Hussein,* p. 211.
9. Flavin, "Cost of War in Persian Gulf Would Be Staggering."
10. D'Amato, "Yes, Hussein Must Be Ousted."
11. Henderson, p. 154.
12. Barnaby, "The Nuclear Arsenal in the Middle East," p. 33.
13. Salinger and Laurent, *Secret Dossier,* pp. 158–59.
14. *Weekly Compilation,* September 17, 1990, p. 1360.
15. Ibid., p. 1362.
16. Drew, "Letter from Washington," p. 107.
17. Woodward, *The Commanders,* p. 324.
18. Ibid.
19. Buchanan, "President's Gulf Decision Day Postponed."
20. Karsh and Rautsi, pp. 229–30.
21. Ibid., p. 252.
22. Pasztor and Davis, "If War Comes the U.S. Hopes to Make It Brief," p. A1.
23. Woodward, p. 251.
24. Apple, "Another Gulf War?"
25. Draper, "Presidential Wars," p. 72.
26. Viorst, "Report from Baghdad," p. 61.
27. *Weekly Compilation,* March 11, 1991, pp. 259–60.

References

APPLE, R. W., JR. "Another Gulf War?" *New York Times,* March 10, 1991, p. 11.

BARNABY, FRANK. "The Nuclear Arsenal in the Middle East." *Technology Review,* May/June 1987, pp. 27–34.

BUCHANAN, PATRICK. "President's Gulf Decision Day Postponed." *Seattle Post-Intelligencer,* September 12, 1990, p. A9.

Committee Against Repression and for Democratic Rights in Iraq (CARDRI). *Saddam's Iraq: Revolution or Reaction?* London: Zed Books, 1989.

D'AMATO, ALFONSE. "Yes, Hussein Must Be Ousted." *New York Times,* August 24, 1990, p. A29.

DRAPER, THEODORE. "Presidential Wars." *New York Review of Books*, September 26, 1991, pp. 64–74.

DREW, ELIZABETH. "Letter from Washington." *New Yorker*, September 24, 1990, pp. 103–12.

FLAVIN, CHRISTOPHER. "Cost of War in Persian Gulf Would Be Staggering." *Seattle Post-Intelligencer*, September 28, 1990, p. A15.

HENDERSON, SIMON. *Instant Empire: Saddam Hussein's Ambition for Iraq*. San Francisco: Mercury House, 1991.

KARSH, EFRAIM, and INARI RAUTSI. *Saddam Hussein: A Political Biography*. New York: The Free Press, 1991.

KHALIL, SAMIR AL-. *Republic of Fear: The Politics of Modern Iraq*. Berkeley: University of California Press, 1989.

MILLER, JUDITH, and LAURIE MYLROIE. *Saddam Hussein and the Crisis in the Gulf*. New York: Times Books, 1990.

PASZTOR, ANDY, and BOB DAVIS. "If War Comes the U.S. Hopes to Make It Brief." *Wall Street Journal* Western Edition, September 6, 1990, pp. A1 and A6.

SALINGER, PIERRE, and ERIC LAURENT. *Secret Dossier: The Hidden Agenda Behind the Gulf War*, trans. by Howard Curtis. New York: Penguin Books, 1991.

VIORST, MILTON. "Report from Baghdad." *New Yorker*, June 24, 1991, pp. 55–72.

Weekly Compilation of Presidential Documents. Washington, D.C., September 17, 1990, pp. 1358–63.

————. Washington, D.C., March 11, 1991, pp. 257–61.

WOODWARD, BOB. *The Commanders*. New York: Simon and Schuster, 1991.

YERGIN, DANIEL. *The Prize: The Epic Quest for Oil, Money and Power*. New York: Simon and Schuster, 1991.

Index

S

T

About the Author

Larry Hedrick is an independent scholar and freelance writer who lives in Seattle. The son of a pilot, he grew up during the cold war on U.S. Air Force bases around the world. His articles have appeared in such publications as *World Monitor*, *Military History*, and *Harvard Magazine*.